Contents

War and welfare

Manchester University Press

War and welfare

British POW families, 1939–45

Barbara Hately-Broad

Manchester University Press
Manchester and New York
distributed in the United States exclusively by Palgrave Macmillan

Published by Manchester University Press
Oxford Road, Manchester M13 9NR, UK
and Room 400, 175 Fifth Avenue, New York, NY 10010, USA
www.manchesteruniversitypress.co.uk

Distributed in the United States exclusively by
Palgrave Macmillan, 175 Fifth Avenue, New York,
NY 10010, USA

Distributed in Canada exclusively by
UBC Press, University of British Columbia, 2029 West Mall,
Vancouver, BC, Canada V6T 1Z2

British Library Cataloguing-in-Publication Data
A catalogue record for this book is available from the British Library

Library of Congress Cataloging-in-Publication Data applied for

ISBN   978 0 7190 7854 5   *hardback*

First published 2009

18 17 16 15 14 13 12 11 10 09   10 9 8 7 6 5 4 3 2 1

The publisher has no responsibility for the persistence or accuracy of URLs for any external or third-party internet websites referred to in this book, and does not guarantee that any content on such websites is, or will remain, accurate or appropriate.

Typeset
by SNP Best-set Typesetter Ltd., Hong Kong
Printed in Great Britain
by the MPG Books Group

List of figures and tables

Figures

Tables

Acknowledgements

As with all works of this nature, the final product has only been possible with support and encouragement from a wide range of sources.

In terms of archival sources, I am particularly grateful to the National Archive, SSAFA, the British Red Cross Archive, the Churchill Archive, the Centre for Oxfordshire Studies, the British War Widows Association Archive, West Yorkshire Archive Services and the Sound Archivists at the Imperial War Museum.

The Royal Historical Society allowed me funding to attend international conferences to present papers on various aspects of this work, and the feedback from these conferences has added to its scope.

Thanks are also due, and gratefully given, to a number of historians working in the field of prisoner of war history who generously shared of their time and knowledge, in particular: Kent Fedorowich, Paul McKenzie, Neville Wylie, David Rolf and Gerry Doud. The project would never have been completed without Bob Moore who has seen it from inception to completion; encouraging, commenting and cajoling as necessary. Whilst their knowledge and comments have undoubtedly improved the work, any omissions or errors remain mine.

A final word of thanks goes to my family and in particular to my son, Luke, whose own interests lie in a very different field but who read and commented on draft chapters with both good grace and acumen. The book is dedicated to my father, who waited a long time for me to find my way.

Introduction

As the war in Europe came to an end in the late spring of 1945, the British government began to implement its plans for the return of servicemen who had fought against Germany to their homes and families. These plans were given added impetus in August when the war against Japan, which had been expected to continue for some years, ended abruptly with unconditional surrender. For many of these men there had been long separations from wives and children as a result of the war, but their role as returning heroes was assured. In contrast, the soldiers, sailors and airmen who had fallen into enemy hands, while also enduring long separation, had also contended with much harsher living conditions and, in the case of those held by the Japanese, almost total isolation from news of the outside world. Moreover, their position as prisoners of war and therefore as military failures precluded their being afforded the same status as their comrades still on active service.

In all, 4,653,000 men joined the British armed services between 1939 and 1945, of whom an estimated 55 per cent were married, giving a total of somewhere in the region of 2.5 million wives separated from their husbands by the exigencies of military service.[1] Given these numbers, it is perhaps surprising how little attention historians have given to this aspect of the social history of the war. While historians and social scientists have examined social change in the twentieth century and the possible role of total war in this process, these analyses have never dealt with the impact of militarisation on British society.[2] Even social histories of the welfare state, although dealing with at least one issue that specifically affected service families, namely the introduction of national Family Allowance, nevertheless make no direct mention of these families.[3] Similarly, political histories refer only in passing to the importance attached by servicemen to state provision of care for their families whilst they were absent and make no mention of any demands for greater provision for families in the post war army.[4] The effect that family welfare was deemed to have on the morale of troops, combined with the fact that conscription would remain in force until well after 1945, should have made this a matter of concern for a significant proportion of the general public, even allowing for decreasing numbers of service personnel following the cessation of hostilities. Instead, questions about the treatment of service families in peacetime, in future wars and in relation to the increasing provisions of the welfare state seem to have been largely overlooked. In fact, changes made to the regulations governing the administration of allowances following the experience of the Second World War were minimal, despite the fact that many families, especially those of servicemen taken prisoner in the Far East, had experienced severe hardships.

Indeed, if the experiences of servicemen and their families have been marginalised in the existing histories, this is even more true of the 135,009 servicemen taken prisoner by the Axis powers and the 37,583 held by the Japanese in the Far East.[5] A consequence of this was that nearly 95,000 women became wives of prisoners of war yet they remain almost completely absent from the social histories of the period, and even from accounts of women's lives in Britain during the Second World War. In fact, although the experiences of prisoner of war families impinge on a wide range of issues related to the social, military and political history of wartime Britain, their history remains largely unwritten, both for this and for every other modern conflict. Thus, McCubbin and Dahl, writing in 1972 about the experience of American prisoner of war families during the Vietnam War, claimed that there was still 'a paucity of research answering questions about how POW families coped' – a claim which remains true to the present day.[6]

This book is designed to remedy this lacuna by examining in detail the treatment of British prisoner of war families by both the government and the armed forces during the Second World War and raises important questions about the state's duty of care towards the families of those taken captive in the service of their country.

During the Second World War there is no doubt that the state recognised the important part that families played in the upkeep of morale amongst servicemen.[7] As one wartime Army Morale Report reported, 'If his family is happy, he has something to fight for: if his family is in distress he cannot give his whole mind and heart to his soldiering'.[8] Without the certainty that their families were being adequately provided for, the efficiency of servicemen as fighting units was perceived to suffer.[9] Worries over wives and families in relation to inadequate allowances, family ill-health and marital infidelity were viewed by the services as distracting men from concentration on duty, thus causing decreased efficiency.[10] Soon after the cessation of hostilities, T.H. Marshall argued that 'total war obliges governments to assume new and heavier responsibilities for the welfare of their people'.[11] Given the necessity first to recruit servicemen and then, following the introduction of conscription in 1939, to retain them, the importance of service families for both political and social history is clear. However, within the British literature on twentieth-century warfare, academic studies that focus on service families are virtually non-existent, and mentions of their concerns within wider studies remain rare.[12] General histories of the army, air force and navy rarely refer to the families of servicemen although Maitland claimed that, by 1885, provision was well established within the army at least.[13] The few specific studies of service families that do exist remain largely narrative and anecdotal.[14] Vera Bamfield's largely uncritical account of family life in the Victorian army emphasises the social and welfare roles played by both the regiment and its commanding officers whilst failing to include any analysis of the situation of army families in terms of overall political or economic policy or wider social issues.

One honourable exception to this general neglect is Myna Trustram's *Women of the Regiment. Marriage and the Victorian Army*, which does devote time to detailing and analysing the position of British army families in relation to wider contemporary social issues. In so doing she provides a comprehensive overview of the British army in the Victorian period, beginning with a review of army attitudes towards wives and families and giving an in-depth analysis of issues affecting army families during the period.[15] Whilst studies of British army families, with the exception of Trustram, may be regarded as more useful in providing a general overview rather than detailed historical evidence, they do help us to form an overall picture of provision for families within the British army in the nineteenth century. No such overviews exist of family life within the navy. The absence of navy families within general histories is, in fact, a precise reflection of contemporary attitudes within the navy itself, where no provision was made for the families of seamen until the start of the First World War. Prior to this, the very existence of wives remained unrecognised by both the Admiralty and navy until men reached the rank of Admiral. Eleanor Rathbone, MP for the Combined British Universities, was told during a visit to the Admiralty in around 1917 that 'a sailor ought not to marry until he was an admiral when perhaps he would need a wife for purposes of hospitality'.[16]

Gillian Thomas's work on state maintenance for women during the First World War provided the first detailed investigation into financial support for families across all the services.[17] This is a rare example of a detailed, analytical investigation of governmental attitudes towards servicemen's dependants. Thomas leans heavily towards a feminist interpretation in her conclusion, concentrating on the continuation of women's economic dependence, the perpetuation of the primacy of a two-parent family model and the 'disposability' of a female labour force which could 'disappear into the family' once their usefulness to the state ended.[18] Nevertheless, many of her assertions remain valid throughout the interwar period, into the 1940s and beyond. As an example, she highlights the fact that state maintenance never became an unquestionable right of service wives, despite the fact that payments were made directly to them. Thomas's work also stresses the continued role of philanthropic organisations in the welfare of service families – again a factor that remained important throughout the period of this book.[19] Although more recent publications on social welfare have looked generally at the development of state assistance for families none has included any discussion of allowances for service families.[20] The same is true of official and general histories of the Second World War, as only those dealing with social policy and welfare make any mention of service families.[21] Titmuss, for example, mentions allowances for children of servicemen, but only as a comparison with those paid to the foster families of evacuees.[22] Parallel studies of this issue for other Western European countries are equally scarce, with Ute Daniel's research in relation to German working-class women in the First World War providing an important exception.[23]

As has already been suggested, if research on British service families generally has been limited, this is even more true for the families of those taken captive. Initially, publications on prisoners of war themselves were largely confined to biographies and auto-biographical memoirs such as *The Great Escape* and *The Wooden Horse*, both of which were also made into well-known feature films.[24] Although a great many of the prisoners appearing in these memoirs undoubtedly had families, concerns for them are rarely expressed, and the voices of those wives and families waiting in Britain for news of their loved ones remain unrecorded.[25] In an unpublished biography held at the Imperial War Museum, Vivienne Chatfield, the widow of a prisoner of war taken captive by the Japanese, noted that, despite the many books written by prisoners of war themselves, 'none has been written by the near relatives of these men who spent long years of waiting for news'.[26]

Instead the narratives concentrate on the immediate experiences of captor and prisoner; day-to-day survival and, especially, escape. Within the field of military history, prisoners of war have only recently been rescued from the oblivion of being 'no longer effective in the business of war and embarrassments to their captors',[27] but even now appear mainly where they have strategic importance to their captors in economic terms or where reciprocity of treatment is involved. As Gerald Davis suggests, 'hostages are only valuable when the other side is sensitive to the fate of its personnel in enemy hands'[28] – a situation that has been only partially resolved by an increasing body of work on the economic relevance of prisoners of war.[29]

Even more general prisoner of war histories, however, contain few references to the families of those captured. A. J. Barker provides an early example of an analytical appraisal of the broader prisoner of war experience, but remains firmly centred on the men themselves, and families are mentioned only in relation to the comfort provided to men by letters and parcels from home.[30] Similarly, David Rolf and David Foy, writing on the British and American experiences respectively, mention families only briefly.[31] This is also true of more recent works by Paul Mackenzie, Bob Moore and Kent Fedorowich that, despite having moved towards a concern with captor policy and behaviour in a variety of situations, still neglect prisoner of war families,[32] as do studies on the experience of military service during the Second World War that deal with the problems associated with the reassimilation of servicemen into civilian and family life.[33] A rare exception is the work of Barry Turner and Tony Rennell, which provides a much fuller account of the effects on both marriages and children of enforced separation, relying largely on interviews with prisoners of war themselves, their wives and their children interspersed with statistical information on divorce and 'sexual aberrations' – largely infidelity.[34] The overall focus of these studies, and of Wootton's *The Politics of Influence*, which deals with ex-service organisations, is the changes engendered as a result of the servicemen's own experience without reference to those of the wider family.[35] Although questions related to demobilisation and 'the return' are not the primary focus of this book, they did have some impact on the ways in which government departments dealt with prisoners of war and their families in the closing stages of the conflict.[36]

Even in the field of women's history, where studies on women during the Second World War have proliferated in recent years, service wives remain neglected.[37] It is tempting to argue that service wives in general, and prisoner of war wives in particular, hold few attractions as a subject for study for feminist historians. The very fact of their financial dependency on male-dominated, and often patriarchal, institutions puts them at odds with a rationale wishing to show British women during the Second World War as gaining greater control of their own lives, branching out into new spheres of employment and enjoying greater self-fulfilment.[38] As this book will make clear, their efforts to secure information on missing menfolk, together with the formation of self-help groups such as local Prisoner of War Committees and their efforts to secure improved treatment for those taken captive, all suggest a highly motivated and articulate group. As Judy Barrett Litoff and David Smith suggest, 'The news that loved ones were prisoner-of-war, missing in action, or killed during battle required women to draw on a previously untapped inner strength.'[39]

However, this view is at odds with many feminist studies which continue to stress the continuing economic dependence and strictures on women in the aftermath of the Second World War. Even Braybon and Summerfield assert that 'After 1945 what was important in life was still emphatically male.'[40] In the light of this, it would seem that prisoner of war and service wives in general should form part of a general debate associated with continued paternalistic practices and economic dependence. Perhaps most important, however, is the fact that, rather than remaining anonymous, prisoner of war and service wives formed a distinct group, with a recognisable and discrete identity, which has nevertheless been overlooked in the historiography of women's wartime history.[41]

This, then, raises the question of how the British government and the British public actually viewed its servicemen who had fallen into enemy hands. Were they regarded as innocent victims of the fortunes of war or, in reality, did the government see captured servicemen as being of no further use to the war effort and, hence, of little military importance? Crucially for this book, governmental attitudes towards prisoners of war themselves would, inevitably, be reflected in the treatment of their families.[42]

To understand the relationships between servicemen's families and the state, it is also necessary to highlight the extremely complex relationships between the various state departments and agencies concerned with the welfare of and information relating to British prisoners of war during the Second World War. Although various writers have attempted to reconcile the relationships of those directly involved in terms of their own fields of research, no attempt appears to have been made to produce an overall chart showing the working relationships of these various agencies.[43] Two official Second World War organisational histories help to shed some light on this issue: an unpublished report on the work of the Prisoner of War Department of the Foreign Office and a report dealing with the work of the British Red Cross and St John War Organisation between 1939 and 1945.[44] Both of these volumes investigate the specific workings of their particular agencies during the war and provide valuable insights into the everyday operations of these central institutions. The volume relating the work of the Red Cross Society and Order of St John was compiled largely from weekly summaries of work at the request of the Society whilst the history of the Prisoner of War Department (PWD) was instigated by the Foreign Office as an enquiry into the workings of one of its own departments. Although it acknowledged that there was no excuse for the Prisoner of War Department not having been established in 1939, it went on to claim that, once the Department did become operational, its relations as an agency of the Foreign Office with the War Office were 'friendly, intimate and efficient'.[45] This view is not, however, substantiated in more recent studies. Rolf in 'Blind Bureaucracy', for example, contends that the Prisoner of War Department at the Foreign Office and the War Office's Directorate of Prisoners of War (DPW) 'failed at times to appreciate their respective spheres of influence'.[46]

One further 'quasi-official' history also needs consideration, namely the historical monograph written by Colonel H.J. Phillimore, commonly referred to as the Phillimore Report. It had been prepared as part of the war histories series and outlined the work of the DPW, within the War Office. It was prepared using information contained in official files, but was never submitted for publication as, in the view of the War Office, it had been written by 'an officer with no War Office experience outside the DPW and without experience in DPW during its formative period at the beginning of the war'.[47]

Given that the secondary sources on the treatment of service dependants in general, and prisoner of war dependants in particular, are distinctly sparse, this book is inevitably highly dependent on primary sources. Evidence for the treatment of prisoner of war families has come from a number of ministry and service archives. Besides those of the War Office, Admiralty and Royal Air Force, information has also been gleaned from files of the Foreign Office, Treasury and Colonial Office, and from those of the Prime Minster's Office. Perhaps the most extensive source is the files of the Unemployment Assistance Board (UAB), which contains some 35 files covering a period up to December 1946 following the administration of both family and dependants' allowances and ending with a consideration of the effect of the National Insurance Act on service dependants' allowances.[48]

This collection, together with Treasury and War Office files, serves to establish the parameters limiting the granting and administration of service allowances together with their development both during the interwar period and throughout the course of the Second World War. As the army had by far the greatest number of personnel involved in the war, the War Office was able to exert some influence on both the Treasury and the Foreign Office in a manner that the other services could not emulate. For example, in discussions on the issue of eligibility for Dependants' Allowances in 1940, although agreement was reached between the Treasury, Ministry of Pensions, Admiralty and Royal Air Force, it was still felt necessary to attempt to reach a unanimous decision rather than take the majority view which went against army opinion.[49] As a further example of the pre-eminence of the War Office, the term 'soldier' is often used as a generic term for all servicemen, as in a UAB pamphlet where it is noted that 'the term "soldiers" should be regarded as including sailors and airmen'.[50]

Beyond the National Archives, sources such as those held by the Soldiers, Sailors and Air Force Families Association (SSAFA) and the British Red Cross have proved useful in providing a more immediate, day-to-day perspective to the implementation of many of the decisions taken by government departments and the historical development of service allowances and their administration during the Second World War.

Documentation on local Prisoner of War Committees is also sparse, although a few have left some traces. For example, the Barnsley and District Prisoner of War Fund dates from 1918, and was formed primarily to 'provide for the needs of British Prisoners of War in the belligerent countries'. The charity also had the express aim of providing grants or loans to the 'spouses and dependants [of prisoners of war] resident within the Metropolitan Borough of Barnsley who are in need of assistance'.[51] Although the Committee continues to meet on a regular basis to the present day, the minutes of meetings and correspondence relating to the Second World War have proved impossible to locate.

One notable exception to this generally bleak picture can be found in the Kirklees Archive in Huddersfield, which holds a number of files relating to the Huddersfield Prisoner of War Committee. This Committee, founded in 1940 by the mother of one of the first Huddersfield men to be taken prisoner, met until November 1946 at which time funds were wound up by donating £8 to the relatives of all local men who had died as a result of their captivity. The archive contains minute books, letters from next of kin and a copy of the booklet provided for the *Daily Telegraph* Prisoner of War Exhibition in May 1944. The same archive also holds copies of the local paper, the *Huddersfield Weekly Examiner*, which carried a regular feature 'News of Some Local Soldiers' giving biographical details of local men reported missing, taken captive or killed in action together with reports of Committee fundraising activities. From these two sources it has been possible to re-create a relatively comprehensive picture of the work of this particular Committee. One possible reason for the existence of this archive lies in the fact that the first batch of Huddersfield prisoners of war included 2nd Lieutenant R.B. Smales of the King's Own Yorkshire Light Infantry, the son of a mayor of Huddersfield, and it was his mother who initiated the founding of the local Prisoners of War Committee. Although impossible to prove, it seems likely that, as a result, this particular Committee attained a higher profile than many in terms of local news coverage and that their records may have achieved a more 'official' status leading to their preservation within the archive. Whatever the reasons for their survival, the material proved a valuable and all-too-rare record of the workings of these local Committees, which provided much-needed support, both emotional and financial, to the families of prisoners of war.

Further information was also found in the archive of the British War Widows, now held at the University of Stafford. This contains letters, newspaper cuttings and newsletters collected by one woman, Iris Strange, herself the widow of a prisoner of war captured by the Japanese, during her long campaign for pensions for war widows.[52] As such, it provides a number of valuable insights into, and personal recollections of, the plight of prisoner of war families, particularly of those taken captive in the Far East. It includes her letters to her husband, captured at Singapore in 1942, letters from wives of other prisoners and newsletters from the Far East Prisoner of War Association (FEPOW).

As with local prisoner of war committees, evidence for help and support for families within the services themselves is also scarce. A number of official sources suggest that support groups were formed, for example in places such as Gosport, which had strong links with one particular service, but the evidence for them remains circumstantial. One explanation may be that much of the support was informal. A study describing the support provided for naval wives in the USA showed that much of it was social in nature: through communal barbecues and unofficial 'phone trees' which remained informal and unrecorded, primarily so that wives did not become the target for exploitation by insurance companies and unscrupulous salesmen.[53]

Whilst this book focuses specifically on the British government and its treatment of prisoner of war families during the Second World War, in order to provide a suitable context it begins by establishing a general framework within which to locate government treatment of prisoner of war families as distinct from service families in general. Chapter 1 outlines the historical development of service allowances and their administration in the period to 1918, their further development during the interwar period and the changes brought about by the advent of the Second World War. Chapter 2 then concentrates on the changes in and administration of allowances during the course of the war itself, most notably the introduction of new levels of allowances in 1942 and 1944. Only then is it possible to focus on the particular difficulties encountered by the families of those taken captive. Chapters 3 and 4 deal specifically with the administration of allowances for the families of servicemen taken captive both by the Germans and by the Italians in Europe and by the Japanese in the Far East. Moving away from financial considerations, Chapter 5 then turns to the equally important provision of information, news and support to the families of prisoners of war through official channels, whilst Chapter 6 deals with the information and support provided by charitable and 'self-help' agencies such as SSAFA and local committees. The final chapter reviews changes to service allowances in the immediate postwar period and considers whether the experience of administering these allowances during the Second World War resulted in any significant changes in the existing administrative systems. In addition, this chapter considers changes in service allowances resulting from the introduction of national Family Allowances and the beginnings of the welfare state.

Bob Moore has suggested that the existence of a substantial body of work already dealing with prisoners of war 'should not be allowed to obscure the fact that there is still much about prisoners of war and their captors of which we have remained ignorant'.[54] One of these aspects is undoubtedly the British government's treatment of the families of those taken captive. To date we have remained ignorant of the modes of administration of allowances and dissemination of information to prisoner of war families and of the underlying government attitudes that informed this administration. In addition, we also know little or nothing about the concerns and opinions of these families, focusing almost exclusively on the men themselves. To provide a balanced overview, it is therefore essential that the ways in which their families coped in their absence must be afforded equal weight to the experiences of the men themselves.

Notes

1 Figures taken from Ferguson, S. and Fitzgerald, H., *Studies in Social Services*. London: HMSO, 1978, p. 3 and Central Statistical Office, *Fighting with Figures. A Statistical Digest of the Second World War*. London: HMSO: 1995. Table 3.4 Strength of the Armed Forces and Women's Auxiliary Services. p. 39.

2 See for example: Marwick, A. (ed.), *Total War and Social Change*. London: Macmillan, 1988; *War and Social Change in the Twentieth Century: A Comparative Study of Britain, France, Germany, Russia and the United States*. London: Macmillan, 1974, and *British Society since 1945*. Harmondsworth: Penguin, 1982; Smith, H.L., *War and Social Change. British Society in the Second World War*. Manchester: Manchester University Press, 1986, and *Britain in the Second World War. A Social History*. Manchester and New York: Manchester University Press, 1996; Addison, P., *Now the War Is Over: A Social History of Britain 1945–1951*. London: BBC & Jonathan Cape, 1985, and *The Road to 1945. British Politics and the Second World War*. London: Jonathan Cape, 1975; Barnett, C., *The Audit of War. The Illusions and Reality of Britain as a Great Nation*. London: Macmillan, 1986; Calder, A., *The People's War. Britain 1939–1945*. London: Granada, 1971; Mommsen, W. (ed.), *The Emergence of the Welfare State in Britain and Germany 1850–1950*. London: Croom Helm on behalf of the German Historical Institute, 1981; Milward, A., *War, Economy and Society, 1939–45*. London: Allen Lane, 1977; Pelling, H., *Britain and the Second World War*. London: Collins, 1970; Brivati, B., and Jones, H. (eds), *What Difference Did the War Make?* London: Leicester University Press, 1995; Ashford, D.E., *The Emergence of the Welfare State*. Oxford: Blackwell, 1986; Hennessey, P., *Never Again. Britain 1945–51*. London: Jonathan Cape, 1992; Titmuss, R.M., *Essays on the Welfare State*. London: Allen and Unwin, 1958; Marshall, T.H., *Class, Citizenship and Social Development*. London: Heinemann, 1977; Birch, R., *The Shaping of the Welfare State*. London: Longman, 1974; Fraser, D., *The Evolution of the British Welfare State*. London: Macmillan,1973; Fussell, P., *Wartime: Understanding and Behaviour in the Second World War*. Oxford: Oxford University Press, 1989; Hall, P., Parker, R., Land, R., and Webb, A. (eds), *Change, Choice and Conflict in Social Policy*. London: Heinemann, 1975; Jeffrey, K., *War and Reform. British Politics during the Second World War*. Manchester and New York: Manchester University Press, 1994; MacKay, R., *The Test of War: Inside Britain 1939–45*. London: UCL Press, 1999; Morgan, D., and Evans, M., *The Battle for Britain: Citizenship and Ideology in the*

Second World War. London and New York: Routledge, 1993; Obelkevich, J. and Catterall, P. (eds), *Understanding British Postwar Society*. London: Routledge, 1994; Thane, P., *Foundations of the Welfare State*. London: Longman, 1982; Wootton, G., *The Politics of Influence. British Ex-servicemen, Cabinet Decisions and Cultural Change (1917–57)*. London: Routledge and Kegan Paul Ltd, 1963; Macnicol, J., *The Movement for Family Allowances 1918–45*. London: Heinemann, 1980.

3 Thane, *Foundations of the Welfare State*. pp. 212–227, and Hall, Land, Parker and Webb, *Change, Choice and Conflict in Social Policy*. p. 157. Generally throughout this book prisoners of war have been regarded as male. During the Second World War only twenty women in all became prisoners of war, all from the Auxiliary Territorial Service including Army Nursing Services. Central Statistical Office, *Fighting with Figures* Table 3.8 Casualties Suffered during the war by the Armed Forces, Auxiliary Services and Merchant Navy, p. 43.

4 Jeffrey, *War and Reform*. pp. 94–96, and Wootton, *The Politics of Influence*. p. 18.

5 Figures taken from Central Statistical Office, Statistical Digest of the War. London and Nendeln: HMSO & Kraus Reprint, 1975 reprint. Central Statistical Office, *Fighting with Figures*. p. 43. Table 3.8 Casualties Suffered during the War by the Armed Forces, Auxiliary Services and Merchant Navy, shows slightly lower figures.

6 McCubbin, H.I., and Dahl, B.B., 'Prolonged Family Separation in the Military: A Longitudinal Study' in McCubbin, H.I., Dahl, B.B., and Hunter, E.J., *Families in the Military System*. Beverly Hills and London: Sage Publications Ltd, 1976. pp. 112–144.

7 Reports of the War Office Morale Committee January 1942 to October 1947. NA/WO32/15772.

8 Report of the War Office Morale Committee November 1943 to January 1944. NA/WO32/15772/50A/.

9 Paper by the Adjutant General on Morale in the Army. 23 February 42. NA/WO32/15772.

10 Financial provision for the wives and families of servicemen was, by 1939, made through Marriage Allowances (known in the navy as Family Allowance). These payments, originating as Separation Allowances during the nineteenth century, formed an integral part of a serviceman's overall pay together with other allowances for heating, light, tobacco and mess charges. However, not all servicemen received all the possible allowances as eligibility depended on a number of factors including whether or not a family lived in service

accommodation, on where the serviceman was posted and, for some items such as clothing, on rank.

11 Marshall, T.H., *Social Policy*. London: Hutchinson & Co., 1975. p. 82.

12 In a number of studies of the Second World War, passing reference is made to service families usually in relation to financial support. See for example: History of the Second World War Series: UK Civil Series. Titmuss, R.M., *Problems of Social Policy*. London: HMSO, 1976. p. 162; Ferguson and Fitzgerald, *Studies in Social Services*. p. 98; and Military Series, Hancock, W.K. and Gowing, M.M., *British War Economy*. London: HMSO, 1949. pp. 169 and 505; Addison, *Now the War Is Over*, pp. 16 and 21–23; Pelling, *Britain and the Second World War*, p. 303; Parker, R.A.C., *Struggle for Survival. The History of the Second World War*. Oxford: Oxford University Press, 1989. p. 293.

13 Maitland, M.D.D., 'The Care of the Soldier's Family' in *Journal of the Royal Army Medical Corps*. August 1950. p. 117.

14 Bamfield, V., *On the Strength. The Story of the British Army Wife*. London: Charles Knight, 1974. For general histories see for example: Barnett, C., *Britain and Her Army: A Military, Political and Social History of the British Army, 1509–1970*. London: Cassell, 2000; Swinnerton, I.S., *An Introduction to the British Army: Its History, Traditions and Records*. Birmingham: Federation of Family History Societies, 1996; Chandler, D., (general ed.), *The Oxford History of the British Army*. Oxford: Oxford University Press, 1996; Preston, A., *History of the Royal Navy*. London: Hamlyn, 1983; Warner, O.M.W., *The British Navy. A Concise History*. London: Thames and Hudson, 1975; Sharpe, M., *History of the Royal Air Force*. Bath: Paragon, 1999; Armitage, M.J., *The Royal Air Force*. London: Arms and Armour, 1995.

15 Trustram, M., *Women of the Regiment. Marriage and the Victorian Army*. Cambridge: Cambridge University Press, 1984.

16 Introduction to a debate in the House of Commons on Service Pay and Allowances 10/09/42. NA/WO32/10448.

17 Thomas, G., *State Maintenance for Women during the First World War: The Case of Separation Allowances and Pensions*. Unpublished PhD thesis, University of Sussex, 1989.

18 Thomas, *State Maintenance for Women during the First World War*. p. 239.

19 Thomas, *State Maintenance for Women during the First World War*. p. 242.

20 Examples of more recent publications into the development of welfare provision in Britain include: Sullivan, M., *The Development of the*

British Welfare State. Hemel Hempstead: Prentice Hall/Harvester Wheatsheaf, 1996; Ungerson, C., and Kember, M. (eds), *Women and Social Policy. A Reader*, 2nd ed. Basingstoke: Macmillan Ltd, 1997; Finlayson, G., *Citizen, State and Social Welfare in Britain 1830–1990.* Oxford: Clarendon Press, 1994; Lowe, R., *The Welfare State in Britain since 1945.* Basingstoke: Macmillan Ltd, 1993, and 'The Second World War, Consensus and the Foundations of the Welfare State' in *Twentieth Century British History.* Vol. 1, 1990. pp. 152–182; Pierson, C., and Castles, F.G., *The Welfare State Reader.* Oxford & Malden, MA: Blackwell, 2000.

21 See, for example: Official Histories of the Second World War Series: Dennison, F.S.V., *Civilian Affairs and Military Government. Central Organisation and Planning.* London: HMSO, 1966; Gibbs, N.H., *Grand Strategy, Vol. 1 Rearmanent Policy.* London: HMSO, 1976; Butler, J.R.M., *Grand Strategy, Vol. 2 Sept. 1939–1941.* London: HMSO, 1957: Gwyer, M.A., *Grand Strategy, Vol. 3 Pt 1, June 1941–August 1942.* London: HMSO, 1964: Butler, J.R.M., *Grand Strategy, Vol. 3 Pt 2, June 1941–August 1942.* London: HMSO, 1964: Howerd, M., *Grand Strategy, Vol. 4 August 1942–Sept. 1943.* London: HMSO, 1972; Ehrman, J., *Grand Strategy, Vol. 5 Aug. 1943–Sept. 1944.* London: HMSO, 1956, and *Grand Strategy, Vol. 6 Oct. 1944–Aug. 1945.* London: HMSO, 1956. Also Liddell Hart, B.H., *Oxford Companion to the Second World War.* Oxford: Oxford University Press, 1995; Lee, L.E., *World War II.* Westport CT: Greenwood Press, 1997; Lukacs, J., *The Last European War. September 1939–December 1941.* London: Routledge & Kegan Paul Ltd, 1976; Parker, *Struggle for Survival. The History of the Second World War*; Wilmot, C., *The Struggle for Europe.* Westport, CT: Greenwood Press, 1952.

22 Titmuss, *Problems of Social Policy.* p. 162.

23 Daniel, U., *The War from Within.*

24 Brickhill, P., *The Great Escape.* New York: Norton, 1950, and Williams, E.E., *The Wooden Horse.* New York: Harper, 1950.

25 One exception to this general trend is Basil Dearden's 1946 film *The Captive Heart.* In this story of POWs held in Europe, concerns and reminiscences of families in Scotland, Wales and southern England are included alongside escapes and camp concerns.

26 Chatfield, V., 'Theirs Not to Reason Why' unpublished autobiography. p. 461. Department of Documents, Imperial War Museum.

27 Barker, A.J., *Behind Barbed Wire.* London: William Clowes and Sons Ltd, 1974.

28 Davis, G.H., 'Prisoners of War in Twentieth-century War Economics' in *Journal of Contemporary History.* Vol. 12, 1977. pp. 623–634.

29   See, for example: Moore, B., 'Turning Liabilities into Assets: British
      Government Policy towards German and Italian Prisoners of War
      during the Second World War' in *Journal of Contemporary History*.
      Vol. 32, No. 1. pp. 117–136; Homze, E.L., *Foreign Labour in Nazi
      Germany*. Princeton: Princeton University Press, 1967; Dallin, A.,
      German Rule in Russia, 1941–1945. London: Macmillan, 1981;
      Lewis, G.G., and Mewha, J., 'History of Prisoner of War Utilization
      by the United States Army 1776–1945.' *Department of the Army
      Pamphlet 20–213*. Washington, 1977; Crew, D.F. (ed.), *Nazism and
      German Society 1933–1945*. London and New York: Routledge,
      1994. pp. 219–273; Frei, N., *National Socialist Rule in Germany. The
      Fuhrer State 1933–1945*. Oxford: Blackwell, 1993. p. 139: Hicks,
      A.L., *Unfinished Business. Prisoner of War Slave Labour*. Oxford:
      Privately printed, 1999; Struve, W., 'The Wartime Economy: Foreign
      Workers, "Half Jews" and Other Prisoners in a German Town 1939–
      1945' in *German Studies Review*. Vol. 16, No. 3, 1993. pp. 463–482;
      Davis, 'Prisoners of War in Twentieth-century War Economics';
      Havers, R., 'The Changi POW Camp and the Burma–Thailand
      Railway' in Towle, P., Kosuge, M., and Kibata, Y., *Japanese Prisoners
      of War*. London: Hambledon and London, 2000. pp. 17–36; Kinvig,
      C., 'Allied POWs and the Burma-Thailand Railway' in Towle, P.,
      Kosuge, M., and Kibata, Y., *Japanese Prisoners of War*. London:
      Hambledon and London, 2000. pp. 37–58, and Daws, G., *Prisoners
      of the Japanese. POWs of World War II in the Pacific*. New York:
      William Morrow & Co. Inc., pp. 141–252.
30   Barker, *Behind Barbed Wire*. pp. 141, 214 and 226.
31   Rolf, D., *Prisoners of the Reich. Germany's Captives, 1939–45*.
      London: Leo Cooper, 1988; Foy, D.A., *For You the War Is Over.
      American Prisoners of War in Nazi Germany*. New York: Stein &
      Day, 1984.
32   Mackenzie, S.P., 'The Treatment of Prisoners of War in World War II'
      in *Journal of Modern History*. Vol. 66, September 1994. pp. 487–520;
      and Moore, B., and Fedorowich, K. (eds), *Prisoners of War and Their
      Captors in World War II*. Oxford: Berg, 1996.
33   See for example: Duchen, C., and Bandhauer-Schoffmann, I., *When
      the War Was Over. Women, War and Peace in Europe, 1940–1956*.
      London and New York: Leicester University Press, 2000; Funch, J.,
      and Summerfield, P., 'Social Reconstruction and the Emergence of
      Companionate Marriage, 1945–59' in Clark, D. (ed.), *Marriage,
      Domestic Life and Social Change. Writings for Jacqueline Burgoyne
      (1944–88)*. London and New York. Routledge, 1991; Reese, P.,
      *Homecoming Heroes. An Account of the Re-assimilation of British
      Military Personnel into Civilian Life*. London: Leo Cooper, 1992;

Howard, K., *Sex Problems of the Returning Soldier*. Manchester: Sydney Pemberton, 1945; Turner, B., and Rennell, T., *When Daddy Came Home. How family Life Changed Forever in 1945*. London: Hutchinson, 1995; Beckh, H.G., 'Reuniting of Families in Europe during and after the Second World War' in *International Review of the Red Cross*. No. 211, 1979. pp. 171–183; No. 216, 1980. pp. 115–128; and No. 227, 1982. pp. 71–85; Swindells, J., 'Coming Home to Heaven: Manpower and Myth in 1944 Britain' in *Women's History Review*. Vol. 4, No. 2, 1995. pp. 223–234; Fishman, S., 'The Cult of the Return: Prisoner of War Wives in France During the Second World War' in *Proceedings of the Annual Meeting of the Western Society for French History*. Vol. 17, 1990; Hartmann, S.M., 'Prescriptions for Penelope: Literature on Women's Obligations to Returning World War II Veterans' in *Women's Studies*. Vol. 5, 1978. pp. 223–239.

34 Turner, B., and Rennell, T., *When Daddy Came Home. How Family Life Changed Forever in 1945*, pp. 141–164.

35 Wootton, G., *The Politics of Influence*.

36 See, for example: Ungerson, C., and Kember, M. (eds), *Women and Social Policy. A Reade*; Taylor-Gooby, P., *Public Opinion, Ideology and State Welfare*. London: Routledge & Kegan Paul plc, 1985; Titmuss, R., *Problems of Social Policy* and *Essays on the Welfare State*; Bruce, M. (ed.), *The Rise of the Welfare State. English Social Policy 1601–1971*. London, Fakenham & Reading: Cox & Wyman Ltd, 1973; and *The Coming of the Welfare State* (4th ed.). London: Batsford Ltd, 1961; Finlayson, G., *Citizen, State and Social Welfare in Britain 1830–1990*. Oxford: Clarendon Press, 1994; Lowe, R., *The Welfare State in Britain since 1945*. Basingstoke: Macmillan Ltd, 1993; Pierson, C., and Castles, F.G., *The Welfare State Reader*. Oxford & Malden, MA: Blackwell, 2000; Mommsen, *The Emergence of the Welfare State in Britain and Germany 1850–1950*; Milward, *War, Economy and Society, 1939–45*; Ashford, *The Emergence of the Welfare State*; Marshall, *Class, Citizenship and Social Development*; Birch, *The Shaping of the Welfare State*; Fraser, *Evolution of the British Welfare State*; Thane, *Foundations of the Welfare State*; Macnicol, *The Movement for Family Allowances 1918–45*.

37 See for example: Braybon, G. and Summerfield, P., *Out of the Cage*. London: Pandora, 1987; Elshtain, J.B., *Women and War*. Brighton: Harvester, 1987; Hartley, J. (ed.), *Hearts Undefeated. Women's Writing of the Second World War*. London: Virago, 1996; Higonet, M.R., Jenson, J., Michel, S., and Weitz, M.C. (eds), *Behind the Lines. Gender and the Two World Wars*. New Haven & London: Yale University Press, 1987; Lang, C., *Keep Smiling Through. Women in*

the Second World War. Cambridge: Cambridge University Press, 1989; Nicholson, M. '*What Did You Do in the War, Mummy?*' London: Chatto & Windus, 1995; Sheridan, D. (ed.), *Wartime Women*. London: Heinemann Ltd, 1990. Sheridan, D., 'Ambivalent Memories: Women and the 1939–45 War in Britain' in *Oral History*. Vol. 18, No. 1, Spring 1990. pp. 32–40; Summerfield, P., 'Women Workers in the Second World War'. *Capital and Class*. Vol. 1, 1972. pp. 27–42, and *Reconstructing Women's Wartime Lives*. Manchester and New York: Manchester University Press, 1998.

38 Sheridan (ed.), *Wartime Women*, and Hartley, J., (ed.) *Hearts Undefeated*.

39 Barrett Litoff, J., and Smith, D.C., 'US Women on the Home Front in World War II' in *The Historian*. Vol. 57, No. 2, December 1995. p. 357.

40 Jolly, M. '*Dear Laughing Motorbyke: Letters from Women Welders of the Second World War*'. London: Scarlet Press, 1997. p. 45; and Braybon and Summerfield. *Out of the Cage*. p. 287.

41 Only in the 1970s did the experiences of prisoner of war wives and their particular problems begin to be recognised as worthy of study in their own right, and then by a discipline other than history. See for example: McCubbin, H.I., Dahl, B.B., Lester, G.R., Benson, D., and Robertson, M.L., 'Coping Repertoires of Families Adapting to Prolonged War-induced Separation' in *Journal of Marriage and the Family*. August 1976, pp. 461–471; MacIntosh, H., 'Separation Problems in Military Wives' in *American Journal of Psychiatry*. Vol. 125, No. 2, 1968, pp. 260–265; Rey, D.R., and Lange, J., 'Waiting Wives: Women Under Stress' in *American Journal of Psychiatry*. Vol. 131, No. 3, March 1974. pp. 283–286; and McCubbin, H.I., Hunter, E.J. and Dahl, B.B., 'Residuals of War: Families of Prisoners of War and Servicemen Missing in Action' in *Journal of Social Issues*. Vol. 31, No. 4, 1975. pp. 95–109.

42 Despite the diverse ways in which men became prisoners of war, including cases where they were surrendered en masse by their commanders, the government made no distinction in the treatment of their families.

43 SHAEF Papers. Tables of Organisation, POW Executive NA/WO219/1402. Imperial POW Committee Minutes NA/WO163.

44 Satow, Sir H., and Sée, M.J., *The Work of the Prisoners of War Department during the Second World War*. London: Foreign Office, 1950; Cambray, P.G., and Briggs, G.G.B., *Red Cross and St. John. The Official Record of the Humanitarian Services of the War Organisation of the British Red Cross Society and Order of St. John of Jerusalem, 1939–1947*. London: Sumfield & Day Ltd, 1949.

45 Satow and Sée. *The Work of the POW Department*. p. 6.
46 Rolf, D., ' "Blind Bureaucracy": The British Government and Prisoners of War in German Captivity, 1939 –1945' in Moore and Fedorowich, *Prisoners of War and Their Captors*. p. 55.
47 Gardner, Ministry of Defence, quoted by Rolf, 'Blind Bureaucracy' fn. 28 p. 65 in Moore and Fedorowich, *Prisoners of War and Their Captors*. As an example of this unreliability, the report refers to the report 'Work in Connection with Prisoners of War from August 1914 to January 1919' as the 'Billfold Report' when the report is actually known as the 'Belfield Report'. Phillimore Report p. 6 NA/WO366/26.
48 NA/AST11/122–157. Files AST11/129 (Territorial Army Proficiency Grants), /130 (Service in HM Forces – 'Normal Occupation' Qualifications'), /141, /147 (Agricultural Occupations), /153 (Personnel of HM Forces and Auxiliary Services: Civil Liabilities Scheme), /154 (Personnel of HM Forces and Other Forms of National Service: Scheme for Resettlement Grants) and /156 (Service in HM Forces: Scope of Position of Commissioned Officers following Discharge) were not utlilised in this study.
49 Records of these discussions can be found in NA/T162/470/E19544/1 and 2.
50 UAB Pamphlet DP25. 18/12/39. NA/AST11/39.
51 Deed of Trust relating to the Barnsley and District Prisoners of War Fund, Borough Secretary's Department, Town Hall, Barnsley, South Yorks.
52 Details of this campaign and the history of service widows' pensions in general can be found in Lomas, J., *War Widows in British Society, 1914–90*. Unpublished PhD thesis. University of Stafford, 1997.
53 O'Bierne, K.P., 'Waiting Wives' in *United States Naval Institute Proceedings*. Vol. 102, September 1976. pp. 28–37.
54 Moore and Fedorowich, *Prisoners of War and Their Captors*. p. 7.

1

'No such useless appendage' – the state and service families before 1939

Traditionally, the British government did not see the wives and families of servicemen as part of the state's responsibility. Instead this responsibility was devolved to the individual services themselves who, in their turn, took steps to limit their involvement with the well-being of wives and families. Although some changes in this attitude became apparent during the nineteenth century, it was only with the deployment of troops in colonial wars at the end of the century and, more forcefully, with the impact of the First World War that this situation began to be reappraised.

From the beginning of the modern British army in the seventeenth century, marriage for soldiers was discouraged and responsibility for the welfare and well-being of servicemen's families was slow to be acknowledged. Indeed, this responsibility was 'not so much evaded as unrecognised' especially for lower ranks with the army expressing the view that 'subalterns must not marry, captains may marry, majors should marry, colonels must marry'.[1] The views of the navy were equally explicit in the late 1880s, as the service officially recognised 'no such useless appendage or encumbrance' as a sailor's wife; at least not below the rank of Admiral, at which stage wives were acknowledged as being a useful accessory for social purposes.[2] Similarly, in the army, increased rank led to increased responsibility for men and a perceived need of a wife to augment the officer's work and 'contribute her special brand of feminine care'.[3] This attitude may well, however, have been attributable to a wish on the part of both services to avoid any responsibility for the welfare of servicemen's families, a responsibility which would have had to have been acknowledged if formal recognition of marriage had been granted.

Despite this official attitude, a study of women at sea in the age of sail records that ships' captains routinely recognised the status of sailors' wives.[4] For example, many captains permitted wives to be ferried out to ships in the Pool of London to spend time with their husbands who were refused shore leave.[5] However, responsibility for the welfare of families was largely regarded by the services as being the province of the serviceman himself. The decision to allot money from pay to families, or not, was left to their discretion and there can be no doubt that a number of men deliberately joined the colours to escape both financial and moral family responsibilities. The words of an eighteenth-century army song tell of men leading happier lives 'by getting rid of brats and wives' as until 1873 soldiers, unlike civilians, could not be charged under the vagrancy laws with failure to maintain their wives and families.[6]

Even in the latter part of the nineteenth century, the only existing provision for family welfare within the armed services was that for army wives 'on the strength' (that is, married with the express permission of the soldier's commanding officer), legitimate children and legitimate stepchildren.[7] However, in the late 1880s and early 1890s, only six men per company of one hundred were granted permission to marry, and then rarely below the rank of Senior Non-commissioned Officer (NCO).[8] Figures for 1861 show that only 48.31 per cent of other ranks under the age of 40 were married compared to 82.59 per cent in the general population.[9] However, the British army was not unusual in this practice. In Canada, where compulsory military service was in force, a similar situation existed and young men were not expected to marry before this service was complete; as late as 1914 permission for other ranks to marry was granted only where there was a vacancy on the married establishment and where the woman was judged to be 'a desirable character'. In practice this resulted in all warrant officer and sergeants being granted permission and only 8 per cent of other ranks.[10] In Britain, the granting of permission to marry was limited not only by the discretion of commanding officers but also by individual regimental practice and the availability of accommodation. In some regiments more soldiers were granted permission to marry than in others. In the Guards, for example, who rarely moved establishments and who were sent abroad only in emergencies, more men were granted permission to marry than was the norm in other regiments who moved more frequently.[11] Sidney Herbert, Secretary of

State for War in 1854, regarded wives as a 'serious evil for a marching army'.[12]

In the late nineteenth century normal practice was still for a number of families, chosen by ballot, to travel with the regiment whenever it was posted away from home, although the Crimea was the last war in which families actually followed their menfolk into a battle zone.[13] The number of families allowed to travel differed according to the actual destination. For regiments leaving for service in India, twelve families were allowed to travel per hundred men; for all other destinations the number of families was limited to six per hundred men.[14] Even recognised 'on the strength' families left behind were not encouraged to remain in the regimental town whilst their husbands were absent. Instead they were provided with a meagre allowance of 1 guinea, plus 5s for every child, to allow them to return to their home parish.[15] In Irish regiments who were 'much married' the situation was often extreme, and from one battalion alone more than four hundred women and their children were sent back to Ireland.[16] Once home, however, there was no guarantee that their relatives would be able to provide for them. With increased industrialisation came a breaking down of the traditional family autonomy in providing care for the very young, the old and the destitute, and the increasing mobility of labour meant that those remaining at home might themselves be in need of care. Many army wives then had to appeal to the Poor Law Commissioners for outdoor relief to allow them to survive until the regiment returned home.[17] Unacknowledged 'off the strength' wives were not granted even this minimal allowance and so were forced to remain, without any means of support, in the regimental towns.

By the latter part of the nineteenth century, the only type of allowance granted to the families of servicemen when separated from their menfolk was a 'one-off' payment to allow them to return to their former homes. No provision was made, by means of an ongoing allowance, for them to maintain the home they had established with their husbands. Although the question of separation allowances had been raised within the War Office, and a Board of General Officers set up in 1810 to investigate the possibilities, no proposals for such allowances were devised for over fifty years.[18] Neither the government nor the services recognised any responsibility to provide continuing support for the families of those fighting for their country. Women were recognised by the army only through the men to whom they were married. As a result, once the men were posted overseas, the women effectively disappeared from official view. Where servicemen themselves had not made financial provision for their families or where this provision fell short of need or broke down completely, families faced destitution. Until the mid-1800s the army argued that a soldier's pay was intended solely for his own upkeep although not to be spent as the soldier wished. Instead it was intended to be used to maintain himself as an efficient fighting member of the service.[19] Compulsory stoppages from service pay to maintain wives and children were not introduced into the Army Act until 1878, and then only to give service wives parity with the non-maintenance claim available to civilians whose husbands did not provide for them.[20]

Given this minimal level of welfare provision, and the vagaries of Poor Law provision, it is clear that many families were forced to rely on philanthropic organisations to avoid hardship, if not actual starvation. Although within the army some provision was made at regimental level, this was largely dependent on the sympathies and traditions of individual regiments. Guards regiments, who had an 'impressive array of funds' at their disposal were, perhaps, the most solicitous of family welfare, setting up a Work Society to provide employment for 'on the strength' wives left behind.[21] In many other cases responsibility for family welfare was often left to the regiment's commanding officer and his wife. Even during the Second World War, these same attitudes were apparent and officers were expected to adopt a paternalistic attitude to the men in their care and, by extension, to their families. However, the very real needs that led to the founding in 1885 of the Soldiers' and Sailors' Family Association (SSFA; after 1919, the Soldiers' Sailors' and Air Force Families Association, SSAFA) suggest that in many cases this informal provision proved inadequate to meet the needs of the families concerned.[22] Given the fact that the very existence of sailors' wives remained unrecognised, it is perhaps not surprising that no similar tradition of care existed in the navy. However, some organisations, such as the Royal British Female Orphan Asylum in Devonport, offered care to the orphans of both soldiers and sailors.

In fact, although service wives remained largely unrecognised whilst their husbands were alive, some provision for widows had existed since 1646. In that year a committee of the House of Commons ordered that an allowance of £40 per week, originally paid to the Earl of Mulgrove, was, following his death, to be made available for the use of soldiers' widows.[23] The impact of this measure is difficult to assess, as there is no further detail of the administration of this allowance or any claims made on it. Although this action does suggest some government acknowledgement of responsibility for army widows that did not exist for wives, it is worth noting that the committee considered that a sum previously allocated to one man was now sufficient to fulfil the needs of all army widows. Whilst husbands remained alive, however, both the government and the services themselves remained reluctant to become involved in what they continued until the end of the Second World War to regard as domestic matters. This applied especially in the case of officers, where such action might be seen as casting doubt on their integrity by suggesting that they had not made adequate arrangements for the care of their families. In fact, by the beginning of the eighteenth century, officers were themselves raising money both officially and unofficially for widows' pensions. All officers were obliged to pay a tax, which was directed into a regimental widows' fund.[24] Additionally, many regiments instituted a 'Widows' Man', whereby a fictitious officer drew statutory pay which was then paid into a widows' fund.[25] For naval widows, however, pensions of any kind were not established in Britain until the late nineteenth century. In comparison, Paul Zumthor notes that in the Netherlands, another major European seafaring nation at the time, pensions had been paid to the widows and orphans of all sailors from the seventeenth century onwards.[26] This provision may, however, reflect the nature of sailors' employment in the Netherlands where employers were more likely to be individual cities or trading companies rather than a national navy.

In 1854, following the outbreak of the Crimean War, there was, for the first time in Britain, an appreciation of 'the non-military factors involved in victory in war', including recognition that the morale and efficiency of an army could be affected by the emotional state of its soldiers.[27] The necessity to recruit an expeditionary force of some 27,000 men led, through sheer weight of numbers, to an increased visibility of service families and a concern that the families of those fighting in a patriotic cause should be seen to be cared for whilst their menfolk were absent. In 1834 a Royal Commission on the Poor Laws and the resulting Poor Law Amendment Act had, in theory, abolished outdoor relief.[28] This abolition was intended to encourage more able-bodied, unemployed men to persevere in their endeavours to find work by making the workhouse the only alternative. However, the Commission failed to take into account the question of destitute women who made up the major proportion of adult recipients. Service wives, in particular, posed a problem in the light of this reform. On the one hand, as able-bodied adults they fell into the category of those expected to find work or obtain relief only in the workhouse. On the other hand, as wives of soldiers defending the Empire, they were seen as deserving of more dignified and considerate treatment than other paupers. In fact the abolition of outdoor relief was largely ineffective and, between 1859 and 1874, most paupers were still provided with relief outside the workhouse.[29] Eventually, in the early 1870s, the regulations were tightened still further sharpening the definition between 'undeserving' poor who could only find relief in the workhouses and the 'deserving' poor who were increasingly cared for by philanthropic agencies.[30] By 1856, 2,794 families of men serving in the Crimea were still able to claim outdoor relief.[31] Trustram claims that 'as helpmates of the defenders of the nation, separated wives and children were seen to be particularly deserving of aid'.[32]

For the first time a cyclical pattern, apparent up to the end of the Second World War, becomes clear whereby provision for families became a matter for public concern when it might affect both recruitment and the efficiency of servicemen. Indeed, provision for families became a particularly important issue when length of service was taken into consideration. Although after 1847 enlistment for life was no longer the norm, length of enlistment still remained at 21 years for the infantry and 24 years for other corps.[33] In this length of service a man could expect to be posted overseas a number of times and so care of his family whilst he was away became especially important. However, this heightened public concern did not lead directly to demands for service welfare provision to become a government concern. Instead, coupled with a general Victorian interest in philanthropic causes, it led rather to an increase in charitable provision, largely through the contemporary perception that philanthropic support arose from 'pure' motives and, as such, was acceptable to families. By contrast, support originating from institutional or governmental sources, be it central government such as the War Office or local government such as the Poor Law Commissioners, was regarded as having a stigma attached to it and was, therefore, less acceptable.[34] Philanthropic agencies claimed to spare families the degradation of accepting such demeaning and impersonal assistance. One must suspect, however, that many destitute and starving 'off the strength' families would have been grateful to receive support from any quarter, impersonal or not.

Both the Central Association for the Aid of Wives and Families of Soldiers Ordered to the East (CA), which operated from 1854 to 1957, and the Royal Patriotic Fund set up in 1854 to provide for widows and orphans of the Crimean War, grew from this concern to help service families who, for whatever reason, were unable to support themselves.[35] At the same time, however, these institutions were at some pains not to undermine the self-help ethic of the period. Skelley records that allowances made by the Royal Patriotic Fund were 'ungenerous' and that most of its income 'went unspent because its Commissioners were so parsimonious'.[36] In addition support was generally not given to families as a right. Instead the CA aimed to provide only temporary relief whilst women were helped to obtain work.[37] In this way families were encouraged to maintain their self-reliance and independence. In contrast, state allowances were viewed by these institutions as lessening the will of families to help themselves, so robbing them of both their will to work and their independence. It should be noted, however, that in all cases children were regarded as truly deserving and received unconditional relief whether or not their mothers were deemed worthy of support.[38]

As a further development of this concern, in 1885 Colonel James Gildea established SSFA to care for the families of both soldiers and sailors.[39] The impetus for this decision was largely a response to the embarkation of large numbers of troops for Egypt following the siege of Khartoum, again raising the profile of service families. Although the principle of self-help remained operative, SSFA was the first organisation to view the poverty of service wives as an outcome of military service rather than as fault on their part. Gildea's particular concern focused on 'off the strength' wives and other dependants, especially aged parents who had been economically dependent on their sons.[40] That having been said, the Association continued to promote independence where possible. All relief was granted temporarily and local committees carried out checks on how aid was spent.[41] Again, officers' wives were encouraged to take part in this provision to help maintain links between the regiment and the families concerned.

In all cases, however, the amount of aid that could be provided by charitable institutions was dependent on the amount of money donated by the public. In times of war, service families achieved a high profile through the need to increase recruitment figures and to ensure that men serving overseas were not rendered ineffective by concern for their families. For Britain, the only major European power without a conscripted army, the question of how to encourage men to volunteer was a critical one.[42] Other European powers, such as the German states, which conscripted men into their armies, were under some obligation to provide for their families as joining the army was not a matter of free choice or even conviction on the part of the men conscripted.[43] Despite this, Daniel suggests that even here the objective of Family Aid was to 'foster the soldiers' readiness for action through financial support of war families'.[44]

In Prussia, then, in the early part of the nineteenth century, although financial provision for service families was on a voluntary basis, it was not the responsibility of the men themselves. Instead it was the responsibility of local communities to provide assistance for the dependants of their conscripted soldiers.[45] However, this provision, and that of the private aid organisations which supplemented it, proved inadequate and, in 1850, a Prussian law ruled that administrative districts and free cities should pay a minimum financial contribution to the families of all conscripts in their charge.[46] In addition to the wives and children of Territorial Army troops or conscript reserves, other dependants such as siblings and children over 14 could receive aid if they could prove that the draftee had previously supported them.[47] In 1867 this law was extended to the North German Confederation and, later, to a number of southern German states.[48] Generally, districts and states were not reimbursed by the Reich for their expenditure on Family Aid, causing conflict with Article 58 of the imperial constitution that stipulated that the Reich should bear the costs of waging war.[49] To correct this anomaly a new draft of the Family Aid Law, the Law Concerning the Support of Families of Conscripted Men, was passed in 1888 which recognised, in theory, the Reich's obligation to reimburse this aid.[50] In addition to increasing the minimum allowance paid to families, the law also increased the categories of dependants eligible for allowances to include parentless grandchildren and illegitimate children not fathered by the conscript brought into the marriage by his wife. Largely, this law remained unchanged throughout the period of the First World War although the minimum level was further increased.[51] In addition aid was also granted to the families of more marginal service personnel, such as cooks employed by the army.[52] In this way, Family Aid in Germany became a much more universal condition than Family Allowances ever were in Britain. By the end of 1915, 4 million families were receiving war-related family support and, by 1917, almost one-third of all German households were receiving government assistance.[53]

On the face of it then, Britain was almost half a century late to acknowledge state responsibility for service families compared with its major protagonist in both World Wars. However, in Germany, acknowledgement of a responsibility to provide Family Aid did not necessarily translate directly into adequate financial support for the families concerned. The main problem was that, although the Reich had made the decision to grant Family Aid, it lacked the necessary administrative structure to be able to deliver the aid itself. Instead responsibility for raising the money required to pay allowances and their administration was devolved to the cities and districts concerned, who took every opportunity to reduce the expenditure required to meet this commitment.[54] Consequently levels of allowances, above the bare minimum laid down centrally, varied from area to area and in many cases service families still suffered severe deprivation as local communities pared down payments wherever possible. As a result many soldiers felt that they had been betrayed by the state and that the implicit contract whereby the government agreed to provide adequately for their families whilst they, themselves, served their country had been broken.[55]

In Britain, where men were free to volunteer or not, a decision to join the armed services must have been influenced by considerations of how their families would fare in the man's absence. As no governmental support in the form of established allowances for families existed in the nineteenth century, the role of philanthropic agencies remained crucial, if not always completely altruistic. As Trustram suggests, 'to help a soldier's dependent relatives was to help the soldier himself and to help the country'.[56] In this way philanthropic impulses may be seen as somewhat self-serving in that they served to ensure that those remaining in Britain were protected by an army who could concentrate their minds on the task in hand. As we shall see in later chapters, the exact correlation between perceived state care of service families and the willingness of men to enlist continued to inform discussions surrounding service families well into the twentieth century. There is no accurate way of estimating the actual number of families in Britain, either 'on' or 'off the strength', who were aided by philanthropic relief or of estimating the actual amount of funds distributed. However, at a time when responsibility for service dependants was gradually being hived off by the Poor Law Commissioners but not yet being fully accepted by the War Office, there can be little doubt that its role must have been substantial. By 1899, SSFA alone had provided assistance for ten thousand families and, with the start of the Boer War in October of that year, further demands were made on its resources as many soldiers about to leave on active service 'rushed into marriage'.[57] During the three years and three months of the war, SSFA gave financial assistance amounting to over £1.25 million to 206,438 dependants and widows.[58]

In general, this pattern of voluntary care remained operative throughout the early years of the twentieth century. Lord Justice Henn Collins's Committee of Enquiry into charitable funds identified three general classes of funds operating at this time.[59] First came funds for the wives and dependants of living soldiers and sailors, with SSFA being the most important organisation operating in this sphere. The other two groups dealt with funds for the dependants of those who had died in service and with funds for the dependants of the sick and wounded who had been invalided or discharged home. Although, as we have already seen, these funds were dependent on public caprice, the scale of fundraising and the amounts raised in times of patriotic fervour should not be underestimated. In January 1901, when SSFA funds were running precariously low, the Princess of Wales made an appeal on their behalf and £300,000 was subscribed.[60] Again, the emphasis was placed on the peace of mind of the servicemen rather than on the needs of the families in their own right. Field Marshal Earl Roberts, on his return from South Africa, commented that 'nothing had cheered the hearts of our soldiers . . . more than the knowledge that those who are nearest and dearest to them are being cared for in their absence by their fellow countrymen and women'.[61]

By 1901, however, and largely as the result of alleged misman-
agement of Royal Patriotic Fund moneys, recommendations were
beginning to be made for the administration of funds to be put on
a more formal basis answerable to central government,[62] an action
that can be regarded as laying the foundation for state welfare
provision for service families. Despite this initiative, however, and
despite claims that the twentieth century 'opened with a wide and
soundly established measure of social care for the soldier's family',
the scope of this provision remained severely limited.[63] 'Off the
strength' army wives, dependent parents and all seamen's wives all
remained totally dependent on charitable provision.

Throughout the Victorian period the relationship between the
army and the wives of its servicemen had remained a source of
conflict. On the one hand, wives and children were seen as a mill-
stone around the army's neck. On the other, a wife and family
provided a means of regularising sexual relations and promoting
the dominant Victorian domestic ideology.[64] With the recognition
of the part played by families in influencing the morale and effectiveness of servicemen, the War Office was forced to reconsider its
responsibilities to families as a means of promoting an efficient
army. As a result payments made to wives moved from the original
granting of a minimal amount, sufficient for them to return to their
home parishes, towards more formalised allowances in times of
separation. In 1871 Separation Allowances were listed in regulations for the first time when wives were granted an allowance of
3d daily for themselves and a further small allowance for any children so that the family could remain in barracks whilst the regiment
moved for training.[65] Still the army remained reluctant to take over
all responsibility for the welfare of families. By 1882 men were
required to allot a portion of their pay towards the maintenance of
their families when separated before any official allowances could
be granted, and this use of allotment as a trigger remained in effect
with the exception of two periods during the World Wars when the
regulation was lifted.[66] However, although families could increasingly look towards the army for welfare, in return the army used
the provision of allowances as a way of regulating families' lives.
Allowances were granted as 'privileges' and 'indulgences' rather
than as a right of the family and could be withdrawn for perceived
misconduct. For example, the 82nd Regiment of Foot kept a 'Wives
Punishment Book' between 1866 and 1895 where misconduct was

listed.[67] Although the most common offences were drunkenness, abusive language and creating a disturbance, allowances were also stopped for refusing to obey a sergeant's orders. In extreme cases, wives could be struck 'off the strength' and forced to resort once again to charity. In Canada at the time, this requirement extended to the granting of pensions. Here widows of permanent soldiers who had died in the North West Campaign in 1885 were granted pensions of half-pay for husbands who had died in action, subject to good behaviour.[68]

In the ten years of peace following the end of the Second Anglo-Boer War, public attention inevitably shifted away from the plight of service families. Although a number of regimental associations were established, by and large their concern was with ex-servicemen, rather than with the families of those still serving.

Despite the fact that the period after the 1906 general election saw a number of major social reforms introduced, these did not extend to service families as a distinct group. The introduction of a first scheme for old age pensions in 1908, unemployment insurance from 1908 and the 1911 National Insurance Act did not form a comprehensive welfare policy, and the Poor Law, albeit that its role had clearly decreased, still had a part to play. Although from 1910 to 1914 the numbers assisted by the Poor Law decreased from 916,000 to 748,000, this change largely reflects the number of elderly men and women who now received old age pensions rather than outdoor relief.[69]

In 1906, the difficulties that had been faced in raising a sufficient army for the South African War, coupled with the greater potential for continental European commitments, led Richard Haldane, the new Secretary of State for War, to announce a series of army reforms. Broadly speaking the main issue faced was that of the 'unpreparedness' of the army in that no effective Expeditionary Force existed and it was estimated at the time that to put 80,000 men on the continent would take at least two months.[70] Haldane aimed to provide an Expeditionary Force that 'could be mobilised and sent to the place where it might be required as rapidly as any German force could be'.[71] Essentially, his reforms amalgamated the existing three strands of the army – the professional, the militia (semi-professional) and the volunteers – into two new strands: the professional and the non-professional comprising the militia, yeomanry and volunteers. As a result, the volunteer organisations, 'possibly the most confused thing we have in the British constitution', largely as a result of being paid in 22 different ways, and everything 'merely for show and not useful for war' were cut down in an attempt to reduce costs.[72] However, neither these major changes to army structure nor an increased focus on naval refurbishment with the introduction of the Dreadnoughts allowed for any attention to be paid to how the families of the families of the servicemen needed for these reforms would be supported if a new conflict arose.[73]

Only with the advent of the First World War, and the necessity for large-scale recruitment, did service families again become an issue for public concern. In *The Politics of Influence*, Wootton suggests that the general unpreparedness of the country for the nature of this war was nowhere more evident that in the 'misfortunes of those families left high and dry by mobilisation'.[74]

As the need to ensure recruitment increased, governmental awareness once again focused on the barrier to enlistment created by the absence of welfare for the families left behind. Sir Arthur Markham, Labour MP for Mansfield, speaking in the House of Commons in August 1914, voiced this widely held concern, stating that it was 'The duty of government to provide sufficient funds so that the wives and children of these men should be maintained in a state of citizenship while their husbands are fighting at the front'.[75] As a result, the distinction between 'on' and 'off the strength' army marriages was abolished on 10 August 1914 and, for the first time, both family and separation allowances were granted to seamen's wives.[76]

The problem now became one of administration rather than conviction. At the outbreak of war, 1,500 soldiers' wives were eligible for allowances; two weeks later this figure had risen to 250,000 for the army alone.[77] By the beginning of September this already overstretched pay system also had to expand further to include provision for navy wives. In addition, payment of funds was often delayed by the fact that voluntary funds, administered by separate bodies, were needed to supplement these flat-rate allowances. Indeed, by July 1916, no fewer than five official bodies were involved in this administration procedure, including the Old Age Pensions Committee, who had overall responsibility for assessing levels of dependency for all dependants other than wives.[78] In the first two years of the war this administrative Gordian knot caused

inevitable delays in payment of allowances with the result that a
number of families remained totally dependent on charitable assistance. However, by 1917, the state was paying a total of 3.5 million
separation allowances regularly.[79] Of these, 90 per cent were paid
to soldiers' families – 47 per cent to wives and 53 per cent to other
dependants, most often dependent mothers who were receiving
allowances for the first time.[80]

In *The Politics of Influence*, Wootton suggests that, during a
major war, areas regarded as 'proper' for government concern
change with the result that people who have previously been ignored
now come 'within the ambit of government for the first time'.[81]
Thomas also argues that a 'relatively coherent system of state
welfare' had been devised for soldiers' and sailors' families.[82]
However, interdependency still existed between state involvement
and voluntary organisations. Contemporary critics argued that the
use of the existing institutional structures of philanthropic organisations to administer an allowance scheme seemed to perpetuate the
attitude that these were given as a charitable act rather than as an
inalienable right.[83] A Ministry of Pensions warrant of 1917 states
that allowances and pensions 'shall not be claimed as a right but
shall be given as a reward for service'.[84] The perception of Family
Allowances in Germany again provides a useful comparison here.
In Germany, the fact that the necessary finance to pay allowances
was raised by the local community led, if anything, to an even closer
monitoring of service wives' behaviour than in Britain.[85] Public
opinion within these communities was particularly critical of any
conspicuous spending, and Daniel quotes an example from Saxony-
Weimar where wives were criticised for going to the theatre as such
spending was 'not compatible with the objectives of assistance'.[86]
At the same time, the state expressed the opinion that Family Aid
was not a state charity but the 'fulfilment of a moral claim' and the
wives concerned therefore came to regard such aid as an entitlement
and developed a 'self-conscious and demanding attitude' towards
the authorities granting it.[87] Daniel goes on to claim that, despite
the fact that service wives may have found humiliating the investigations into their financial circumstances necessary for aid to be
granted, they nevertheless gained greater confidence from their
status as war wives.[88] Although in Britain such financial investigations were unnecessary for wives to be able to claim Family
Allowance, at the same time allowances never became a right, and

wives were never able to express dissatisfaction with allowances in a similarly forthright manner.

Gradually, however, a slow change took place in public perception of where responsibility for the welfare of service families lay, and public perception of stigma attached to accepting state welfare shifted. Philanthropic relief, originally seen as more acceptable, now became less so, to the extent that families who, largely through administrative ineptitude and delays in the payments, had been dependent at some stage of the war on Poor Relief, were able to ask for their names to be removed from the records.[89] SSFA, which had previously stressed that their assistance should be viewed as 'help given by friends to friends' now recognised that charitable funds were in danger of being regarded as being given for the benefit of one class 'at the discretion of a different class'.[90] With the looming General Election of 1918, the whole question of state care of service families took on an extra importance. Politicians assumed that men returning from active service would not vote to retain a government that had failed in its promises to take care of their families whilst they were serving their country. As a result of this sustained postwar interest in service families, the level of weekly allowances continued to increase until January 1919.[91] This resulted in an overall increase for army wives without children of 12 per cent, from 11s in 1914 to 12s 6d, with no distinction made between 'on' and 'off the strength' wives.[92] In real terms, however, these increases fell a long way short of allowing army families to keep pace with a rising cost of living. Between 1914 and 1919 the purchasing power of the pound fell by over 50 per cent.[93]

For navy wives without children the increase was, on the face of it, much more dramatic – from no allowances at all in the first part of 1914, to 11s per week in January 1919 although, as we have already seen, this level of allowances still did not provide for an adequate standard of living.[94] Despite this, the government regarded itself as having been 'exceedingly generous throughout the war' although separation allowances in the UK remained consistently lower than those paid by Canada, Australia and the United States to the families of their servicemen.[95] In Germany, although the minimum level of Family Aid increased by over 100 per cent during the course of the war, inflation was much greater and many of the agencies responsible took every step possible to minimise the actual amount they paid to service families.[96] One such strategy was to include all earned income against Family Aid payments, despite the fact that such a strategy was in direct contradiction to the state's policy that those receiving aid should not be discouraged from taking up employment in war industries. As a result many urban families in particular, faced with spiralling cost-of-living increases, were unable to make ends meet.[97] Bessel claims that the deterioration in German civilian diet 'clearly affected' mortality levels during the second half of the First World War, citing the rise in deaths amongst women from both tuberculosis and pneumonia together with the figure of 102,130 women who died in the influenza epidemic of 1918.[98]

By the end of October 1920 the British government had ended payment of all Separation Allowances. The term, however, continued in common usage up to 1939, causing widespread confusion. In the introduction to a House of Commons debate in December of that year a note on the nomenclature reads 'the term "separation allowance", though widely used in connexion [*sic*] with serving soldiers, does not seem to have any precise meaning'.[99] In the army, it was replaced by a Marriage Allowance, payable to the wives and children of regular soldiers, a move that the navy soon followed.[100] However, the confusion that had resulted from the lack of preparation for the administration of service allowances during the war was not totally forgotten, at least not by the philanthropic organisations which had been caught up in its effects. Sir George Wickham Legg, Secretary of SSAFA, writing to the Ministry of Pensions in 1924, recollected 'the chaotic state of affairs in regard to the issue of Separation Allowances at the outbreak of war in August 1914'.[101] Sir George Chrystal, Wickham Legg's correspondent at the Ministry, agreed with this recollection, regarding it as 'essential that advances should be forthcoming without delay in the event of men being called up'.[102] Wickham Legg's suggestion was that, in the event of a future war, Local War Pensions Committees should administer allowances, but this was strongly opposed by the Treasury.[103] Their view was that there was little danger of a similar situation recurring. As Marriage Allowance was now granted as a norm to regular servicemen, the administrative machinery for this was already in place and there was no certainty that Dependants' Allowances, payable to other dependants such as parents, would necessarily be granted in a future war. The War Office, in particular, regarded it purely a matter of ensuring that 'its machinery was in perfect working order' to guarantee that payment of allowances would be made promptly.[104]

On the question of Dependants' Allowances, the Interdepartmental Committee on Dependants' Allowances in Future Emergencies stated, in July 1925, that 'as long as only the regular forces are concerned, there will be no need for an allowance'.[105] However, this Report dealt only with dependants of 'other ranks'. In April 1926 the committee re-assembled to consider provision for dependants of officers together with the rates and conditions applicable to such allowances should the need arise.[106] No decisions were made at this meeting and, in fact, the question of Dependants' Allowances was never fully resolved and continued to be the subject of numerous inter-departmental discussions throughout the 1920s. The Ministry of Pensions also voiced concern about the granting of such allowances. Under the proposed scheme, allowances might be given to dependants who were not eligible for pensions, and the Ministry felt that this might create a *prima facie* case for the granting of pensions to these dependants.[107] In these discussions political awareness of the high profile of service families in time of war is clearly acknowledged. The Army Council in particular argued that, in the case of a future 'great' war, dependants' allowances and pensions were bound to be an important issue with all provision being 'subject to public criticism'.[108] In addition they suggested that it would not be enough to satisfy the 'peacetime demands of reason' but that any scheme must also 'make allowance for individuals on whose behalf war-time public opinion was likely to be sentimental'.[109]

All parties involved in these discussions felt that the huge expansion in personnel which would take place in the event of a future war necessitated that any scheme should have unanimous rather than majority agreement.[110] In particular, the huge expansion in army personnel that would take place in the event of a future war gave the opinions of the War Office added weight. In the light of this, no decisions could be taken which ran counter to War Office opinion. This dominance was reinforced when it was agreed that the Treasury and War Office, without consultation with the other services, should undertake preliminary discussions to outline an agreement. However the matter was not regarded as one of great urgency. Leslie Hore-Belisha, at the time Financial Secretary to the Treasury, suggested that such discussions should be postponed as the Treasury would be 'fully occupied with the Budget and Finance Bill'.[111] In the light of the contemporary economic situation this was a more than reasonable suggestion. With unemployment standing at three million and an estimated budget deficit for the year 1931–32 of £120 million, the government's attention was focused on more immediate national economic problems than preparation for a possible future conflict.[112]

Following the budget of 1933, representatives of the Treasury, the War Office and the Ministry of Pensions met again in an attempt to resolve the problem of how allowances should be administered in future conflicts, but their differences still proved irreconcilable.[113] So great was the disagreement that the War Office went so far as to produce two different drafts of a booklet covering the regulations governing dependants' allowances – one based on their own view and the other on that of the Treasury. Despite a professed opinion of the War Office that the departments concerned ought to be able to settle the matter 'without inflicting it on the Cabinet', no final decision had been made by June 1938.[114] With the likelihood of conflict increasing, charitable institutions again voiced their concern regarding arrangements for the administration of allowances. SSAFA went so far as to enquire of the Prime Minister whether, on the outbreak of war, the government actually proposed to grant Dependants' Allowances. This enquiry elicited the frosty reply that 'consideration had, of course, been given to this and similar matters' although it was 'impossible to give any indication of what the details of policy were likely to be.'[115]

The aim of both governmental discussions and concern from charitable organisations had been to settle the question of eligibility for, and administration of, service allowances so that the 'chaotic' situation, which had ensued in the First World War, was not repeated. Instead, fourteen years later, the situation remained unresolved. Not only were there no clear guidelines formulated for the administration of dependants' allowances, there were not even clear indications as to whether these allowances would be granted at all and, if granted, to whom.

The introduction of the Military Training Act, on 27 April 1939, further complicated the already confused picture. Regular servicemen were considered to have joined the services knowing the conditions under which they would be expected to serve, including those relating to families and allowances. Although wives and children received Marriage Allowance as a matter of course, arrangements for other dependants were the sole responsibility of the serviceman himself. However, the government recognised that amongst the 200,000 or so conscripts about to be 'swept willy-nilly into the services' some would already be the sole support for dependent relatives other than wives and children, and provision would have to be made to sustain these existing arrangements.[116] Accordingly, Dependants' Allowances were granted to cover this situation, although the calculations for these allowances were by no means straightforward. Indeed, the Defence Department of the Government of India, when considering the development of its own system for the administration of Dependants' Allowances in February 1941, examined the rules and systems in force in the UK and concluded that they were 'too complicated for application to India'.[117] Rates were calculated on the amount the serviceman had been contributing towards the upkeep of the dependant prior to conscription and were dependent on the men continuing to contribute an allotment from their pay of no less than 3s 6d per week.[118] If this condition was met, allowances then fell within three bands. For those who had been contributing more than 3s 6d per week but no more than 9s, an allowance was paid at the rate of 7s per week making a total of 10s 6d. For those who had been contributing more than 9s but no more than 15s, the allowance was 12s making a total of 15s 6d. For those contributing more than 15s per week, an allowance was given of 17s making a total of £1 0s 6d.[119] The proviso was also added that, in cases where dependants lived with others, such as other family members or lodgers, who might contribute to the total income of the household, no allowance would be paid if this income, after allowances for rent and other fixed costs, exceeded 15s per head.[120] Conversely, where a dependant lived alone, or in a household without other income, a special rate of £1 0s 6d was granted if it could be proved that the serviceman had been contributing at least this level of support before conscription.[121]

With the introduction of conscription, the question of Marriage Allowances also had to be re-assessed. In the regular forces this allowance was not paid to the families of army and air force servicemen under the age of 26 or families of sailors under the age of 25, although the Chancellor had already agreed to a reduction of these ages to 23 across the services.[122] Whilst regular servicemen were expected to take this factor into consideration when contem-

plating marriage, this could not be applied to men now being
conscripted. Indeed, the whole issue of the qualifying age for marriage allowances in the service had been a matter of some public
debate. The *News of the World*, in August 1937, carried an article
by a former Coldstream Guard asking 'Why prevent a healthy and
fit man from marrying until the age of 26'. The same article then
went on to claim 'surely a man in the army has as much right to
marry as a civilian'.[123] In fact, the Treasury estimated that one in
every 40 men in the general population in the 20–21 age group was
married.[124] The withholding of Family Allowance from the wives
of conscripted men under the age of 23 was recognised as being
likely to have a detrimental affect on morale. A paper for Cabinet
consideration in May 1939 stated that

> The Secretary of State for War is faced with the problem of raising
> some 75,000 recruits for the Regular Army in the near future and,
> though the number of married men in these low age groups is not
> great, it cannot be denied that the existence of a few married men
> ineligible for family allowance might have an adverse effect on
> recruiting quite out of proportion to their number.[125]

It should be noted that, although the decision had been taken by
the government a month earlier to introduce conscription, in this
paper the Treasury still referred to 'recruits' and a necessity to
persuade men to enlist although in the discussions of arrangements
for men called up under the Military Training Act a month earlier
they had referred to men being 'swept willy-nilly' into the services.
At the same time, allowances could not be granted to the wives of
conscripts under the age of 23, if they were denied to those of
regular servicemen below this age. As a result, in May 1939 the
qualifying age for Family Allowance across the services was lowered
to the age of 20.[126]

These adjustments to allowances were accordingly codified into
a white paper 'Allowances for Families and Dependants of Men
Serving in HM Forces during the Present War', presented to
Parliament on 28 November 1939 by Leslie Hore-Belisha, then
Secretary of State for War.[127] For Family Allowance, known in the
navy as Marriage Allowance, the qualifying age limit was suspended for the duration of the war. In all cases allowances remained
dependent on the serviceman allotting a portion of his pay to
his family according to rank and rate of pay. For example, for a

serviceman being paid less than 17s 6d per week but not less than 14s, the minimum allotment to family was set at 7s per week. This rose in stages to the rank of Warrant Officer Class I and II where minimum allotment was set at 28s per week.[128]

Dependants' Allowances were granted to wives, legitimate, legitimated and statutorily adopted children or legitimate stepchildren for whom Family Allowance was not issued, together with fathers, mothers (if the father was either not alive or incapable of self-support owing to infirmity or age), grandparents, step-parents, grandchildren, brothers and sisters (including half-brothers and sisters) plus foster parents, if they had supported the serviceman whilst a minor for no less than five years.[129] As can be seen from this list, once the decision had been taken to grant Dependants' Allowances, eligibility for these allowances was extended dramatically from that granted during the First World War. Whilst not made explicit in the regulations governing allowances, the intent was clear that this provision would also cater for illegitimate children although some administering authorities did not make such payments willingly. For example, a letter from the UAB District Officer in Dundee to the Secretary of the UAB at the Ministry of Pensions in London in May 1940 indicated that payments to illegitimate children were being refused and applicants advised to apply to the War Service Grants (WSG) Advisory Committee.[130] This Committee, an advisory committee of the Minister of Pensions, known until December 1939 as the Military Service (Special Allowances) Advisory Committee, had been established to administer special allowances which could be claimed in cases of financial hardship which were not covered by either Family or Dependants' Allowances. The Committee also dealt with other financial problems, that had arisen following the introduction of conscription for the families of those who were not regular servicemen. Many families had existing financial commitments based on their previous civilian wages, which they could not meet on service pay. Applications could be made to the Committee for additional payments of up to £2 per week to meet commitments such as hire purchase agreements, insurance payments or education expenses undertaken before call-up.[131] In contrast to cases where pension payments had come into effect, in these instances the Military Service (Special Allowances) Advisory Committee accepted that 'The separation of the man from his home is only temporary and the wife cannot be expected to reduce the standard of living to conform to the standard which might be expected in a permanent situation'.[132]

Administrators also had problems with another category of service dependants, namely those women who came to be known as 'unmarried' wives. In a number of cases, a man joining the forces claimed Family Allowance for a woman who later proved not to be his legal wife. Often these cases came to light only when the legal wife later made a claim for Family Allowance from the same man. Usually in these cases a man, separated from his legal wife, had established a home with another woman. Here the services found themselves in a difficult situation. On the one hand they did not wish to be seen as denying allowances to legal wives. On the other hand the War Office stated quite clearly that allowances were paid for 'the maintenance of the soldier's home and, in time of war in particular, made to enable the home to be kept up, to which the soldier would return when released from service'.[133] In the cases in question, clearly, the home to which the soldier would be returning was not that occupied by his legal wife. Despite many attempted solutions, the heated feelings surrounding these particular allowances meant that by 1942 the situation had still not been resolved and, indeed, resurfaced in postwar discussions on service allowances.[134] As a War Office spokesman suggested, 'This is a very tangled question in which the advocates of morality may possibly take one view and those of humanity another'.[135] In the event the War Office eventually took the humane view that allowances should be made, utilising both Family and Dependants' Allowance, to both women, stating 'in both cases we should relieve the hardship due to the man's being called up'.[136]

Similarly complex cases also arose in April 1940 when the Ministry of Pensions had to deal with a number of cases of hardship resulting from men being called up who were not wage earners at that time but who would have been within a 'measurable period'.[137] By and large these were sons who were undertaking an apprenticeship at the time of their call-up and who would have contributed to the upkeep of their parents after their training. In a number of these cases War Service Grant was allowed, limited to examples where serious financial hardship had resulted from debts incurred to meet training costs or where 'sacrifices' had been made and parents were now 'deprived of any reasonable prospect of comfort'.[138] As the *Yorkshire Post* suggested in June 1941, 'No scheme, however elastic, can hope to cover the multitudinous individual cases by a rigid laying down of regulations'.[139] For those involved in the drafting of these regulations, the task of attempting to cover all eventualities must have seemed analogous of that of Jason trying to sow the dragon's teeth.

In all cases, however, the whole system for claiming allowances often led to confusion for families and delays in the granting of allowances. For Family Allowance, a claim had to be submitted by the serviceman and then processed by the Regimental Paymaster, in the case of the army, and by the Director of Navy Accounts or the Director of Accounts, Air Ministry in the cases of the navy and the air force respectively.[140] Once this claim had been processed, a book of weekly drafts was sent to a nominated Post Office and a confirmatory form issued to the wife concerned. On presentation of this form at the relevant Post Office, signed and witnessed, the wife was issued with the book of drafts from which she could draw her allowances weekly, in advance. In an attempt to ensure that allowances were issued as quickly as possible once a man had been called up, claim forms were issued at the time of medical examination to be handed in, ready completed, when the man joined his regiment. In December 1939, this system was altered so that the completed form could be handed in at medical examination to further speed up the process. In cases where a man enlisted voluntarily, forms were originally given out at the time of enlistment, but this procedure was also changed so that forms could be given out at recruiting centres.[141]

For Dependants' Allowances, claims had to be provided both by the man himself, who had to consent to deductions from his pay, and from the dependant involved, giving details of their financial circumstances.[142] As all such claims were subject to investigation to confirm levels of dependency, these allowances took rather more time to process. As a result of this, delays occurred and many people applied to the UAB for temporary help under the government scheme for the prevention and relief of distress arising out of the war, which had originally been envisaged as providing temporary assistance to those whose homes had suffered bomb damage.[143] Relief was often granted until such time as allowances were cleared when the money would be recouped from the backdated allowances. Although these payments were supposedly strictly termed an 'interim payment', attempts to reclaim such temporary aid were largely unsuccessful as many recipients persisted in regarding them as an advance on their allowances rather than a separate payment.[144] However, it remains almost impossible to distinguish whether this was due to deliberate attempts to defraud the system, a failure to understand a far from accessible system or even the result of non-delivery of mail as a result of frequent relocations and evacuations. One example is that of the mother of a naval rating who claimed Dependants' Allowance on the grounds that her husband earned only 70s per week.[145] On investigation it was discovered that her husband's earnings were actually £7 per week, an amount well above the level of eligibility for such an allowance. Although an overpayment of approximately £20 had occurred before the true facts of the situation were discovered, it was impossible to reclaim the overpayment as the only person who could give evidence against the woman was her husband, and this was inadmissible in law. It should, however, also be noted that, given the social norms of the period, it was also quite possible that the woman was ignorant of the true level of her husband's income until the investigation took place.

In some cases, however, wives and dependants did make great efforts to pay back these advances, often at considerable hardship to themselves. In October 1939 Family Allowance drafts for a discharged air force aircraftman were not immediately withdrawn. As a result the wife of the aircraftman continued to draw an allowance of £1 16s 6d up to March 1940, an overpayment of £36 6s. When applied to for repayment, the wife agreed to make payments at £1 per week until the full amount had been repaid.[146]

The UAB also played a vital role in the normal administration of Dependants' Allowances by carrying out the investigations into family circumstances necessary before such an allowance could be granted.[147] Completed forms for Dependants' Allowance, as was the case originally for Family Allowances, were forwarded to the Regimental Paymaster. However, in December 1939 these arrangements were changed, as they had been for Family Allowances, so that forms completed at the time of medical examination could be send direct to the local office of the UAB in an attempt to speed up investigations.[148] There can be no doubt that often these investigations caused resentment. Although families or dependants may well have supported the enlistment of their breadwinners, many felt that they now had a clear right to allowances as recompense. Any enquiry into their financial circumstances could appear as a suggestion that they were deliberately trying to defraud the services, and the details required by the investigators meant that other members of the household also had to answer searching questions as to their financial status.

Although by April 1941 the regulations governing the award of Dependants' Allowances had been revised so that the UAB was no longer required to ascertain the actual amount of income of all members of the household, the investigation remained searching.[149] The form itself was divided into six parts. Details of the dependants themselves, their wives or husbands and all their children under 16 years of age, both resident in the house and evacuated, plus any children to whom the dependants stood in the relationship of parent, had to be entered in Section A. Two further sections required details of the gross income, and its source, for each member of the household plus details of their relationship to the dependant. Household members who had no or 'insubstantial' resources were also required to state how long they had been resident in the household and how they had been maintained before the serviceman was called for service. The dependants themselves also had to provide details of any income from capital such as Post Office savings or government stock and to state if they actually paid the rent and whether or not this included furnishings, light and heat. Where the dependant was a boarder, the actual amount paid in board and lodgings was required.[150] Even in cases where these details were fully completed, difficulties often arose when the investigators tried to verify the information.

In June 1939, the District Officer of the UAB in Leeds reported local difficulties in assessing incomes in households where some members were employed intermittently in local collieries.[151] The problem arose because the local colliery company, Airedale Collieries Co. Ltd, proposed to make a charge of 6d for each enquiry. The local UAB had refused to pay this fee, taking the view that 'employers should be ready to do without payment something which is in the public interest'.[152] Although the Colliery Company eventually 'expressed their willingness to co-operate', their attitude had resulted in yet another delay in the payment of allowances to needy families.[153] In other cases resolution of the problems proved to be impossible. In the case of dependants of crofters from the

Scottish Isles claiming either Dependants' Allowances or WSG allowances, no accurate way was ever established to verify the previous earnings of the crofts.[154]

Regardless of the allowances being applied for, all claims depended on the correct and speedy completion of application forms often without advice or support. Although an air force form of the time suggests that representatives from the British Legion or SSAFA would be 'pleased to assist applicants in completing the form', no advice is given on how or where to contact such representatives.[155] For men in the throes of leaving home, the extra time needed to contact these agencies may not have been available and there can be no doubt that many forms were completed incorrectly, causing delays and inaccuracies in the payment of allowances. In November 1939, *The South Wales Daily Herald* reported a number of such cases.[156] As a result of these cases the War Office sent officials to the area to investigate the situation and a system was devised whereby the British Legion was supplied with allowance forms and assisted applicants with their completion. Although in this instance the War Office reacted swiftly and visibly, it had been necessary for the situation to be highlighted by an outside agency before action was taken.[157] By the end of 1939, these problems were more widely acknowledged, with the UAB advising both the War Service Grants Committee and the War Office that many dependants 'may well feel dismay at the idea of completing it [the application form] unaided'.[158] To improve the situation, the Board suggested that a leaflet should be enclosed with each form informing applicants that their officers could help with its completion and listing the names and addresses of appropriate offices. No thought appears to have been given to the fact that many of the applicants may have had poor literacy or numeracy skills which, in addition to making it impossible for them to complete the form, would also have precluded them from reading the leaflet.

The single case of an Able Seaman serving on HMS *Kenet* at Portsmouth highlights not only the hardship which could result from inaccurate completion of forms but also the hardships many families encountered with the change from civilian to service pay.[159] While the serviceman in this case had been in civilian employment, he had been earning £4 1s 9d per week. As a naval reservist he now contributed £2 15s to his family's upkeep made up of 25s allotment from pay plus 30s Marriage Allowance based on a claim for six children. A letter from his wife to the UAB set out the outgoings for the family, totalling them as 38s 9d per week, leaving 16s 6d for food. Based on the figures given in her letter, the wife's calculations were actually incorrect as the amount left after outgoings was only 16s 3d. An investigating officer who visited the family reported that there were, in fact, seven children in the family and the wife was heavily pregnant so that additional expenses relating to her confinement would accrue in the near future. This case illustrates clearly the need families experienced for help in the completion of claim forms to ensure that they were receiving the full amount due to them. If the form had been completed correctly the family could have claimed in the region of an extra 1s 6d per week bringing the total left after outgoings to 18s. Although the wife in this case is making a claim for extra support, nowhere does she give any estimate of the true cost of keeping her family. However, the amount she was receiving to keep a family of eight in 1939 was only 11s 6d above the level calculated by Rowntree in 1936 as necessary to maintain a family of five above the poverty line despite the fact that the cost of living index had risen by 11 points in the intervening period.[160]

Nor were there any obvious means for claiming allowances if men left without handing in their claim forms. Except in the case of War Service Grants, no provision was made for a situation in which the men concerned were not readily contactable. However, it was suggested that, in cases where normal procedure could not be followed, it had 'always been the intention that . . . claims may be made by the wife or dependant as if the member of the Forces were himself applying'.[161] In all these cases the onus was on the claimant to prove that dependency had previously existed and, in addition, permission would need to be granted by the man concerned for stoppage of allotment from his pay. No provision was made for a situation in which contact with the men involved might be difficult or impossible. As we shall see in Chapter 3, these issues had serious financial implications for the families of those later taken prisoner of war.

The decision then to introduce conscription in 1939 and the subsequent mass mobilisation of manpower led to major administrative problems in the administration of service allowances. The Treasury view that, as Marriage Allowance was now the norm, there would be few problems with administration, although correct for regular servicemen, took no account of the possible effects of conscription. However, few of the problems associated with the granting and administration of service allowances faced in the Second World War had not already surfaced in the First. 'Unmarried' wives, dependent parents and other problems associated with the conscription of large numbers of a normally civilian population had all been encountered between 1914 and 1918. In particular, delays in payment of allowances due to the sheer weight of numbers involved had been common. In many of these cases, families had turned to charitable organisations for support and financial assistance. Lord Derby, speaking at the 37th Annual Meeting of SSAFA, recorded that he had

> ...no hesitation in saying that although there was undoubtedly at the commencement of the [Great] War a considerable amount of distress to families of soldiers suddenly summoned to the Colours, that distress would have been ten times greater if it had not been for the work of this Association.[162]

Despite this experience and the continuing concern expressed by charitable organisations during the 1920s that adequate arrangements had not been made for the administration of allowances in the event of a future war, the government and the services maintained a complacent attitude. In the light of this, Bamfield's statement that 'no organisation of any kind anywhere can have fulfilled the needs, physical and emotional, of its members as has the army' seems extraordinary.[163]

The state's declared intention to make claiming for and administration of allowances as quick as possible ignored the potential for delay at every stage of the process which was readily apparent to outside agencies. Although, as we have seen, a newspaper article of the time suggested that 'no scheme, however elastic, can hope to cover the multitudinous individual cases by a rigid laying down of regulations', the failure of the government to benefit from the experience of the First World War contributed greatly to what quickly became an administrative nightmare.[164] As in 1914, the sheer scale of the problem was overwhelming. Between the outbreak of war and November 1939 alone, 300,000 Family Allowances were granted.[165] The difficulties encountered and delays in granting allowances are clearly demonstrated by the fact that, by the end of 1941, applications for War Service Grant, to provide for families whose allowances were delayed, were running at over 15,000 per week.[166] Far from the situation being dealt with solely by the War Office ensuring that its machinery was in perfect order, as had been suggested in 1924, only a few months into the conflict the services were already having to rely heavily on philanthropic organisations to keep the machinery working at all. General Sir Ronald Adam, Adjutant General to the Forces, speaking to the SSAFA Conference of County Secretaries in 1944, acknowledged this debt, saying 'We do realise in the War Office the tremendous burden we have thrown on your shoulders – a bigger burden than we ever expected you would be asked to bear. It ought to have been foreseen'.[167]

In later chapters we shall see how this administrative burden in relation to allowances was added to with work concerned more specifically with the financial plight of prisoner of war families.

Notes

1   Wootton, *The Politics of Influence.* p. 12; Trustram, *Women of the Regiment.* p. 195.
2   Barnes, A., 'History of SSAFA' in *SSAFA News.* Winter 1984/85. SSAFA Archive.
3   Trustram, *Women of the Regiment.* p. 195.
4   Cordingly, D., *Heroines and Harlots. Women at Sea in the Great Age of Sail.* London, Basingstoke and Oxford: Macmillan, 2001.
5   Cordingly, *Heroines and Harlots.* p. 28.
6   Winstock, L., *Songs and Music of the Redcoats.* London: Leo Cooper, 1970. Quoted in Trustram, *Women of the Regiment.* p. 50.
7   During the course of this study no sources have come to light showing regulations of guidelines governing officers' decisions in this matter.
8   Skelley, A.R., *The Victorian Army at Home. The Recruitment and Terms and Conditions of the British Regular 1859–1899.* London: Croom Helm Ltd, 1977. p. 30.
9   Trustram, *Women of the Regiment.* Table 3.2 Proportion of officers and men serving in the British army who are married and the propor-tion of men married in the general population of England and Wales, 1851, 1861 and 1871. p. 34.
10 Morton, D., *Fight or Pay. Soldiers' Families in the Great War.* Vancouver and Toronto: University of British Columbia Press, 2004. pp. 5 and 11.
11 Skelley, *The Victorian Army at Home.* p. 32.
12 Bamfield, *On the Strength.* pp. 13 and 24.
13 Trustram, *Women of the Regiment.* p. 85.

14 Trustram, *Women of the Regiment*. p. 86.
15 Trustram, *Women of the Regiment*. p. 86.
16 Morton, *Fight or Pay*. p. 9.
17 Army Regulations, 1760–1807 quoted in Trustram, *Women of the Regiment*. p. 86.
18 Trustram, *Women of the Regiment*. p. 142.
19 Trustram, *Women of the Regiment*. p. 55.
20 Trustram, *Women of the Regiment*. p. 64.
21 Trustram, *Women of the Regiment*. p. 166.
22 Barnes, 'History of SSAFA'.
23 Bamfield, *On the Strength*. p. 213.
24 Bamfield, *On the Strength*. p. 213.
25 Bamfield, *On the Strength*. p. 213. For a more detailed study of the development of widows' pensions in the British Armed Forces see Lomas, *War Widows in British Society, 1914–90*.
26 Zumthor, P., *Daily Life in Rembrandt's Holland*, trans. S. Watson Taylor. Stanford, CA: Stanford University Press, 1994. p. 244.
27 Anderson, O., 'Early Experiences of Manpower Problems in an Industrial Society at War: Great Britain 1854–1856' in *Political Science Quarterly*. Vol. 82, 1967. p. 544. Quoted in Trustram, *Women of the Regiment*. p. 39.
28 Fraser, D., 'English Poor Law' in Mommsen (ed.), *The Emergence of the Welfare State in Britain and Germany*. p. 22.
29 Fraser, 'English Poor Law'. p. 22.
30 Fraser, 'English Poor Law'. p. 22.
31 Trustram, *Women of the Regiment*. p. 153.
32 Trustram, *Women of the Regiment*. p. 181.
33 Skelley, *The Victorian Army at Home*. p. 251.
34 Trustram, *Women of the Regiment*. p. 163.
35 Trustram, *Women of the Regiment*. p. 172; and Thomas, *State Maintenance for Women during the First World War*. p. 20.
36 Skelley, *The Victorian Army at Home*. p. 217.
37 Trustram, *Women of the Regiment*. p. 172.
38 Trustram, *Women of the Regiment*. p. 172.
39 Barnes, 'History of SSAFA'.
40 Barnes, 'History of SSAFA'; and Trustram, *Women of the Regiment*. p. 179.
41 Trustram, *Women of the Regiment*. p. 180.
42 Skelley reports that, despite concern over recruitment figures, all politicians believed that the introduction of conscription would be tantamount to political suicide. None of the major enquiries into army recruitment in the late nineteenth century considered it as a

reasonable alternative to enlistment. Skelley, *The Victorian Army at Home*. p. 262.

43 Daniel, *The War from Within*. p. 181.

44 Daniel, *The War from Within*. p. 181.

45 Daniel, *The War from Within*. p. 174.

46 Daniel, *The War from Within*. p. 174.

47 Daniel, *The War from Within*. p. 175.

48 Daniel, *The War from Within*. p. 175.

49 Daniel, *The War from Within*. p. 175.

50 Daniel, *The War from Within*. p. 176.

51 Unlike Britain, Germany applied different minimum rates for summer and winter conditions during the First World War (in 1914 6–9 Marks in summer and 9–12 Marks in winter) although this differentiation was dropped at the end of the war. Daniel, *The War from Within*. p. 177.

52 Daniel, *The War from Within*. p. 177.

53 Bessel, R., *Germany after the First World War*. Oxford: Clarendon Press, 1993. p. 30; and Daniel, *The War from Within*. p. 178.

54 Daniel, *The War from Within*. p. 176.

55 Bessel, *Germany after the First World War*. p. 43.

56 Trustram, *Women of the Regiment*. p. 182.

57 Barnes, 'History of SSAFA'.

58 Barnes, 'History of SSAFA'.

59 Report of the Committee of Enquiry into Charitable Funds, 1900. p. 5. NA/CD196.

60 Barnes, 'History Of SSAFA'.

61 Barnes, 'History Of SSAFA'.

62 Thomas, *State Maintenance for Women during the First World War*. p. 25.

63 Maitland, Major D.D., 'The Care of the Soldier's Family' in *Journal of the Royal Army Medical Corps*. August 1950. pp. 107–125.

64 Trustram, *Women of the Regiment*. p. 29.

65 Trustram, *Women of the Regiment*. p. 90.

66 Trustram, *Women of the Regiment*. p. 91.

67 Trustram, *Women of the Regiment*. p. 40.

68 Morton, *Fight or Pay*. p. 12.

69 Pugh, M., *State and Society. British Political and Social History 1870–1992*. London and New York: Arnold, 1994. p. 116.

70 Sommer, D., *Haldane of Cloan. His Life and Times, 1856–1928*. London: George Allen & Unwin, 1960. p. 169.

71 Sommer, *Haldane of Cloan*. p. 170.

72 Haldane, R.B., *Army Reform and Other Addresses*. London: T. Fisher Unwin, 1907. 'On the Reform of the Army, 25 February 1907'. In 1906, British military expenditure ran at £30 million compared to German expenditure of £31 million.

73 Haldane, *Army Reform and Other Addresses*. p. 3.

74 Wootton, *Politics of Influence*. p. 18.

75 Extract from Hansard, 09 August 1914. NA/AST11/123.

76 Thomas, *State Maintenance for Women during the First World War*. p. 28.

77 Wootton, *The Politics of Influence*. p. 18.

78 Thomas, *State Maintenance for Women during the First World War*. p. 26.

79 Thomas, *State Maintenance for Women during the First World War*. p. 26.

80 Thomas, *State Maintenance for Women during the First World War*. p. 26. Thomas gives no indication of how the remaining 10 per cent of separation allowances were distributed.

81 Wootton, *Politics of Influence*. p. 26.

82 Thomas, *State Maintenance for Women during the First World War*.

83 Thomas, *State Maintenance for Women during the First World War*. p. 239.

84 Pensions for Seamen and Marines Disabled and the Families and Dependants of those Deceased in Consequence of the Great War 1916–1917. NA/PIN15/168.

85 Daniel, *The War from Within*. p. 182.

86 Weida Board of Aldermen (Saxony-Weimar) quoted in *Vossische Zeitung* 22 August 16. Quoted in Daniel, *The War from Within*. p. 182.

87 Daniel, *The War from Within*. p. 185.

88 Daniel, *The War from Within*. p. 186.

89 Barnes, 'History of SSAFA'.

90 Bernard Bosanquet, General Secretary, SSFA, speaking at a meeting of the Charity Organisations Society in Oxford, 1915. Quoted in Wootton, *Politics of Influence*. p. 82.

91 Thomas, *State Maintenance for Women During the First World War*. p. 96.

92 Thomas, *State Maintenance for Women During the First World War*. p. 98.

93 Butler, D. and Butler, G., *British Political Facts, 1900–1994*. London: Macmillan Ltd, 1994. National Income, Taxes and Prices. p. 383.

94 Thomas, *State Maintenance for Women during the First World War*. p. 98.

95 Thomas, *State Maintenance for Women during the First World War.* p. 98.

96 Allowances increased from 9 Marks summer allowance and 12 Marks winter allowance in August 1914, to 25 Marks for wives plus 15 Marks for supported children by the end of the war. Daniel, *The War from Within.* p. 177.

97 Details of increases in average food prices in cities, together with tables showing expenditure in worker households are included in Bessel, *Germany after the First World War.* pp. 1–48. German widows of the First World War faced even greater hardships in the Weimar era. See Hausen, K., 'The German Nation's Obligations to the Heroes: Widows of World War I' in Higonnet, M.R., Jenson, J., Michel, S. and Weitz, M.C., *Behind the Lines. Gender and the two World Wars.* New Haven and London: Yale University Press, 1987. pp. 126–140.

98 Bessel, *Germany after the First World War.* p. 39.

99 Introduction to House of Commons Debate on 1939 Army Regulations. 12 December 39. NA/AST11/138.

100 Introduction to House of Commons Debate on Service Allowances. 12 December 39. NA/AST11/138.

101 Letter Sir George Wickham Legg, General Secretary, SSAFA, to Chrystal, Ministry of Pensions. 27 February 24. NA/T162/470/E19544/1.

102 Letter Chrystal, Ministry of Pensions, to Longhurst, Committee of Imperial Defence. 07 March 24. NA/T162/470/E19544/1.

103 Letter Millar, Assistant Secretary, Treasury, to Widdows, Assistant Secretary, Financial Section, War Office. April 1924. NA/T162/470/E19544/1.

104 Letter Millar, Assistant Secretary, Treasury, to Widdows, Assistant Secretary, Financial Section, War Office. April 1924. NA/T162/470/E19544/1.

105 Report of the Inter-departmental Committee on Dependants' Allowances in Future Emergencies. July 1925. NA/T162/470/E19544/1.

106 Report of the Inter-departmental Committee on Dependants' Allowances in Future Emergencies. April 1926. NA/T162/470/E19544/1.

107 Report of the Inter-departmental Committee on Pensions. 14 November 31. NA/T162/470/E19544/2.

108 Letter War Office to Treasury regarding the reaction of the Army Council, the Board of the Admiralty and the Air Council to the Report of the Inter-departmental Committee on Pensions. 14 November 31. NA/T162/470/E19544/2.

109 Unsigned letter War Office to Treasury. 14 November 31. NA/ T162/470/E19544/2.
110 Report of the Inter-departmental Committee on Pensions. 14 November 31. NA/T162/470/E19544/2.
111 Letter, Hore-Belisha, Financial Secretary, Treasury, to Duff Cooper, Financial Secretary, War Office. 10 January 33. NA/T162/470/ E19544/2.
112 Figures taken from Pugh, M., *State and Society. British Political and Social History 1870–1992*. London and New York: Edward Arnold, 1994. pp. 167 and 168.
113 Report of Meeting on Administration of Allowances in the event of a Future War. Undated but probably late May/early June 1933. NA/ T162/470/E19544/2.
114 Letter Duff Cooper, Financial Secretary, War Office, to Hore-Belisha, Financial Secretary, Treasury. 21 July 33. NA/T162/470/ E19544/2.
115 Letter Rae, Staff Officer, Treasury, to Controller, SSAFA. 08 August 38. NA/T162/470/E19544/2.
116 Fighting Services Separation Allowances. Arrangements for men called up under Military Training Act 1939. NA/T162/573/ E3886601.
117 Decoded telegram from the Defence Department of the Government of India to Co-ordinating (Inter-Departmental) Committee on Dependants' Allowances. 15 February 41. NA/AST11/146.
118 Fighting Services Separation Allowances. Men called up under the Military Training Act, 1939. NA/T162/573/E38866/01.
119 Fighting Services Separation Allowances. Men called up under the Military Training Act, 1939. NA/T162/573/E38866/01.
120 Fighting Services Separation Allowances. Men called up under the Military Training Act, 1939. NA/T162/573/E38866/01.
121 Within six months the regulations governing the awarding of Dependants' Allowances had changed. The minimum level of allotment from pay was raised to 7s per week, resulting in the scrapping of the lowest level of allowance payments. Allowances were then paid at two rates only – 12s and 17s per week – with the special rate for dependants living alone remaining unchanged. Regulations governing the Granting of Dependants Allowances. NA/AST11/124.
122 Memo on the proposal to grant Marriage Allowance to men below 26 years of age. 26 January 34. NA/WO32/3169.
123 *News of the World*. 29 August 37. Papers of Leslie Hore-Belisha, Churchill Archive HOBE 5/1.
124 Fighting Services Separation Allowances. Men called up under the Military Training Act, 1939. NA/T162/573/E38866/01.

125 Paper for Cabinet Consideration. 03 May 39. NA/T162/573/ E38866/01.

126 Paper for Cabinet Consideration. 03 May 39. NA/T162/573/ E38866/01.

127 White Paper 'Allowances for Families and Dependants of Men Serving in HM Forces during the Present War'. 28 November 39. Copies of this White Paper are included in both NA/T162/573/ E38866/01 and NA/WO32/3169.

128 White Paper 'Allowances for Families and Dependants of Men Serving in HM Forces during the Present War'. 28 November 39. NA/T162/573/E38866/01.

129 White Paper 'Allowances for Families and Dependants of Men Serving in HM Forces during the Present War'. 28 November 39. NA/T162/573/E38866/01.

130 Letter District Officer, Unemployment Assistance Board, Dundee, to Secretary, Unemployment Assistance Board, London. 13 May 40. NA/AST11/124.

131 Military Service (Special Allowances) Advisory Committee. NA/ AST11/124.

132 Notes on Service Pay and Allowances. 26 May 43. NA/AST11/155.

133 Register No. 46/Gen/1395. 04 September 41. NA/WO32/9818.

134 Discussions on this topic involved not only the Treasury and services but also the Secretary of State for War and Lady Astor, who objected strongly to the term 'unmarried wives', stating that such women were 'no wife at all' and preferring the term 'unmarried housekeeper'. Notes on meeting held in the Secretary of State for War's Office. 24 January 40. NA/WO32/4679.

135 Minute Sheet. 08 December 39. NA/WO32/4679.

136 Unsigned note, War Office to Unemployment Assistance Board. 02 December 39. NA/AST11/123. By a strange anomaly, air force officers were able to claim allowances for separated wives and the children of divorced wives, but ordinary airmen were not. A letter from the Air Ministry states that they are 'at a loss to defend the present position which seems to be without rhyme or reason'. Letter Air Ministry to Grigg, Permanent Under-secretary of State, War Office. 21 June 42. NA/WO32/9981.

137 Report of Inter-departmental Committee on Dependants' Allowances. NA/WO32/9444.

138 Letter Andrews, Secretary SSAFA, to Dyer, War Office. 11 March 44. NA/WO32/10449.

139 *Yorkshire Post*. 25 June 41. NA/AST11/136.

140 Notes on the claiming of Family Allowance. December 39. NA/ AST11/123.

141 Notes on the claiming of Family Allowance. December 39. NA/
     AST/123.
142 Notes on the claiming of Family Allowance. December 39. NA/
     AST11/123.
143 Confidential notes on Family Allowances, Dependants' Allowances
     and War Service Grants. 28 November 39. NA/AST11/123.
144 Confidential notes of a meeting of the Unemployment Assistance
     Board. 28 November 39. NA/AST11/123.
145 Details of this case history are given in: Letter Admiralty to Logan,
     Unemployment Assistance Board. 30 July 42. NA/AST11/149.
146 Confidential Notes on Family Allowances, Dependants' Allowances
     and War Service Grants prepared by the Unemployment Assistance
     board following a meeting 28 November 39. NA/AST11/123.
147 Confidential notes of a meeting of the Unemployment Assistance
     Board. 28 November 39. NA/AST11/123.
148 Confidential notes of a meeting of the Unemployment Assistance
     Board. 28 November 39. NA/AST11/123.
149 Revisions to the Regulations Governing the Award of Dependants'
     Allowances. 08 April 41. NA/AST11/125.
150 Revisions to the Regulations governing the award of Dependants'
     Allowances. 08 April 41. NA/AST11/125.
151 District Officer, UAB Leeds, to Secretary, UAB London. 24 June 39.
     NA/AST11/133.
152 District Officer, UAB Leeds, to Secretary, UAB London. 24 June 39;
     Letters Pontefract Collieries and Glass Houghton and Castleford
     Collieries Ltd to Relieving Officer, UAB Pontefract 22 June 39; Letter
     UAB London to War Office. 29 June 39. NA/AST11/133.
153 Further difficulties arose with the verification of earnings for other
     specific groups and with claims from dependants in foreign locations.
     See, for example, a claim from a parent resident in Palestine, where
     the Assistance Board asks for help from the Colonial Office as 'obvi-
     ously this is not a case in which the Assistance Board can make any
     personal investigation'. NA/AST11/150.
154 Notes on attempted verification of earnings of crofters. Undated but
     probably mid-1942. NA/AST11/149.
155 RAF Form, Dependants' Allowances – Notes for the guidance of
     applicants. Undated, but probably late 1939. NA/AST11/124.
156 *South Wales Daily Herald.* 06 November 39. NA/AST11/134.
157 *South Wales Daily Herald.* 06 November 39. NA/AST11/134.
158 Letters Brockie, Area Officer, Unemployment Assistance Board, to
     Simes, War Service Grants Committee, and Monk, Senior Staff Clerk,
     War Office. 04 December 39 and 05 December 39 respectively. A
     copy of the required form, completed on behalf of Patrick Dailly of

Dundee, a Private in 270th Troop 100 AA Light Batallion, dated 28 November 39, is included in this file and demonstrates its complexity. NA/AST11/135.

159 Details of this case history are included in: Letter Admiralty to Logan, Unemployment Assistance Board. 30 July 42. NA/AST11/149.

160 Rowntree, in his study of poverty in York in the years 1935–36, calculated that a family of five would require a weekly income of £4 3s 6d to remain above the poverty line. Pugh, *State and Society*. p. 96.

161 White Paper 'Allowances for Families and Dependants of Men Serving in HM Forces During the Present War'. 14 November 39. NA/AS|T11/123.

162 37th Annual Meeting of SSAFA. SSAFA Annual Reports June 1923. p. 16.

163 Bamfield, *On the Strength*. p. 209.

164 Article from *Yorkshire Evening Post*. 25 June 41. NA/AST11/136.

165 Letter UAB to Dancyger, Senior Principal Officer, Ministry of Pensions. 20 February 42. NA/AST11/136.

166 Letter UAB to Dancyger, Senior Principal Officer, Ministry of Pensions. 20 February 42. NA/AST11/136.

167 Minutes of Emergency Conference of County Secretaries, SSAFA Annual Reports. 26 April 44. p. 6. SSAFA Archive.

2

'An untidy arrangement' – service Family and Dependants' Allowances, 1939 to 1945

During 1940 the strength of the armed forces in Britain rose by over 1,340,000, with the great majority of this increase, over one million, being within the army.[1] As a result the number of allowances rose in proportion and, towards the end of 1940, the problems associated with delays in the payment of allowances reached such proportions that the War Office requested a Major-General Buckley, who had formerly had 'considerable experience of examining the organisation of commercial firms', to tour regimental Pay Offices and report on their operating systems.[2] At the time, responsibility for the delays was being laid at the door of the UAB, although they, themselves, felt that their turnaround time for the investigations of claims for allowances was not unreasonable.[3] Most cases were dealt with within six days of receipt although some delays, beyond the control of the Board, did arise, often caused by inability to locate and interview the claimants.[4] In the week of 1 November 1940, investigations were carried out into 21,287 claims, of which 5,272 were 'fruitless visits'.[5] Largely these unsuccessful visits were occasioned by claimants having subsequently taken up employment which meant that they were not at home when the investigating officer called or by claimants having changed address without notifying the Board.[6] As a result of Major-General Buckley's report, the Inter-departmental Committee on Army Allowances and War Service, consisting of representatives from the UAB, War Office and Ministry of Pensions, was established to ascertain 'whether appreciable delays occur in settling claims for Dependants' Allowances and War Service Grants and, if such delays do occur, to suggest remedies which may appear appropriate'.[7]

The final report of this Committee, known as the Malpass Report, was delivered in March 1941 and made a number of suggestions to ensure claims were dealt with all possible speed. Firstly the Committee established that postal delays were one of the main factors delaying the processing of claims.[8] The average delay in transmission of any item of mail was found to be four days and, as investigation reports were normally forwarded three times, delays of up to twelve days could easily result. To expedite this situation, the Committee suggested that the Post Office should send claims direct to UAB Area Offices rather than sending them first to the District Offices, as had been common practice.[9] Within the Area Offices themselves, most delays were attributable to the difficulties outlined above of establishing contact with the dependants. In one in every three cases the dependant was absent at the time of the visit.[10] However, it was noted that in some cases unavoidable delays were brought about by the sheer complexity of the cases. The cases of claims involving crofters, already mentioned in Chapter 1, where there were grave difficulties in assessing former earnings, prove a case in point here. Overall, however, delays were found to be less than one week, which was not viewed as excessive. An undated, and unsigned, note on the draft report of the Committee suggested that Sir Frederick Bovenschen, Joint Permanent Under-secretary of State at the War Office, would 'no doubt' not only make the amendments recommended but, at the same time, 'pray again for the salvation of the Service from outside so-called business experts'.[11]

However, as a result of the investigation, a reminder was issued to all officers to the effect that cases under investigation were not to be viewed as 'merely paperwork' as they concerned 'living persons whose well-being and happiness often depended on an early decision being given'.[12] For the first time since 1916 the service hierarchies, and the War Office in particular, had been brought into direct contact with large sectors of the general public whose motivation, concerns and prior knowledge of service life were rather different from those of the career servicemen they normally dealt with, and, as we shall see in subsequent chapters, their response was not always sympathetic.

Besides these investigations into the mechanisms for the payment of Dependants' Allowances, throughout the course of the Second World War the question of whether or not service pay and allowances were adequate and their regular reviews continued to pose problems. Initially, all three services had expressed an intention to review allowances every six months as set out in Defence Procedure

Circular No. 33, but by May 1940 only the Admiralty and Air Ministry had carried out such reviews.[13] For the army, faced with much larger numbers of claimants, staff levels rendered the task impossible.[14] As a result, allowances had failed to keep pace with cost of living increases and, from as early as March 1940, campaigns had begun claiming that existing levels of Family Allowances were inadequate.[15] As in the First World War, women themselves played a large part in demands for adequate allowances.[16] Wives of servicemen were often instrumental in beginning campaigns for increased allowances. The *Ilford Recorder*, for example, ran a series of articles beginning on 7 March headlined 'Ilford Wives lead fight of Bigger Allowances'.[17] Five local service wives, led by Miss Sylvia Pankhurst, formed a deputation to lobby MPs and protest that existing allowances were inadequate, stating that 'Women in Ilford are being forced below the poverty line because their husbands had joined the Services'.[18] The women demanded a six-point charter for service dependants including speedy delivery of application forms for grants, cases to be dealt with more 'expeditiously' and an increase in war pensions.[19]

In the First World War, however, large labour organisations with some influence at government level, such as the War Emergency Workers National Committee, had also become involved in such campaigns.[20] Between 1939 and 1945 no such labour involvement was apparent. Campaigns, begun locally by wives themselves, relied on capturing the attention of local MPs and newspapers to publicise them and move them into a wider arena. As both the government and the services were sensitive to problems of desertion and lack of effectiveness of troops when the well-being of their families was in doubt, if local campaigns managed to capture the interest of national newspapers they did acquire some degree of influence. However, despite the fact that national figures, such as Sylvia Pankhurst, and prominent MPs, such as Eleanor Rathbone, maintained an interest in service families throughout the period of the war, no popular national champion appeared to keep the topic permanently in the public mind. Virtually every campaign for increases in pay and allowances had to start from scratch at a local level and gradually build its support until it gained national attention. But, whilst dependants could make at least make their discontent known, servicemen themselves found it more difficult to articulate their discontent with pay and allowances.

Generally, those serving in the armed forces could not campaign for increases to pay. Fred Bellinger, Labour MP for Bassetlaw, raised this point in a House of Commons debate on service pay and allowances in 1942, claiming that 'service lips are sealed by King's Regulations'.[21] In fact Parliament was the only institution that could speak on behalf of servicemen in this matter and, traditionally, all claims for increases to pay had to be debated and agreed on the floor of the House. With the outbreak of war, the perceived motivation for joining the services became patriotism and a wish to serve one's country and in the light of this to cavil at existing rates of pay might be regarded as disloyal. This point is made explicitly on the cover of a report into army pay and allowances in 1944, which carries the following excerpt from an address to servicemen quoted in Thomas Hardy's novel *The Trumpet Major*.

> If the love of true Liberty and honest Fame has not ceased to animate the Hearts of Englishmen, Pay, though necessary, will be the least part of your Reward. You will find you best Recompense in having done your Duty to your King and Country, . . . , in having protected your Wives and Children from Death, or worse than Death, which will follow the success of such Inveterate Foes.[22]

However, for those conscripted into the armed forces, the decrease in family income as a result of the change from civilian wages to service allowances was often dramatic and led to severe hardship as the number of families claiming additional War Service Grants to supplement their allowances has shown.[23] Conscripted servicemen were, therefore, caught in a dilemma. Although their level of service pay took no account of financial commitments undertaken before their conscription, at the same time they were unable to take any action to bring about an increase in pay to allow them to meet these commitments. All action to increase allowances came from independent campaigns in response to financial difficulties faced by families and as such was always retrospective. Families had to be in need and facing hardship before they attracted the attention of MPs or philanthropic campaigners. No structure existed to ensure that families had sufficient allowances from the outset to ensure an adequate standard of living.

In November 1940 both Family and Dependants' Allowances were increased, at least partly in response to local and national campaigns, although, for Dependants' Allowances in particular, the increases were also influenced by the principles underlying the Determination of Needs Act.[24] These increases resulted in an overall increase in expenditure on Family Allowances alone of £7 million per annum but were not at a consistent level across the services.[25] In the army and navy increases were dependent on level of pay, whilst in the air force increases were dependent on rank. In order to show the scale of increases afforded through the course of the War, Table 1 gives an overview of the changes in Family Allowance awarded to the lowest paid army ranks. Whilst an increase of £7 million at first sight appears to suggest a substantial increase to allowances, this increase was, however, spread over an increase in total strength of armed forces of 1,345,000 between September 1939 and September 1940. Given these increased numbers claiming allowances and the rise in the cost of living in the same period, the increases were not even sufficient to allow families to maintain their existing standard of living.

Consequently, campaigning for increased pay and allowances continued throughout 1941. In October, the Minister for Pensions, speaking in a secret session in the House of Commons, declared his awareness that there had been 'a demand for a general all-round increase in pay and allowances'.[26] This, however, was deemed to

Table 1: Changes in service Family Allowances (minimum other ranks) 1939–45

Date	Wife	Wife + 1 child	Wife + 2 children	Wife + 3 children	Wife + 4 children
Prewar	24s	29s 0d	32s 0d	34s 0d	35s 0d
Nov. 1939	24s	29s 0d	33s 0d	36s 0d	39s 0d
Nov. 1940	25s	32s 6d	38s 0d	42s 0d	46s 0d
Feb. 1942	25s	33s 6d	40s 0d	45s 0d	50s 0d
May 1944	Not given, probably unchanged	35s 0d	47s 6d	60s 0d	72s 6d
Proposed postwar	31s	42s 0d	53s 7½d	64s 1¼d	75s 9d

Note: Rates quoted are per week. Allowances before February 1942 include the relevant minimum allotment from husband's pay. Allowances after that date include the standard reduced allotment of 3s 6d per week. All figures taken from NA/T162/692/45396/1.

be so costly that it was 'almost impossible to contemplate at the present time'.[27] And, for the first time, explicit comparisons began to be made between the rates of pay of civilian and munitions workers and service pay, as well as comparisons with the pay of the armed forces from Dominion countries.[28] Major Milner, Conservative MP for Leeds, South East, speaking in the same debate made it clear that he felt that

> The munition worker or civilian worker will still be far better paid and his family better fed and clothed than the soldier's wife and family can hope to be [. . .] and still there will be men from Canada, Australia and New Zealand fighting alongside our men but drawing twice and in some cases three times as much.[29]

The campaign for increased pay and allowances also continued in the pages of both national and local newspapers. In December 1941 both *The Star* and the *Yorkshire Evening Post* carried articles campaigning for higher allowances for service wives. The article in *The Star*, headlined 'Army Wives Must Have A Fairer Deal', was written by Irene Ward, Conservative MP for Wallsend, demonstrating the continued interest of local MPs in the plight of service wives.[30]

Although an attempt was made in 1941 to focus increases on those most in need, the system by which hardship was determined remained extremely complex, even in the eyes of the service departments themselves. By October of that year, the War Office was forced to recognise that this complexity meant that, although efforts were being made to ensure that claims were dealt with as promptly as possible, 'some time may elapse before claims can be disposed of'.[31] As a result, the Treasury, perhaps following the War Office lead in employing the services of a previously independent expert, commissioned a report from a former employee of Standard Cables into the procedures for claiming and administering Dependants' Allowances and WSG.[32] This report suggested that, because of the way the procedure for investigating claims had been established, with the UAB making preliminary investigations into household income but the Treasury and Service Departments maintaining responsibility for the final accuracy of the figures, a wasteful 'double check' was operating.[33] If the UAB was made responsible for final accuracy, although service pay offices would make the award, issue allowance books and ensure allotments from pay were authorised, this 'double check' would be eliminated. The service departments,

however, after perusing the report came to the decision that following this course would make no appreciable savings.[34]

By the end of 1941 establishment concerns over the effects that
worry about home and family might have on both the morale and
the effectiveness of servicemen led to the War Office contacting all
army commanders asking them to make regular monthly reports
on factors concerning their troops.[35] Reports on the effect of conditions affecting families and allowances were specifically requested.
From these reports an overall Morale Report was compiled quarterly throughout the remainder of the war and up to January
1948.[36] In April 1942 the first meeting of the War Office Morale
Committee took place, to consider the findings of these reports.[37]
In a report predating the establishment of the Committee, the
Adjutant-General had suggested that 'the loss of Malaya, Hong
Kong and the withdrawal in Burma, were all due to the low morale
of the troops'.[38] He added that he felt the war would be won or
lost on morale, an issue the British Army was 'too apt' to ignore
as 'Morale is a psychological problem like sex, and therefore the
Britisher is almost ashamed to talk about it'.[39]

From the outset, the role played by home and wives in the maintaining of morale was acknowledged. Item 14 in the report of May
to July 1942 details the 'influence of women', listing a number of
ways in which wives could adversely affect morale.[40] These included
persuading their husbands to be AWOL or overstay their leave and
dissuading husbands from volunteering for dangerous duties in
addition to themselves taking 'French leave' from their factory
work to go on holiday with their husbands. The perennial question
of the 'fickleness' of women also surfaces in this first report. Women
were regarded as 'almost invariably' preferring the company of the
RAF, US or Dominion troops and even civilian workers to that of
soldiers as the British soldier 'had less money to spend on them'.[41]
In fact, for the whole six years it operated, the War Office Morale
Committee had little good to say about the wives of soldiers. The
Victorian view of army wives as a 'serious evil' clearly persisted
well into the twentieth century.[42] Whilst there can be no doubt that
a number of these accusations were well founded, the army gave
no thought to ways in which it could alleviate this drain on morale
by providing the families concerned with extra support. Instead
wives were issued with suggestions on how not to worry their
menfolk. For example, women were advised to limit their news in

letters to the positive aspects of home life such as flowers they had grown and books they had read rather than telling their husbands about how frightened they had been by bombing or if they had been ill.[43] A suggestion, in May 1942, that women should tell their husbands about films they had seen was enlarged on three months later to suggest that they include whom they had seen the film with.[44] Presumably this suggestion was made to reassure their husbands that they had been with girlfriends or family members and not for wives to confirm that they had been going out with other men.

With the entry of the USA into the war in Europe, comparisons between British service pay and that of not only Dominion but also American troops continued to inform discussions on levels of pay and allowances. The Treasury, however, took the view that to use other countries as a 'yardstick' by which to measure British service pay would lead to a 'breakdown in the financial front which would be as dangerous to our war effort as any military defeat could be'.[45] Generally, rates of pay within the different countries were felt to 'reflect the circumstances of that country, the standard of living, the difficulty of obtaining recruits'.[46] Table 2 shows comparative rates of pay and allowances between British, Dominion and US troops in 1942.

In fact, although absolute rates of pay were often higher for Dominion and American troops, for their families the administrative procedures by which allowances were granted often negated these benefits. Under the American system married 'other ranks', except for the three highest ranks, were not recognised for Family Allowance.[47] To qualify for allowances US troops were required to contribute a minimum of $22 per month, approximately £5 10s, to their dependants, who then received $28 from the government.[48] As Barrett Litoff and Smith report, 'the meagre allotment checks provided by the [American] government did not cover the expenses of most service wives'.[49] In Britain allotments varied with rank in the army and navy and with level of pay in the air force but were generally in the region of 7s per week.[50] Canadian troops however, had to allot 50 per cent of their total pay, equivalent to approximately 3s per day, to qualify for allowance.[51] Not only was the level of allotment required from British troops higher than that from Americans, the problem of 'disposable income' too continued to be problematic for the whole of the Second World War, and the

Table 2: Comparative rates of pay and allowances for British, Dominion and American servicemen 1942

Rank	British		American		Canadian		Australian		New Zealand	
	Single	Married + 2 children	Single	Married + 2 children	Single	Married + 2 children	Single	Married + 2 children	Single	Married + 2 children
Private	2s 6d to 4s 3d	7s 8d to 9s 5d	9s 11d	18s 3d	5s 10d	14s 9d	5s 2d	11s 7d	6s 7d	12s 2d
Lance corporal	4s 3d to 4s 9d	9s 5d to 9s 11d	10s 9d	19s	6s 9d	15s 8d	5s 2d	11s 7d	7s 1d	12s 8d
Corporal	5s 0d to 5s 6d	10s 2d to 10s 8d	13s 1d	21s 5d	7s 8d	16s 7d	8s 8d	15s 1d	8s 1d	13s 8d
Sergeant	6s 6d to 7s 0d	11s 8d to 12s 2d	15s 6d	23s 10d	9s 11d	18s 10d	9s 7d	16s	9s	14s 7d
Warrant officer class II	9s 0d	14s 7d	22s 8d	28s 4d	13s 6d	22s 5d	10s 4d	16s 9d	11s 6d	17s 1d
Warrant officer class I	12s 6d	18s 7d	27s 5d	33s 2d	19s	27s 11d	12s 2d	18s 7d	12s 6d	18s 1d
2nd Lieutenant	11s	18s 6d	27s 4d	33s 4d	–	–	–	–	15s 6d	21s 1d
Lieutenant	13s	20s 6d	30s 4d	36s 4d	24s 10d	33s 9d	13s 11d	20s 4d	16s 6d	22s 1d
Captain	Figure not given	24s	36s 5d	42s 5d	32s 3d	41s 2d	17s 5d	23s 10d	20s	25s 7d
Major	28s 6d	36s	45s 7d	55s 0d	38s	47s 5d	22s 9d	29s 2d	26s 4d	31s 11d
Lt Colonel	43s	50s 6d	53s 1d	62s 7d	49s 8d	58s 7d	27s 2d	33s 7d	33s 6d	39s 1d

Note: rate of exchange: £1 Sterling = $4.025 USA, $4.43 Canadian, £1.25 Australian. Figures taken from:NA/T162/692/45396/1.

Prime Minister expressed 'deep concern' about the troubles that could arise from this.[52] By early 1942 a single American soldier had a disposable income in the region of 10s per day, even if he made allotment to dependants, compared to that of a British private of 3s per day.[53] Rates of disposable income for married soldiers were 6s 6d and 2s 6d respectively.[54] These comparative rates were deemed to place American troops in a much stronger position 'for the purposes of attracting the opposite sex', and examples rapidly come to light of 'bitter remarks about Americans and women' in Northern Ireland.[55] Again, Table 2 illustrates these differences by showing comparative rates of pay for British, US and Dominion troops in 1942.

Similarly, letters from troops in the Middle East expressed concern that Canadian and American troops were 'occupying' Britain whilst they were being sent to Libya and Egypt.[56] The government, whilst recognising that it would be 'out of the question to fix the scales of pay of the Armed Forces by reference to those of other countries where the cost of living and scales of pay in general are considerably higher',[57] nevertheless recognised the necessity for taking some action in this matter, particularly in view of the fact that the number of American troops in Britain was likely to increase dramatically within a short space of time.[58] To this end they decided to appeal to British women, as part of their war effort, to 'not encourage troops of any nationality to indulge in ostentatious expenditure in public places'.[59] There appears to be some confusion as to where this suggestion originated and whether or not it was ever put into practice. Although War Office files attribute it to the Ministry of Information and are not clear as to whether or not it was implemented, Reynolds, in *Rich Relations*, attributes it to the War Office and claims that it was never taken seriously.[60]

However, even if the suggestion was carried out, army perception at least seems to have been that the appeal fell on deaf ears. In the months immediately afterwards, reports of the Army Morale Committee continued to suggest that women 'almost invariably' preferred the company of American or Dominion troops who had a greater level of disposable income than British soldiers.[61] Whilst Canadian rates of pay also were higher than those of British troops, the situation here was ameliorated as the Canadian government agreed to hold back a portion of the pay of their servicemen in credits.[62] The US War Department, however, was reluctant to do this, suggesting two other measures to ease the situation.[63] Firstly, they suggested that US troops should be paid twice a month to reduce the amount of cash available to them to spend in any one night on the town. Secondly, they agreed to attempt to encourage troops to invest part of their pay in war bonds, insurance or army savings schemes. Although Sir Kingsley Wood, Chancellor of the Exchequer, saw these suggestions as being 'very helpful' in principle, their actual effectiveness is open to doubt.[64] By September 1942, GIs were routinely spending two-thirds of their disposable pay and largely ignoring official saving schemes.[65]

Unfavourable comparisons were also made, both by the public and in the press, between service pay and that earned by civilian, and particularly munitions, workers.[66] Hancock and Gowing, in the official *History of the Second World War* volume dealing with the British war economy, claim that this public criticism led directly to a debate in the House of Commons in late 1941 which in turn put in motion revisions to pay and allowances.[67] In January 1942 the Secretary of State for War, speaking in the House of Commons, referred to a suggestion that some explanation needed to be given for the 'disparity between the earnings of munitions workers and the emoluments of the forces'.[68] A draft White Paper on Emoluments of the Armed Forces in July 1942 reported that it was a 'common thing' to hear service pay compared unfavourably with that of industrial workers.[69] Although there 'had been no evidence of serious discontent in the Services with the existing scale of allowances', pressure for increases had come from 'outside the Services' largely directed towards removing the 'alleged discrepancies' between service pay and that of munitions workers.[70] The paper went on to state that the comparison was not valid as industrial workers received all their pay in cash whilst servicemen received allowances for clothing, food and accommodation in addition to their pay.[71] In addition, a soldier was liable to tax only on pay and not on benefits in kind or allowances whereas married civilian workers were liable for tax on any income above £3 per week.[72] This meant that a married sergeant in the army might have a total cash income for himself and his wife of £4 3s 6d exempt from tax and in addition to allowances covering his own keep and clothing.[73] In a letter to the Secretary of State for War, the Treasury suggested that, in reply to unfavourable comparisons between civilian pay and service emoluments, stress should be given to the 'preferential position enjoyed by the Forces in relation to income tax'.[74] However, the War Cabinet agreed that a final revision of the White Paper should be made to avoid making direct comparisons between the real incomes of civilians and servicemen. The final version contained the statement that

> The object of this paper is to set out some of the factors which should be borne in mind in any attempt to measure the real value of the remuneration of all kinds received by members of the Services. Any direct or immediate comparison of pay between the soldier and the civilian is impossible since their systems of remuneration are essentially different.[75]

Although the general purpose of this White Paper on Service Pay and Allowances was primarily to dispel unfavourable comparisons between service pay and civilian wages, described by the Treasury as 'a particularly annoying line of claptrap', more concrete adjustments to allowances and pay were also included.[76] Qualifying allotments from soldiers to enable their families to receive Family Allowance were reduced from 7s per week to 3s 6d at a cost of £17.5 million per annum.[77] This proposal, put forward originally by the Labour Party Parliamentary Services Committee, received 'a good deal of support' in debate and compared favourably with the rates required of US and Dominion troops of the equivalent of 3s 6d and 3s 8d per day respectively.[78] However, the matter did result in some discussion. The reduction would effectively mean that the lowest-paid ranks would now not pay any allotment whilst the higher ranks would still maintain a minimum payment. Although this was regarded as an 'untidy arrangement', it was deemed preferable to removing all responsibility for families from the men themselves.[79] In addition, minor adjustments were made to child and dependants' allowances amounting to £5 million per annum.[80] The total cost of all changes to allowances and pensions, and including the instigation of a system of postwar credits for other ranks, was estimated to be in the region of £55 million per annum – an expenditure likely to rise to £60 million per annum with continued expansion of the armed forces but which, the Chancellor felt, would 'no doubt' be 'cheerfully and patiently borne'.[81] From the outbreak of war in 1939 and including the implementation of the changes proposed in the 1942 White Paper, the cost of improvements to the conditions of service for members of the armed forces, excluding any improvements to pension rates, totalled £93.25 million.[82]

However, in the same period the strength of the armed forces had risen by over 320 per cent whilst the purchasing power of the pound had decreased by almost one-third.[83] Perhaps not surprisingly then, the White Paper received a very poor reception in both Parliament and the press. 'The Forces Programme' on the BBC on the evening of 15 September described its reception as 'as bad as ever scorched a White Paper black'.[84] Similarly, the Army Morale Reports for this period, although initially suggesting that there had been little pressure for increased pay and allowances before the White Paper, now reported a 'unanimous' reaction that the increases were 'not satisfactory'.[85] Generally, soldiers were reported as stating that they felt they had been given the minimum increase possible and families continued to suffer.[86] In Leeds a survey carried out after these increases had been implemented showed that one of the main causes of poverty was 'being a soldier's wife'.[87] One-fifth of all soldiers' wives were claimed to be living in poverty, largely those with children who were too young for the mothers to go out to work, with an average shortfall of income against expenditure of 15s 6d per week.[88]

In the light of this discontent, in October 1942 the question of exactly how service pay and allowances were negotiated was again raised by Fred Bellinger, who led a deputation from the Serving Members Committee to meet with the Lord President and Lord Privy Seal and discuss the matter.[89] As already outlined, the only existing channel for these negotiations was through the House of Commons, and MPs felt that 'the constant repetition of Parliamentary Questions and debates on the subject of service pay and allowances was most undesirable from almost every point of view'.[90] Instead a Committee of the House was suggested as a means of bringing the mechanism for negotiating service pay closer to that which existed in industry. A number of objections were raised to this proposal, largely by the services themselves, who felt that the introduction of a Standing Committee would widen the gulf between the services and the government and encourage a flow of grievances.[91] In addition, the Committee would come to be seen as being the decision-making body rather than just a channel for communication. In November the government decided not to adopt the proposal for the Standing Committee.[92] Instead, a Cabinet Committee of Under-secretaries from the Treasury, Ministry of Pensions and all three Service Departments was set up to examine questions relating to service pay and allowances as they arose.[93]

Sir Stafford Cripps, the Lord Privy Seal, felt that the 'improvements' provided by the 1942 White Paper had given 'substantial justice' to all ranks of the services.[94] However, throughout the remainder of 1942 and the whole of 1943, financial worries continued to play a large part in the reports of the Army Morale Committee.[95] The 1942 revisions, aimed largely at narrowing the gap between service and civilian pay, had been intended to be final but civilian wages continued to rise, once again widening the gap. By July 1943 commanders were reporting that men's letters no longer contained many complaints about pay and allowances, but this was felt to be 'because they were tired of complaining about them' rather than because the grievances had been met.[96] However, in October, commanders themselves were suggesting that the whole question of Family Allowances needed reviewing and were particularly concerned with reports of families who were just making ends meet but could not save anything for emergencies.[97] Discontent also continued to be expressed with levels of service pay compared to that in industry. Ministry of Labour figures showed that average industrial earnings in July 1943 were £6 1s 3d per week.[98] Service wages consisted of allowances for all meals, clothing, accommodation and amenities in addition to Family or Dependants' Allowances where applicable, exemption from tax as outlined above and health and unemployment insurance plus a cash wage of £1 1s per week.[99]

As a result the Treasury concluded that the 'real' value of service pay was often above that of civilian wages.[100] However, it also concluded that, even taking into account payment of WSG, existing rates of Family Allowance, especially for the families of lower-paid servicemen, 'did not enable the wife with children to live at the same standard as that enjoyed by the families of munitions workers'.[101] Because of this, increases to Family Allowances would now 'merit consideration'.[102] At the time 1.8–2 million Family Allowances were being paid across the three services and the cost of increasing minimum income for all wives to £1 12s per week, without increasing required allotment, was likely to be in the region of £5 million.[103] Despite the fact that the Lord President of the

Council, together with the Foreign Secretary, the Chancellor and MPs who had expressed interest in the matter now began discussions into these possible increases, the feeling persisted that the government had only acted under pressure from outside sources. Irene Ward, a persistent critic of government policy in this and other fields, suggested that the feeling in the country was that 'the government never comes forward with proposals but waits for agitation'.[104]

Two schools of thought existed in relation to levels of service pay.[105] The first continued a train of thought outlined earlier that, in times of war, defence of one's country and duty took precedence over absolute levels of pay. Together with financial considerations raised by the necessities of a war economy, this resulted in an attitude whereby, if an existing pay system met the necessities of daily life, it would be 'an extravagant use of public funds to make available to servicemen and their families more than the bare necessities'.[106] The second school of thought, however, suggested that the labourer was always worthy of his hire. Service families should, in the light of this, be granted pay and allowances that would 'bring them above the mere subsistence level'.[107]

As the level of both public debate and that within the House of Commons became increasingly heated, it became clear to the government that it could not rely on the first school of thought. The army had claimed that soldiers were upset by allegations that their families were 'starving or at any rate ill-provided for' and this view had been reinforced by the opinion of SSAFA, which was dealing with the day-to-day problems of families whose allowances were delayed or inadequate.[108] The War Office, therefore, argued that a speedy end to the discussions was necessary to put servicemen's minds at rest, suggesting that they could imagine 'nothing more damaging to the spirit of the troops who are about to be engaged than acrimonious debate in the House of Commons'.[109] In the event W.D. Kendal, Independent MP for Grantham, introduced an amendment to the government's proposed motion to investigate levels of service allowances, stating that:

> This House is of the opinion that the pay and allowances of members of His Majesty's Army are inadequate to enable them or their families to maintain a decent standard of living and that, therefore, it is urgent that immediate increases be made in such payments and allowances.[110]

This amendment, which would have forced the government to acknowledge that existing levels of service pay were inadequate, was narrowly defeated, after a lengthy debate.[111]

At all costs the government deemed it necessary to 'avoid a hasty and ill-considered decision . . . on the lines of the equally hasty and ill-considered conclusion reached in September 1942'.[112] To prevent this a paper, known as the Holland Report, was prepared by the Adjutant General's office on existing rates of pay and allowances.[113] The report firstly analysed the finances of 'other ranks' army families and came to the conclusion that, without other income, families 'cannot maintain a decent standard on the allowances, qualifying allotments and voluntary allotments available to the private soldier'.[114] For officers the Report assumed that their families would 'follow the way of life of a middle class family enjoying an income of some £600 per year'.[115] Difficulties in maintaining this lifestyle were largely experienced only by junior officers. However, the case of officers' families proved to be 'very much more complicated' as, during war, Family Allowance for officers did not vary with rank so any flat rate increase would apply both to those in need and to higher-ranking officers' families, who were already adequately provided for.[116] The Report concluded that 'the basic rates of Family Allowance are below the normal rates of bare subsistence'.[117] The increases suggested would amount to a cost of in the region of £20 million per annum, a cost that the Prime Minister regarded as 'not unreasonable'.[118]

In the resultant White Paper, the main suggestions dealt with increases to Family and Children's Allowances for the families of 'other ranks', and with introducing a common basis for allotments across the services.[119] Minimum payments for WSG were also increased, as were allowances for officer's families.[120] Although, as already discussed, such an increase benefited all officers, increases were greatest for junior officers with families. Overall the cost of the changes, which were to be implemented from May 1944, was estimated to be in the region of £50 million in the first year.[121]

The First Lord of the Admiralty, introducing the revised rates of allowances on behalf of all three services in a broadcast on 20 December 1944, spoke of the changes having come about as the result of a 'comprehensive' review of all service rates of pay and allowances in relation to workers in industry.[122] For 'the first time in history' there was now a 'reasonable equity' between pay in the armed forces and that in industry and broad 'equality between the services'.[123] The review was sited in a wider government initiative to make the services a more attractive career so as not to have to 'rely on an large unemployment list as a recruiting ground for the forces of the crown'.[124]

There was, however, no suggestion that increased levels of Children's Allowances would continue beyond the period of the war itself. Just as discontent existed among some servicemen at their levels of pay compared to that of civilian workers, so some civilian workers expressed discontent with the services' system of Children's Allowances.[125] These were regarded as rewarding those who had large families as the levels of allowance increased with the number of children. In fact the government, whilst considering these particular changes as being appropriate in a time of conscription when older men with existing families were taken into the forces, did not consider that such changes would be 'suitable as a permanent part of the pay code'.[126] In addition, under the Family Allowance Act, for the first time Family Allowances within the services became liable for income tax when the serviceman's pay reached taxable level.[127] Within the army, the new rates of pay and allowances were 'accepted as not unreasonable'.[128]

Overall the review was seen as establishing the fundamental points of 'a broad equality of treatment between the three services and a substantial correspondence at a suitable point between Service pay and industrial wages'.[129] No further changes to allowances or pay were envisaged in the near future except in the event of a 'marked alteration in the economic situation of the country generally'.[130]

As we have seen, the problems of attempting to draft regulations covering all eventualities continued for the whole period of the war. From 1940 onwards, however, the difficulties associated with pay and allowances became increasingly focused around the question of the comparison between service and civilian pay. Issues surrounding family welfare in terms of levels of income continued to inform comments in the Army Morale Reports throughout the period of the war although no specific information is given in relation to the morale of those taken prisoner of war. The information contained in the reports was gathered by divisional and district commanders, and no comparable system was established for camp leaders in prisoner of war camps to collect information.[131] Despite the fact that in 1940 large numbers of men from the British Expeditionary Force had been taken captive, the plight of their families did not feature in any of the discussions of that year surrounding pay and allowances. The fall of Singapore in 1942 and the subsequent ill-defined status of those missing in the Far East posed even more problems for families but again these problems were not specifically addressed in discussions on service allowances in either 1942 or 1944. By late 1944 reports of the Army Morale Committee showed that concerns of servicemen in general regarding their families were becoming subsumed by other concerns.[132] Concerns more directly related to a return to civilian life such as re-establishing family life and housing and employment feature more prominently in later reports. Similarly, comments in the 1944 White Paper suggest that the services too were beginning to focus their concerns on recruitment and pay for the postwar services.[133]

In contrast to the situation in Britain, in France the financial concerns of prisoner of war families achieved a much higher profile. In France the prisoner of war issue weighed heavily, with the national economy suffering as a result of a greatly reduced workforce, particularly in rural areas, and, given the high numbers involved, almost every family having a relative who was held captive or, at least, knowing someone who was. Furthermore, prisoners of war in France had a political importance unknown in Britain as the Vichy government considered their liberation essential.[134] Immediately after the outbreak of war, the Third Republic acted to provide for the families of all servicemen: career officers, non-commissioned officers and other officers with a minimum of two years' service were entitled to a monthly salary, of which up to three-quarters could be paid directly to their wives or parents.[135] Soldiers whose families had depended on them for financial support were entitled to claim allowances made up of a daily sum for their wives or dependent parents plus an additional sum for each child.[136] As with Dependants' Allowances in Britain, these allowances were subject to investigation but in France this was to determine need rather than prior levels of support.[137] With the fall of France in June 1940, the great majority of these allowances became payable to the families of prisoners of war. As a result, whereas campaigns in Britain were waged for higher allowances for all servicemen, those in France were directed explicitly towards better allowances for prisoner of war dependants.[138]

Despite this, in July 1941 the Family and Health Secretary, Jacques Chevalier, wrote that 'a prisoner's family with children is condemned to the most severe deprivation'.[139] Assertions were made, firstly by Chevalier and later by Maurice Pinot, in charge of the Commissariat Général aux Prisonniers de Guerre Repatriés, that this deprivation led directly to POW wives turning to prostitution as a means of eking out their meagre allowances.[140] Pinot asserted that, in Paris by December 1941, 75 per cent of all prostitutes were prisoner of war wives.[141] Fishman asserts that the accuracy of these figures is impossible to determine and that they were used largely as a scare tactic to gain increases in allowances for prisoner of war families.[142] Although the tactic was eventually successful, the proposed changes took over a year to implement and allowances were finally increased only under pressure from Pierre Laval, Head of the Vichy government from April 1942.[143] Laval, like many in the British government, recognised important political benefits to be gained by demonstrating concern from service families in general.[144] In France, however, as a result of the particularly large number of women who were wives of prisoners of war, this group gained a political importance not afforded to them in Britain. Despite this higher political profile and the resultant increases in allowances, Sarah Fishman reports that, of the prisoner of war wives she contacted for her study, none reported living on allowances alone; 80 per cent reported also being in some form of employment either in or outside the home.[145]

In Britain the suggestion of wives turning to prostitution to supplement their allowances never appeared as an issue in political debates or in local campaigns to increase allowances. Even in cases where complaints were made against wives, these were usually based on allegations of cohabitation or neglect of children. However, there can be little doubt that, for many, allowances proved barely adequate to provide for a family. Mrs Parkes, whose husband was taken prisoner in January 1941, recorded 'you'd got to be very, very careful because what little bit you'd got you'd got to pay yer rent and, er, of course there wasn't a lot of food you could get'.[146] Although between 1939 and early 1946, allowances for a wife with two children rose by over 65 per cent, in the same period the purchasing power of the pound fell by almost exactly the same amount.[147] In real terms then, service families as a whole were very much worse off than the families of those employed in, for example, engineering and shipbuilding, whose wages had risen by almost 180 per cent.[148]

Despite the fact that many of the problems faced by service dependants in Britain during the Second World War had already been apparent between 1914 and 1918, few remedies had been developed in the intervening years. Perhaps the fact that, although many families had faced hardship during the First World War, few had actually starved, meant that the need to devise solutions to the problems of administering large numbers of allowances and ensuring that they were at an adequate level was not regarded as vital. In Germany, where many service families and war widows had faced destitution and starvation both during and immediately after the First World War, such solutions had been devised with 'relatively generous' allowances being given to soldiers' wives 'in an effort to maintain morale among troops'.[149] Indeed, during the first six months of the war, the number of working women declined by some 400,000 and, even in 1940 when labour shortages in Germany were critical, it proved impossible to recruit soldiers' wives into work as the allowances they received were so generous.[150] Koonz suggests that labour market experts at the time went so far as to suggest decreasing the benefits paid to soldiers' wives in an effort to encourage them to take up paid employment.[151]

In Britain, however, the administration of allowances staggered on, with the amounts granted being neither totally adequate nor at a level low enough to cause national outrage. And, for those like Mrs Parkes, whose husbands were taken captive, the general problems of inadequate allowances, inefficiently administered, were exacerbated by the interpretation of regulations governing the admission and administration of Family and Dependants' Allowances with regard to the families of those taken prisoner of war.

Notes

1 Central Statistical Office, *Fighting with Figures. A Statistical Digest of the Second World War*. London: HMSO, 1995. Table 3.4 Strength of the Armed Forces and Women's Auxiliary Services. p. 39.
2 Letter War Office to Reid, Area Officer, UAB. 06 November 40. NA/AST11/143.
3 Letter Reid, Area Officer, UAB, to Bovenschen, Deputy Undersecretary of State, War Office. 22 November 40. NA/AST11/143.

4 Letter Reid, Area Officer, UAB, to Bovenschen, Deputy Under-secretary of State, War Office. 22 November 40. NA/AST11/143.
5 Letter Reid, Area Officer, UAB, to Bovenschen, Deputy Under-secretary of State, War Office. 22 November 40. NA/AST11/143.
6 Report of the Inter-departmental Committee on Army Allowances and War Service Grants (Malpass Report). Introduction. 31 March 41. NA/AST11/143.
7 Report of the Inter-departmental Committee on Army Allowances and War Service Grants (Malpass Report). Introduction. 31 March 1941. NA/AST11/143.
8 Report of the Inter-departmental Committee on Army Allowances and War Service Grants (Malpass Report). Introduction. 31 March 1941. NA/AST11/143.
9 Report of the Inter-departmental Committee on Army Allowances and War Service Grants (Malpass Report). 31 March 1941. NA/AST11/143.
10 Report of the Inter-departmental Committee on Army Allowances and War Service Grants (Malpass Report). 31 March 1941. NA/AST11/143.
11 Note to the Draft Report of the Inter-departmental Committee on Army Allowances and War Service Grants. Undated but probably early April 1942. NA/AST11/143.
12 Report of the Inter-departmental Committee on Army Allowances and War Service Grants (Malpass Report). 31 March 42. p. 6. NA/AST11/143.
13 Letter UAB to Crombie, Assistant Secretary, Treasury. 24 May 40. NA/AST11/124.
14 Letter UAB to Crombie, Assistant Secretary, Treasury. 24 May 40. NA/AST11/124.
15 Between 1939 and 1940 the actual purchasing power of the pound fell by 20 per cent. Butler and Butler, *British Political Facts*. p. 383.
16 Thomas, *State Maintenance for Women during the First World War*. Chapter 2.
17 *Ilford Recorder*. 07 March 40. NA/AST11/135.
18 Thomas, notes that, although no archival material exists, Sylvia Pankhurst had been instrumental in the formation of the League of Rights for Soldiers and Sailors' Wives and Female Relatives in the East End of London during the First World War. Thomas, *State Maintenance for Women during the First World War*. Chapter 2. During the Second World War, she revived this role, becoming honorary secretary of the Women's War Emergency Committee which campaigned, amongst other matters, for separation allowances for wives and allowances to the mothers of single men

in the forces. Pugh, M., *The Pankhursts*. London: Allen Lane, 2001.
p. 451.

19 *Ilford Recorder*. 07 March 40. NA/AST11/135.

20 Thomas, *State, Maintenance for Women during the First World War*.
Chapter 2.

21 Fred Bellinger, Labour MP Bassetlaw, speaking in a debate in House
of Commons. 10 September 42. NA/WO32/10448.

22 Extract from 'Address to all Ranks and Descriptions of Englishmen',
circa 1814, quoted by Hardy, T., *The Trumpet Major*, and used on
the cover of *An Examination of Army Pay and Allowances*. 1944.
NA/WO32/10975.

23 Confidential notes on Family Allowances, Dependants' Allowances
and War Service Grants. 28 November 39. NA/AST11/123.

24 Means tests for Dependants' Allowances differed from those generally used by the UAB for Unemployment Assistance and to supplement Old Age Pension in that they dealt with the general financial
position of the whole household rather than with individual need.
Draft White Paper on Service Pay and Allowances. 01 April 44. NA/
WO32/9444.

25 Draft White Paper on Service Pay and Allowances. July 42. NA/
T162/692/E45396/1.

26 Minister of Pensions speaking in Secret Session, House of Commons.
16 October 41. NA/AST11/136.

27 Minister of Pensions speaking in Secret Session, House of Commons.
16 October 41. NA/AST11/136.

28 Secret Session of House of Commons. 16 October 41. NA/AST11/136.

29 Secret Session of House of Commons. 16 October 41. NA/AST11/136.

30 Articles in *The Star* and the *Yorkshire Evening* Post, both 09
December 41. NA/AST11/136.

31 Army Council Instructions No. 532 of 1941. By October 350,000
claims had been made for Dependants' Allowances. Of these, 150,000
were ultimately accepted and 200,000 denied. However, with
changing rules governing allowable income, most of the cases previously rejected now became eligible for re-application. NA/
WO32/9444.

32 Report by Mr Chalk, previously of Standard Cables. September
1942. NA/AST11/151.

33 Report by Mr Chalk, previously of Standard Cables. September
1942. NA/AST11/151.

34 The debate may, however, have continued into better ways to administer these allowances and grants as the matter re-surfaced in a review
of WSG in July 1947. NA/AST11/125.

35 First Meeting of the War Office Morale Committee. 01 April 42. NA/
WO32/15772.

36 Final Report of the War Office Morale Committee. 10 February 48. NA/WO32/15772.

37 First Meeting of the War Office Morale Committee. 01 April 42. NA/WO32/15772.

38 Adjutant General, Paper on Morale in the Army. 23 February 42. NA/WO32/15772.

39 Adjutant General, Paper on Morale in the Army. 23 February 42. NA/WO32/15772.

40 Report of the War Office Morale Committee. May–July 1942, Item 14. NA/WO32/15772.

41 Report of the War Office Morale Committee. May–July 1942, Item 14. NA/WO32/15772.

42 Trustram, *Women of the Regiment*. p. 24.

43 *The Prisoner of War*. May 1942. British Red Cross Archive.

44 *The Prisoner of War*. May 1942 and August 1942. British Red Cross Archive.

45 Treasury Draft Statement on Pay and Allowances. Undated. NA/T162/692/45396/2.

46 Comparative rates of pay UK, USA and Dominions. 09 February 42. NA/T162/646/E44411/1and2.

47 Unsigned copy of letter from Treasury to Rt Hon. Sir Kingsley Wood, Chancellor of the Exchequer. 23 June 42. NA/T162/E45396/1.

48 Unsigned copy of letter from Treasury to Rt Hon. Sir Kingsley Wood, Chancellor of Exchequer. 23 June 42. NA/T162/E45396/1.

49 Barrett Litoff and Smith, 'US Women on the Home Front'. p. 355.

50 Fighting Services Separation Allowances. Men called up under the Military Training Act, 1939. NA/T162/573/E38806/01.

51 Unusually, New Zealand troops had to make allotments from pay whether or not they were married. If single their allotment was made to a nominee, bank or insurance company. Table III Comparison of Rates of Pay and Family Allowance with Amercian and Dominion Overseas Rates. Non-tradesmen. NA/T162/692/45396/1.

52 Letter Rt Hon. Winston Churchill, Prime Minister, to Rt Hon. Sir Kingsley Wood, Chancellor of the Exchequer. 13 July 42. NA/T162/692/E45396/1.

53 Note Rt Hon. Sir Kingsley Wood, Chancellor of the Exchequer, to Rt Hon. Winston Churchill, Prime Minister. 13 July 42. NA/T162/692/E45396/1.

54 Note Rt Hon. Sir Kingsley Wood, Chancellor of the Exchequer, to Rt Hon. Winston Churchill, Prime Minister. 13 July 42. NA/T162/692/E45396/1.

55 Minute Sheet 1. 20 July 42. NA/WO32/10477.

56 Minutes of meeting of Executive Committee of the Army Council. 17 July 42. NA/WO32/10477.

57 Notes for the Press. August 1942. NA/T162/692/E45396/1.

58 Minutes of meeting of Executive Committee of the Army Council. 17 July 42. NA/WO32/10477.

59 Minutes of 68th meeting of the Executive Committee of the Army Council. 17 July 42. NA/WO32/10477. Further army discussions on this matter can also be found in NA/WO32/15772.

60 Reynolds, D., *Rich Relations. The American Occupation of Britain 1942-1945*. New York: Random House, Inc., 1995. p. 153.

61 The Report of the War Office Morale Committee, May–July 1942, suggested that women also preferred the company of the air force and civilian workers for the same reason. NA/WO32/10477.

62 Unsigned copy of letter from Treasury to Rt Hon. Sir Kingsley Wood, Chancellor of the Exchequer. 23 June 42. NA/T162/E45396/1.

63 Reynolds, *Rich Relations*. p. 153.

64 Reynolds, *Rich Relations*. p. 153.

65 Reynolds, *Rich Relations*. p. 153.

66 Draft White Paper 'Emoluments of the Armed Forces'. July 42. NA/T162/692/E45396/1.

67 Hancock, W.K., and Gowing M.M., *History of the Second World War. British War Economy*. London: HMSO, 1949. p. 505.

68 Secretary of State for War speaking in the House of Commons. 01 January 42. T162/646/E44411/1 and 2.

69 Draft White Paper 'Emoluments of the Armed Forces'. July 42. NA/T162/692/E45396/1.

70 Draft White Paper. 'Emoluments of the Armed Forces'. August 1942. NA/T162/692/E4596/1. See also NA/WO32/10488.

71 Draft White Paper 'Emoluments of the Armed Forces'. July 42. NA/T162/692/E45396/1.

72 Draft White Paper 'Emoluments of the Armed Forces'. July 42. NA/T162/692/E45396/1.

73 Draft White Paper 'Emoluments of the Armed Forces'. July 42. NA/T162/692/E45396/1.

74 Letter Treasury to Sir Edward Bridges, Secretary of State for War. 30 July 42. NA/WO32/10488.

75 White Paper on Service Pay and Allowances. August 1942. NA/WO32/10488.

76 Unsigned letter Treasury to BBC. 15 September 42. NA/T162/692/45396/2.

77 Unsigned copy letter War Office to Clough, Principal, Treasury. 19 January 43. NA/T162/692/45396/2.

78 Letter Sir Edward Bridges, Secretary of State for War, to Rt Hon. Sir Kingsley Wood, Chancellor of the Exchequer. 01 January 42. NA/T162/646/E44411/1 and 2.

79 Letter Sir Edward Bridges, Chancellor of the Exchequer, to Miss Culhane, UAB. 29 August 42. NA/T162/692/E45396/1.

80 Letter Sir Edward Bridges, Chancellor of the Exchequer, to Miss Culhane, UAB. 29 August 42. NA/T162/692/E45396/1.

81 Fighting Service – Revision of Pay and Allowances. 1941-42. NA/T162/646/E44411/1 and 2.

82 White Paper Service Pay and Allowances. August 1942. NA/T162/692/45396/2.

83 Figures calculated from *Fighting with Figures*. Table 3.4 Strength of the Armed Forces and Women's Auxiliary Services. p. 39; and *British Political Facts*. Select Statistics: National Income, Taxes and Prices. p. 383.

84 Forces Programme, 15.45-18.00. 15 September 42. NA/T162/646/E44411/1 and 2.

85 Item 4, Report of the War Office Morale Committee. August–October 1942. NA/WO32/15772.

86 Item 4, Report of the War Office Morale Committee. August–October 1942. NA/WO32/15772.

87 No details are given of how the how the survey was conducted or by whom. Douie, V., *The Lesser Half: A Survey of Laws, Regulations and Practices Introduced during the Present War, Which Embody Discrimination against Women*. London: Women's Publicity Planning Association, 1943. p. 45.

88 Douie, *The Lesser Half*. p. 45.

89 Proposals for the establishment of a Joint Standing Committee on Service Pay and Allowances. 19 October 42. NA/T162/647/E45846.

90 Proposals for the establishment of a Joint Standing Committee on Service Pay and Allowances. 19 October 42. NA/T162/647/E45846.

91 Proposals for the establishment of a Joint Standing Committee on Service Pay and Allowances. 19 October 42. NA/T162/647/E45846.

92 Note of Government decision. 25 November 42. NA/T162/647/E45846.

93 Note of Government decision. 25 November 42. NA/T162/647/E45846.

94 Statement by Lord Privy Seal on improvements to service pay and allowances contained in White Paper, 1942. April 44. NA/T162/801/E45396/01/1.

95 Statement by Lord Privy Seal. April 44. NA/T162/801/E45396/01/1.

96 Report of the War office Morale Committee. May–July 1943. NA/WO32/15772[43A].

97 Report of the War Office Morale Committee. August–October 1943. NA/WO32/15772[46A].

98 Memo, Clough, Principal, Treasury, to Financial Secretary, Treasury. February 44. NA/T162/801/E45396/01/1.

99 Memo, Clough, Principal, Treasury, to Financial Secretary, Treasury. February 44. NA/T162/801/E45396/01/1.

100 The Treasury also noted that army rations included larger portions to meet the nutritional requirements of soldiers according to the duty on which they were employed – and that 'amenities' included cheap cigarettes, ENSA and free leave travel. NA/T162/801/E45396/01/1.

101 Memo, Clough, Principal, Treasury, to Financial Secretary, Treasury. February 44. NA/T162/801/E45396/01/1.

102 NA/T162/801/E45396/01/1.

103 Letter Ministry of Pensions to Wilson Smith, Assistant Secretary, Treasury. 07 March 44. NA/T162/801/E45396/01/1.

104 Letter Irene Ward, MP, Combined Universities, to Foreign Secretary. 12 March 44. NA/T162/801/E45396/01/1. See also NA/WO32/10448.

105 Minute Sheet Register No. 30/GenA/87. 03 March 44. NA/WO32/10975.

106 Prime Minister's Personal Minute. 07 March 44. NA/WO32/10448. See also NA/WO32/10975.

107 Prime Minister's Personal Minute. 07 March 44. NA/WO32/10448. See also NA/WO32/10975.

108 Report of the War Office Morale Committee. February–April 1944. NA/WO32/15772.

109 Letter War Office to Treasury, marked Top Secret. 28 March 44. NA/T162/801/E45396/01/2.

110 Parliamentary Debates (Hansard) House of Commons Official Report. Vol. 397 No. 40. 02 March 44. NA/WO32/10975.

111 Following a discussion of approximately six hours, the amendment was defeated by 63 votes to 40. Hansard. Vol. 397, No.40. NA/WO32/10975.

112 Debate in House of Commons. 02 March 44. NA/WO32/10975 and Minute Sheet 30/GEN/9952. 03 March 44. NA/WO32/10448. The 'hasty and ill-considered' decision of 1942 had been made against War Office opinion.

113 Holland Report. March 1944. NA/WO32/10975.

114 Item 5. Holland Report. March 1944. NA/WO32/10975.

115 Item 6. Holland Report. March 1944. NA/WO32/10975.

116 Items 8 and 9. Holland Report. March 1944. NA/WO32/10975.

117 Holland Report. March 1944. NA/WO32/10975[6A].

118 Prime Minister's Personal Minute. 07 March 44. NA/T162/801/E45396/01/2.

119 White Paper, 'Service Pay and Allowances'. April 1944. NA/T162/801/E45396/01/1.

120 White Paper, 'Service Pay and Allowances'. April 1944. NA/T162/801/E45396/01/1.
121 White Paper, 'Service Pay and Allowances'. April 1944. NA/T162/801/E45396/01/1.
122 Broadcast by the First Lord of the Admiralty. 20 December 44. NA/162/801/E45396/01/5.
123 Broadcast by the First Lord of the Admiralty. 20 December 44. NA/162/801/E45396/01/5.
124 Broadcast by the First Lord of the Admiralty. 20 December 44. NA/162/801/E45396/01/5.
125 Inter-departmental Committee on postwar pay, allowances and pensions. December 1945. NA/WO32/11565.
126 White Paper, PostWar Code of Pay, Allowances and Service Pensions and Gratuities for Members of the Forces below Officer Rank. December 1945. NA/T213/7/DP611/37/06.
127 Broadcast by the First Lord of the Admiralty. 20 December 44. NA/162/801/E45396/01/5.
128 Report of the War Office Morale Committee May–July 1944, Appendix 'A' Finance. NA/WO32/15772[59A].
129 Broadcast by First Lord of the Admiralty. NA/T162.801/E45396/1/5.
130 Broadcast by First Lord of the Admiralty. NA/T162.801/E45396/1/5.
131 Letter War Office to All Army Commanders. 30 December 1941. NA/WO32/15772.
132 War Office Morale Committee Reports November 1944–November 1945. NA/WO32/15772.
133 White Paper, Increased Financial Provision for Members of His Majesty's Forces and their Families with Certain Changes in War Pensions. April 1944. NA/T162/801/E45396/01/1, 2, 3, 4 and 5 and Minute Sheet 1. 20 February 44. NA/WO32/10972.
134 Fishman, *We Will Wait*. p. 30.
135 Fishman, *We Will Wait*. p. 46.
136 Fishman, *We Will Wait*. p. 46.
137 Fishman, *We Will Wait*. p. 46.
138 Fishman, *We Will Wait*. p. 46.
139 Fishman, *We Will Wait*. p. 47.
140 Fishman, *We Will Wait*. p. 49.
141 Fishman, *We Will Wait*. p. 48.
142 Fishman, *We Will Wait*. p. 50.
143 Fishman, *We Will Wait*. p. 52.
144 Fishman, *We Will Wait*. p. 51.
145 Fishman, *We Will Wait*. p. 58.
146 Parkes, IWM Sound Archive 12864/1.
147 Butler and Butler. *British Political Facts*. p. 383.

148 *Fighting with Figures.* p. 237. Table 12.5 Average Weekly Wages in Certain Industries.
149 Mason, T., *Social Policy in the Third Reich*. Oxford: Berg, 1993. p. 236.
150 Mason, *Social policy in the Third Reich*. p. 236. Mason records that separation allowances were as much as 85 per cent of the family's previous income.
151 Koonz, C., *Mothers in the Fatherland. Women, the Family and Nazi Politics*. London: Methuen, 1998. p. 396.

3

'Dead, missing or prisoner of war?' – classifying men lost in action

As we have already seen, despite the warnings from the experience of the First World War and the concerns of a number of charitable institutions, when war broke out in September 1939 the authorities concerned found themselves, once again, unprepared for the sheer scale of the burden that administering service allowances in a time of war would entail. By the end of 1939 large numbers of service families were already facing hardship as a result of delayed payments. At the end of May 1940 when some 34,000 British and Commonwealth troops were taken captive following the British retreat from Dunkirk, the families of these servicemen faced even greater problems in trying to ensure financial security.

From the outset it seemed clear that the government intended that Family and Dependants' Allowances should continue for any period during which the soldier was a prisoner of war.[1] This is confirmed by a War Office minute following the outbreak of war in September 1939, which stated that pay, Family Allowance and Dependants' Allowances should continue during any period of captivity for both officers and other ranks.[2] However, different scales of allowances were applicable depending on whether the serviceman was deemed to be missing, prisoner of war or killed. For many families the point at which a missing breadwinner changed from being categorised as 'missing' to 'presumed dead' or 'prisoner of war', apart from the huge emotional upheaval involved, was often critical in terms of family budgeting. As has already been shown, Family Allowance rates were often substantially higher than pensions as wives of missing servicemen were 'under a greater obligation to try to maintain the normal standard of the home than was the wife who knew she had become a widow and would, therefore, have to conform to a new and lower standard'.[3] So critical was this difference for some families that R.F.L. Watkins, a member of the Territorials, wrote that men often used to leave their identity tags off when they went into battle. If they were killed they would then be reported 'missing' and their families would continue to receive allowances for a time before being reduced to a widow's pension.[4]

In a letter to the Treasury, Humphreys-Davies, Under-secretary at the War Office, set out the agreed position regarding allowances for men reported missing.[5] For the families and dependants of both officers and men, pay and allowances continued to be issued at normal rates for the first four weeks unless the man was reported dead during this time. For the next thirteen weeks, the appropriate allowances plus two-sevenths pay (for officers) or compulsory allotment (for men) were issued.[6] Dependants of officers who were not entitled to pensions did not receive any allowances. In the case of families of officers reported killed, married allowance plus two-sevenths of pay was issued for thirteen weeks although no allowances were issued to dependants.[7] For the families of other ranks reported killed, widows and dependants eligible for pensions continued to receive a temporary allowance pending the award of pension for a total period of thirteen weeks.[8] In the first four weeks this temporary allowance amounted to Family or Dependants' Allowance plus actual allotment from pay. After this time it decreased to allowance plus allotment at the qualifying level. For those dependants outside the pensionable categories, allotment at qualifying rate was issued for four weeks only.[9]

Although the regulations were by no means straightforward they appeared, at least in theory, to cover all possible eventualities. However, once war was actually declared, two major problems arose particularly concerning the determination of allowances payable to the families and dependants of servicemen taken captive. Many servicemen later notified as being prisoners of war were initially recorded as missing before their true status was clarified. For these families the length of time before the serviceman's fate was ascertained became a critical factor in determining their entitlement to allowances. This can be demonstrated most easily in relation to the navy where the exact fate of men lost on the high seas was particularly difficult to determine. Before 1942, the normal procedure had been to assume that seamen lost in battle on the high seas were extremely unlikely to have survived if no information as to their whereabouts had been received within the four-week period.[10] Unless survivors had been picked up by another ship, which would have forwarded information, they were most likely to have drowned. In July 1942 HMS *Exeter*, *Jupiter*, *Electra*, *Encounter* and *Stronghold* had all been lost in battles in the Java Seas.[11] However, given the geography of the area, it seemed likely that most of the crew members, particularly of the *Exeter* and *Jupiter* who had survived the initial battle, would have been able to reach the Java coast. Although this change in perception of the fate of sailors did prompt calls for a change in procedure, some within the navy felt that there was 'no reason' for change.[12] Others considered that an extended missing period should be implemented as the Japanese had not adhered to the 'normal civilised procedure' of allowing the Red Cross to ascertain details of prisoners in their hands and so notification might not be immediately forthcoming.[13] By the end of July 1942 this second attitude had prevailed and an extended missing period was granted to personnel missing from these ships plus sailors from HMS *Thanet* and HMS *Perth*, both of which had also been lost in the area.[14] By November 1943 this decision had been vindicated. At the fourth meeting of the Interdepartmental Prisoner of War Co-ordinating Committee (Finance), the Admiralty reported that an 'unexpectedly large' number of naval personnel reported missing in the Java Sea were now confirmed as being captives of the Japanese.[15] In the case of officers, 50 per cent of the total number originally reported missing had survived.[16]

Once the procedural decision was taken, however, the administration of such allowances did not automatically run smoothly. As was often the case, decisions taken at one level did not always filter through immediately to those applying them. The wife of Chief Petty Officer Butland, missing from HMS *Electra*, still had her allowances reduced to pension rates after the statutory seventeen weeks, and had the 'missing' rate reinstated only after attention was drawn to her case by the *London Evening News*.[17] As we have already seen in a number of instances, the intervention of the press was again required to expedite the situation.

Indeed, from the beginning of the war, difficulties had arisen around the issue of precise dates when families were notified that servicemen were posted 'missing'. Although specific periods were set out when allowances should change from full pay plus allowances to allowance plus allotments and then to pension rates,

Service Departments and families did not necessarily receive this information at the same time.[18] To use the navy again as an example, in the case of officers there was often a discrepancy between the date on which the officer was known by the Admiralty to be missing and the date on which his family received such notification.[19] For operational reasons, it was often considered politic by the navy not to allow the loss, or otherwise, of particular vessels to become common knowledge. For example, in early 1941 a German radio broadcast claimed the loss of HMS *Illustrious* in the Mediterranean.[20] A later broadcast by Sir Walter Monkton, KC, Director General of the Ministry of Information, reported that, at the time, it had been tempting to set the record straight by releasing the information that the vessel had not in fact sunk.[21] However, as the Ministry of Information felt that this was exactly the information which German agencies were trying to obtain, silence was maintained until the *Illustrious* had been sufficiently repaired in Malta to leave under its own steam.[22] No mention is made of whether or not any consideration was given to the feelings of the families of the seamen on this vessel who must have believed that their loved ones had been lost. This policy somewhat backfired in 1941 when the medium Helen Duncan released the news of the sinking of HMS *Barham* during a séance in Portsmouth before the Admiralty had released the news to the families concerned.[23] Mrs Duncan was regarded as such a threat to security that she was later tried in 1944, initially on a charge of conspiracy, and eventually convicted under the 1735 Witchcraft Act.[24]

Obviously, a widow could not be expected to make any financial arrangements until she was officially notified of her husband's death. As a consequence the Treasury agreed that pay and allowances should be continued up to the date at which their families were notified that they had been killed rather than being stopped from the date at which the authorities received such information.[25] Similarly, the period during which payment of temporary allowances commenced was also calculated from the date of notification of death to the widow herself rather than notification to the appropriate government department.

Problems also arose, again apparently largely unforeseen, from the lack of official notification of the death of a serviceman if the wife subsequently wished to remarry. If the woman in question wished to remarry another serviceman, a possibility existed in the eyes of the Treasury that one woman might in this way be claimed as a legitimate dependant by two men.[26] The War Office generally gave allowances for second marriages only if a period of seven years had elapsed from the time when the former spouse was known to have been alive.[27] However, the Co-ordinating (Inter-departmental) Committee on Dependants' Allowances, meeting in April 1942, considered whether or not it was realistic in time of war for service departments to grant allowances for second marriages only if the woman had formally been notified that her first husband was dead.[28] At the time there was no agreement on this issue as differing views existed within the Committee as to how far the service departments should become involved in the moral issues that these remarriages raised. Some members felt that there was no need to 'look beyond the marriage certificate'. That is, if a marriage certificate existed then the serviceman had a right to claim allowances, but no agreement could be reached.[29] Although an Assistant Secretary in the Administration and Clerical Section of the War Office, acting as Chairman of the Committee, felt that the matter should be referred to a 'higher authority' there is no information as to whether this higher authority was envisaged as being governmental or spiritual.[30] The matter then disappeared from the files, but it becomes clear that no solution was agreed upon as it resurfaced in October 1945. At this time both the War Office and the Admiralty were in agreement that it was 'not unreasonable' for a woman whose allowances had been reduced to pension rates to assume that the authorities regarded her husband as dead even although no formal notification of death may have been received.[31] Although the Air Ministry still had continued reservations, the matter once again disappeared.[32]

In fact, the whole question of women remarrying on the assumption that their husbands were dead, when they were actually prisoners of war, continued to present a problem throughout the war and in the years immediately after. One example will serve to illustrate this point. In March 1942 Bombardier Ford of the Maritime Regiment was reported killed in the Far East and his wife officially notified of his death in July.[33] In September of the same year Mrs Ford remarried a Private Appleton and Family Allowance was issued to her in respect of this marriage from 27 September.[34] However, in June 1943 Mrs Appleton, as she now was, received a postcard from Bombadier Ford informing her that he was in fact a prisoner of war in Japanese hands. The War Office decreed that in these 'distressing circumstances' it was up to Mrs Ford to 'make up her own mind as to her future' and she decided that she would carry on living with Private Appleton even if this had to be on an 'irregular basis'. As she had married in good faith following official notification of her husband's death, the War Office requested permission from the Treasury to continue her payments of Family Allowance in respect of her new marriage. Although the Treasury agreed to this, it asked the War Office to note that this decision should be seen as being 'without prejudice to any general decision on policy that we may wish to take if an appreciable number of similar cases come to notice'.

In the Treasury files this case is referred to as an 'Enoch Arden' case after the Tennyson poem of the same title.[35] In this poem two childhood friends, Philip Ray and Enoch Arden, compete for the hand of Annie Lee with whom they have grown up. Annie marries Enoch but he later goes to sea to earn sufficient money to support his family. Following reports of Enoch's death at sea, Annie then marries Philip. However, Enoch is not dead. He returns to their village but, on seeing Annie and his children happy with Philip, he determines not to spoil their happiness and leaves without speaking to them. The fact that this type of case had been given a name suggests that Mrs Appleton was not an isolated example, and the Treasury was reluctant to commit itself to a policy without specific information as to the likely overall financial implications. This attitude was again apparent when the question of extended allowances for servicemen whose status was not confirmed came under consideration. In some ways their caution was justified. Recovery of 'overpayment' of allowances claimed for a bigamous 'wife' could not be made under the normal articles of payment. Instead they could be recouped only by a penal deduction from wages under Section 25 of the Army Act or by sentence of a court-martial.[36] War Office records for the period 1941 and 1947 show no such cases where overpayment was successfully recovered.[37]

Vivienne Chatfield, herself the widow of a Far East prisoner of war, states that there were many unpleasant shocks of this nature for returning prisoners as 'many [wives] had remarried when their husbands were missing, and others were living with other men'.[38] However, it should not be assumed that failing marriages or bigamous relationships were solely the prerogative of those taken captive and their families. Many of the general histories concerning the return of servicemen to Britain after the end of the war contain similar testimony.[39] A survey conducted in Birmingham during the last two years of the war estimated that one-third of all illegitimate births were to married women and, of these, half were to servicemen's wives.[40] Divorce figures for adultery in the years 1939–45 show a fourfold increase, with 58 per cent of cases being brought by husbands.[41]

Problems also arose in relation to notification dates and the veracity of confirmation of status of servicemen from the 'unexpected developments in France and Belgium' as, following the evacuation from Dunkirk, large numbers of British servicemen became trapped behind enemy lines without any reliable information as to their fate.[42] In many cases the only information available was from other servicemen who had escaped into unoccupied France and reported that several of their comrades were alive but hidden with French families.[43] In these cases the rules were adapted so as not to jeopardise the situation of the man himself or of the family hiding him and no further enquiries were made. Instead allowances continued at full rates for two and a half months from the date when the man was reported as having last been seen alive, after which time each individual case was reviewed.[44] By August 1941, 49 men had been reported missing but alive behind enemy lines in France or Belgium.[45] Of these men, fourteen eventually found their way back to British territory and reported their escape.[46] Fifteen of the remainder were captured by the Germans and in March 1943 were prisoners of war. Eight were interned in Vichy France and later became prisoners of war in Italian hands.[47] In another six cases, relatives submitted further letters written by the men involved to support claims for continuing allowances rather than reduction to pension rates.[48] In the remaining six cases, no news was received following the original report of their still being alive.[49] Thirty other cases also came to light, mainly of escaped prisoners of war, but also of some servicemen missing in Greece in similar circumstances, and a number of men were known to have escaped from prisoner of war camps and remained at large for at least one year and, in one case, for three years.[50] Again, in the great majority of these cases no further action was taken to try to verify the situation in case the man's position in hiding was jeopardised.

By March 1941 it had become clear, to the War Office at least, that the period of seventeen weeks during which allowances and allotments were continued was insufficient time to ascertain whether a serviceman was dead or a prisoner of war, even in Europe.[51] Indeed reports that men were prisoners of war in German hands were still being received for some men ten months after they had been reported missing during the evacuations from Belgium and France.[52] The War Office now suggested that this period for continuing allowances should be extended to 26 weeks.[53] This was still less than the time allowed in the First World War when, although allowances continued only for two months for married officers and single officers with pensionable dependants, they were continued for 30 weeks for other ranks. However, in March 1940 the likelihood of large numbers of men being taken captive was not seen as being likely. Humphreys-Davies, Assistant Secretary at the Treasury, regarded it as 'unnecessary and undesirable to legislate for the future on the assumption that the British Army habitually throws away its arms' and is, by implication, taken prisoner.[54] Instead, it was suggested that provision should be made for 'special cases', where men previously reported missing were subsequently found to be alive and at large in Belgium and France.[55] Despite the matter being referred to an Inter-Departmental Conference on 20 March 1941, the Treasury held to this position.[56]

The entry of Japan into the war and the fall of Hong Kong on 25 December 1941 again opened the matter for discussion. Within the War Office, the feeling was that, although most of the garrison here would eventually prove to have been taken prisoner of war, the length of time anticipated for the Japanese to formally notify the authorities of this fact would mean that, under existing rules, many families would be reduced to the equivalent of pensions unnecessarily.[57] In the light of this, the Army Council anticipated 'a strong and growing body of public criticism' and proposed that the seventeen-week period for the continuation of allowances be extended by a further thirteen weeks.[58] The position was to be reviewed if the Army Council received definite information regarding the fate of 80 per cent of the garrison within the first eight weeks of this extended period. Although some concern was expressed that the public should understand the 'differentiation in treatment' between personnel missing at Hong Kong and those

captured in Libya, in February 1942, the Treasury agreed to sanction the situation in the Far East as 'a special case'.[59] The rationale
for this was that where men were lost in 'small batches', as was the
case in Libya, information as to their status was almost always
available 'within a comparatively short time'.[60] As a result, extension of allowances was required only in cases where large numbers
of men had been lost at the same time and notification was likely
to be delayed.[61] On the basis of this decision the War Office then
requested that further 'special cases' should be considered if other
areas of the Far East fell under Japanese control.[62] For example, in
the case of Malaya, the War Office argued that, as three months
after the fall of Hong Kong 'not a single name [had] been transmitted by the Japanese Government', there were no grounds for hoping
that the position would be any different in the case of Malaya.[63] In
fact this example was seen as being even more delicate in that many
families from Malaya had been evacuated to Australia where they
would be in contact with families evacuated from Hong Kong and
any difference in treatment would be immediately apparent.[64]

As Hong Kong had fallen on 25 December 1941 families and
dependants would have automatically received allowances in full,
including any voluntary allotments in issue, up to 30 April 1942.
Following agreement by the Treasury, these allowances were now
extended to 30 July 1942, that is for a further thirteen weeks.[65]
Singapore had fallen on 15 February 1942, and, allowing five days
for official notification, temporary allowances would anyway continue up to 20 June.[66] In Java, which was reported as having surrendered on 10 March 1942, under the normal regulations
allowances would continue up to 15 July.[67] In these later cases, the
normal time for the issue of temporary allowances had not yet
expired so the Treasury saw no reason to extend them. A handwritten, and unsigned, note in the margins of a letter on the subject
accuses the War Office of making such proposals on 'sentimental
grounds'.[68] Not an attitude many service families would have attributed to it.

Instead of formulating an overall policy, the Treasury argued
that agreement with the Japanese to allow for telegraphic notification of prisoners of war had changed the situation from the time
of the fall of Hong Kong. Unlike the Foreign Office, who saw the
Japanese as extremely inefficient in giving these notifications, the
Treasury, without giving specific examples, claimed to have 'found

them quite the reverse in many other things'.[69] Consequently, they
regarded it as 'not impossible' that their prisoner of war information service would prove to be efficient, at the same time noting
that the War Office offered the 'usual threats of Ministerial action'
if the War Office's proposals were not agreed to.[70] The possibility
was also raised that most families from these locations, rather than
being in Australia as had been assumed, would, in fact, be returned
to Britain.[71] They would then compare their own situation favourably with that of families of men reported missing in Libya rather
than unfavourably with those reported missing in Hong Kong.
Nevertheless, some extension was reluctantly agreed to and the
Treasury suggested that allowances in all Far Eastern cases should
be extended to the date approved for Hong Kong.

The War Office argued that to implement such a decision to
agree a common date would effectively give families concerned with
the fall of Singapore seven weeks less on temporary allowances than
those from Hong Kong.[72] A further complication was also raised
in that, whereas there was little doubt about who was actually in
Hong Kong at the time of its fall, there was greater confusion in
the case of Singapore. Large numbers of reinforcements reached
there late in the campaign, moving under rules of secrecy.[73] As a
result many relatives did not have definite knowledge that their
menfolk had actually been in Singapore. In response, the Treasury
attempted to clarify their position by stating that it had been their
intention that 'in all Far Eastern cases where the normal period, or
the extended period in the case of Hong Kong, expired before the
31 July, full allowances should nevertheless be continued to that
date'.[74] Even then, temporary allowances would not necessarily
cease at that date as the particular circumstances would be taken
into consideration nearer the time.

By the third week in June 1942, when normal temporary allowances were due to cease for the families of those missing from
Singapore, the War Office had received only one official list of 343
prisoners of war taken at Hong Kong.[75] Although the Japanese
government had promised that a list of names of 280,000 would
be sent by way of ships carrying evacuated diplomatic staff from
Japan, this list would not be available until after the first exchange
in Lourenço Marques.[76] In view of this, the War Office saw no
prospect of being able to inform the majority of the next of kin
within 'any reasonable interval' after the 31 July.[77] As a result, the

Army Council requested that normal allowances should be continued for a further thirteen weeks, adding the question of how cessation of these allowances would be construed by relatives.[78]
Transfer to pension rates after this period of time would, they
thought, be viewed by some, if not the majority of, families as
'unofficial' notification of death.[79] Inevitably, the lack of information available to the relatives of those missing in the Far East
through official channels meant that any changes of this nature
would be immediately seized on. The Treasury, as usual more concerned with financial savings than family well-being, viewed further
extensions as 'entirely wrong' and claimed that if it had known how
long the situation would go on for it would have approved an
extension only for a maximum period of three months.[80]

Eventually, however, the question of administrative costs helped
to sway the Treasury from this opinion. Even if 80 per cent of those
missing were eventually found to be alive, some twenty thousand
remaining cases would still need to be transferred to pensions or
allowances equal to pension.[81] As it would be a 'difficult matter' to
change all these dependants of men not reported captive from temporary allowances to pensions in a short space of time, the Treasury
agreed that there should not be any reduction in temporary allowances before the end of October 1942, a total of 43 weeks from
the fall of Hong Kong.[82] Extensions beyond this period would still
be considered, if necessary, to ease the administrative work involved.
In respect of the effect on public morale and possible repercussions
in terms of popular support for the war effort, the War Office had
on this occasion a better than normal grasp of public opinion, and
certainly a better understanding than the Treasury. In a letter to
the Treasury, it claimed the matter as one 'which could not be dealt
with solely in the light of reason and logic'.[83] It also thought it
necessary to take into account 'the force of public sentiment as it
has been and will be expressed, in this connection, in Parliament
and elsewhere'.[84] In contrast, a handwritten margin note to this
letter, added by the Treasury, asks 'Do the general public believe
this?'[85]

The economic argument put forward by the War Office hinged
on the assumption that at least 80 per cent of those originally notified as missing would eventually be found to be prisoners of war.
For these men no extra costs would have actually been accrued as
families and dependants of prisoners of war were entitled to full

allowances anyway. On the basis of this assumption the War Office estimated that the extra cost of extending the payment of temporary allowances until 31 October 1942 would 'certainly be less than £20,000'.[86] Again administrative factors came into play. The prospect of having to issue 45,000 new allowance books for 31 July 1942, when it was not known for certain who was to be issued with allowances and who with pensions, certainly added weight to the argument for continuing temporary allowances until definite information was available about the majority of those missing.

By 7 December 1942, a year after hostilities in the Far East had begun, only 2,200 army personnel had been reported by the Japanese as having been taken prisoner – accounting for slightly fewer than 6 per cent of all those originally posted missing.[87] Judging by the Japanese performance to date there seemed little prospect of others being notified before the middle of January 1943 when the next deadline for expiry of temporary allowances came into effect. As a result the Treasury again sanctioned an extension, this time of 26 rather than the anticipated thirteen weeks.[88] However, the Far East was still regarded as a special case and the Treasury declined to authorise the War Office, Air Ministry or Admiralty to extend payment of temporary allowances in other cases beyond the normal seventeen-week period.[89] They argued that to discriminate between cases in Europe would lead to complaints from those whose allowances were not extended and that it would be difficult to convince them 'that they are being fairly dealt with'.[90] Initially, both the Air Ministry and Admiralty saw this as fair. However, neither of these services wished to resist the War Office, because of the much greater number of soldiers concerned. As a result, in November 1942, the Treasury agreed to extend the normal period of payment of temporary allowances from seventeen to 26 weeks in all cases from the date of notification of casualty for other ranks.[91] Payment of temporary allowances to dependants of officers remained at thirteen weeks.[92]

There can be no doubt that the lack of a coherent policy on length of payment of temporary allowances and the length of time taken to make decisions on these matters did have an effect on the finances of the families concerned. Corporal D. Hanks, of the 2nd Battalion Highland Light Infantry, was notified as missing in June 1942.[93] In a formal letter of 30 June 1942 his wife was notified that her current allowance of 35s 6d per week would continue until 25

October 1942. If no news of her husband had been received by that time the War Office would then make a decision regarding further allowances. A letter of 28 November 1942 from the War Office to the Treasury seems to suggest that Mrs Hanks may have complained to the Treasury about not knowing what her future arrangements were to be. In fact she had not been told what would happen once the temporary allowance expired as the War Office was trying to obtain sanction from the Treasury to continue this allowance. Its letter noted that 'I hope that what has happened in this case will help to convince the Treasury of our difficulties in dealing with this type of case if we do not get quick decisions from you'. By 25 October the Treasury still had not reached a decision and Mrs Hanks's temporary allowance ceased. She was then paid an allowance at pension rates of 19s per week until the Treasury reached its decision. As this decision reinstated her temporary allowance, a book of drafts then had to be reissued for Family Allowance at the original rate. The Treasury's indecision had resulted in the extra administrative work involved in issuing two allowance books in addition to a reduction in Mrs Hanks's income of 16s 6d per week while their decision was pending. There is no suggestion that she was then reimbursed for the period during which her allowance was unnecessarily reduced.

The whole issue of reducing the allowances paid to the families of men who were posted 'missing' was viewed by the War Office as likely to cause 'serious financial embarrassment', especially to wives and children of officers.[94] If the allotment portion of the allowances ceased after four weeks and lower temporary allowances were issued, the reduction of income could be up to £30 per month for the families of higher-paid officers. This could lead to particular problems for the families of naval personnel who had traditionally been able to make allotments to other payees than bank accounts. Not only had families been able to draw directly on these funds but payments had also been made directly to outside agencies such as insurance companies.[95] If such payment of insurance premiums was interrupted, because of a reduction in funds available, then the whole policy would be forfeit. At a meeting of the Imperial Prisoners of War Committee in early June 1942, Admiralty representatives suggested that the families of naval officers missing in the Far East should receive temporary allowances assessed on married allowance plus any allotment that the officer was 'already making to the family at time of casualty'.[96] As naval officers were perceived as normally allotting 'considerably more' than the two-sevenths of pay allowed for by temporary allowances, a reduction to this level would represent a serious cut in family budget.[97] Again the navy saw this as especially hard where men would probably ultimately be found to be prisoners of war and the reductions unnecessary. The War Office objected strongly to this proposal as the army pay system did not allow officers to make allotments through official channels.[98] As a result there was no official means within the army of verifying existing levels of contribution and in this objection the Air Ministry supported them, as a similar situation operated within the air force. Again, owing to weight of numbers, the Treasury, whilst feeling a 'very considerable sympathy' for the Admiralty view, none the less supported the War Office standpoint.[99]

In the face of continuing problems with information from the Far East, the period for the payment of temporary allowances to dependants of men missing in the Far Eastern theatre of war continued to be extended throughout late 1942 and early 1943. In June 1943 the War Office set out the existing position for all areas concerned.[100] In Malaya extensions were proposed which would bring the period of payment of temporary allowances up to 69 weeks or to 30 September 1943, whichever was sooner. In this area the Japanese were reporting names of prisoners of war 'roughly by areas of internment in alphabetical order' so that an almost complete list had been received, albeit in stages.[101] However these lists did not cover those prisoners, possibly up to 50 per cent of the total, who had been moved to Siam and Indo-China from where almost no names at all had been forthcoming.[102] It was hoped that, as the Japanese lists for Malaya were almost complete, they might then turn their attention to Siam and Indo-China next and there was 'some reason' to hope that the bulk of names would be received by the end of the year.[103] Because of this expectation a new proposal was made that temporary payments should be made to dependants of all those missing in Malaya and Singapore up to 95 weeks in total, but not beyond 31 January 1944.[104]

In the Dutch East Indies uncertainty about the overall situation had led to those servicemen known to have been in this area not being posted missing until 1 February 1943 (i.e. approximately twelve months after the fall of Singapore).[105] Accordingly, temporary allowances were due to expire after the normal 26 weeks at the end of August. Of those missing, one-third of army personnel had been reported as prisoners of war, with a slightly higher figure for the air force. The general feeling within the War Office was that allowances to the dependants of these men should be extended to the same date as those for dependants of missing from Malaya or for 43 weeks, whichever was the shorter.[106] Originally service personnel reported missing in Burma had also been included in the Malayan category, and all those reported missing in either Burma or India before 31 October 1942 were still included in this category.[107] For the families of those missing in these areas in later campaigns, between 1 November 1942 and 31 May 1943, estimated by the army to be probably less than a thousand men, temporary allowances were extended to 52 weeks in all, without any over riding date for cessation of payment.[108] As these were the most recent casualties, and as they were furthest from Tokyo, it was assumed that prisoners here would be amongst the last to be officially reported.[109]

These suggestions were all agreed by the Treasury in June 1943 and the *ad hoc* situation for the extension of temporary allowances continued throughout 1944 and up to the beginning of 1945, by which time the War Office was dealing with nearly three thousand cases of missing personnel.[110] In the case of allowances for dependants of navy personnel in particular, pressure was still being exerted on the Treasury by the services to continue allowances 'so long as names of prisoners were coming through'.[111] In this way, government handling of some families may be regarded as being dictated by the provision of information by the Japanese.

Although, as had been assumed by the services, many of those notified missing did indeed later turn out to be prisoners of war, naturally a number of servicemen were officially declared dead during the extended period of allowances. In these cases the Treasury had envisaged that a period of six weeks would be needed to make arrangements for a changeover from allowances to pension in order to ascertain eligibility for pension and the rate payable. Initially it was suggested that allowances should be continued during the changeover period rather than an immediate reduction to pension rates. However, the War Office had already put in hand preliminary enquiries in the cases of all men declared missing so that the results of these enquiries would be immediately available to the Ministry of Pensions should the men subsequently be notified dead. As a result of these enquiries the War Office envisaged that cases needing investigation from scratch would be few and could be dealt with within the six-week period.[112] The Treasury, rather unusually given its normal lack of sympathy for widows, in this case saw it as important to give dependants three months' notice of cessation of allowances, especially where these had been extended for long periods of time, to allow for new financial arrangements or cutbacks to be implemented.[113] In the light of this, for all allowances due to end on the current proposed date of 30 June 1945, reviews needed to be completed by February and would have to be based on data available at the end of January to allow time for circulation of information.[114] On the other hand, if reviews of naval allowances were postponed until April, as the Admiralty was suggesting, allowances for these cases would have to be extended beyond the end of June. Therefore, it would have been manifestly impossible for the Secretary of State for War to announce in February that army and air force allowances were going to be terminated if the Admiralty was not going to review the position until April.[115]

In the event, the Secretary of State for War, Sir John Grigg, made a statement to the House of Commons in March 1945 regarding allotments and allowances for dependants of both officers and men, for all three services, missing in the Far East.[116] After outlining the normal position, Sir John continued by explaining that, because of the 'extreme delays' by the Japanese government in reporting the names of those held prisoner of war, extensions to the missing allowance had been approved for an extended period. In the case of men reported missing following the fall of Hong Kong, normal allowances had ended in May 1943 and lower rates paid as the length of elapsed time was such that men still missing from this theatre of war had to be assumed dead. For men missing in other areas in the Far East the position had been reviewed in the light of all available information. Most of those reported as missing in the fighting in Malaya, in the Netherlands East Indies and in Burma before November 1942 had now been reported as prisoners of war either by official notification or through communications received from the men themselves. Because of this level of notification the government was forced to accept that a 'considerable number' of those still missing following these campaigns would not still be alive.[117] In the light of this conclusion it had been decided that temporary allowances for those still missing from these campaigns would cease on 31 July 1945 for other ranks and on 1 August 1945 for officers. For the families and dependants of all these men, continuing allowances at the lower pension rate would be paid. Despite his earlier assertion that many of those missing could not still be alive, Sir John nevertheless stated that this did not mean that the death of the missing man had automatically been presumed or that efforts to trace him would cease. Out of a total of 2,054 men missing in campaigns after November 1942, only nineteen had been officially notified as being captives of the Japanese by July 1945 and, at the end of October 1944, the War Office suggested a further 26-week extension of temporary allowances to 31 January 1946.[118] Ironically, by the time these decisions were implemented, the war was in fact on the point of ending.

Although many of those reported as missing in the Far East did later prove to have been taken captive, nearly thirty thousand men were killed in this particular theatre of war. Consequently, a number of families must have been granted continued missing allowances when they should have been paid lower pension rates, and the Treasury and Service Departments faced the problems of whether to try to reclaim such allowances and if so how. In fact, even where families were officially notified of the death of a serviceman, the authorities often perceived potential dangers of overpayment. Mrs Fuller, the widow of Airman Sgt L.E. Fuller was officially notified of her husband's death in early 1943.[119] By October 1944 five applications had been made to Mrs Fuller for the return of her RAF order book that was valid up to February 1945 and, in the eyes of the issuing paymaster, allowed for the possibility of 'serious fraudulent encashment of orders'. The Postmaster at the Bramford Road Office in Ipswich where the orders were due for encashment stated clearly that the book was 'not to hand' and so it was assumed that Mrs Fuller had retained the book and might possibly be continuing to draw her allowance. However, a later note in November 1944 records that the book had in fact been handed to the postmaster at Bramford Road in May 1943 and the book was finally forwarded to the Air Ministry in Worcester in November 1944. Far from having fraudulent intentions, Mrs Fuller's lack of reply was, as the Ministry of Pensions suggested, 'a stony silence as a protest against what she may regard as our incompetence'. For a recent widow struggling to cope with the death of her husband and the reduction in her income, the continual badgering for the return of an order book which she had promptly returned in the correct way must have seemed final proof that the government and services held the families of their servicemen in very low regard indeed. However, where overpayments did occur, there is no evidence to show that the services or the Treasury made any attempt to reclaim them. Perhaps it proved too difficult to establish an exact date when the man had died and so calculate the extent of overpayment. Perhaps the experience of trying to reclaim overpayment of allowances for bigamous 'wives' had alerted the authorities to the difficulties implicit in such action. Given the case of Mrs Fuller, it seems more likely that the action had a practical basis rather than that the Treasury balked at trying to reclaim overpayments from grieving widows.

Decisions affecting the families of British servicemen also had wider ramifications in that they could also affect the families of Dominion and Empire servicemen. The India Office, for example, saw any British decision regarding the dependants of those missing in Burma in particular as important as it would apply also to the families of those missing from British service establishments in India.[120] It considered that the way in which the families of those missing following a mass surrender were dealt with would be 'of great psychological importance from the recruiting point of view', thus echoing the Secretary of State's statement of 1939.[121] However, the War Office had discovered that there was no regular allotment system in operation for the families of men of the Indian Brigade missing following the fall of Hong Kong and Singapore and, in the light of this, agreed to pay families the amount reckoned to have been generally remitted to them by the men: 50 per cent of pay – much higher than the amount normally allotted by British troops.[122] In the case of families of men missing at Hong Kong these allotments would have ceased on 1 May 1943. By this time only 184 out of a total of three thousand men of the Brigade known to have been in Hong Kong and Singapore had been reported by the Japanese government as prisoner of war and it appeared that the Japanese were deliberately withholding the names of Indian servicemen.[123] In the light of this, allowances for the families of Brigade servicemen missing from Hong Kong and Singapore were extended up to 31 December 1943. However, by the beginning of December, despite all efforts made by the government of India to obtain names, the total number of servicemen confirmed as captive from Hong Kong was only 364, with no names at all reported for Singapore.[124] A further extension to allowances of six months was proposed with subsequent automatic extensions of six months for as long as the total reported remained at less than 50 per cent of the total missing. By June 1944 only 463 of the 1,700 missing at Hong Kong and 1,804 of the 3,600 missing in Malaya were confirmed as being prisoners of war.[125] Although the latter figure was hoped to show some change in the attitude of the Japanese government in the notification of status of Indian troops, 50 per cent were still unaccounted for. At this time the maximum of 50 per cent being allotted to families from pay was increased to 60 per cent following a similar increase already implemented within the Indian army.[126]

Again the actions of the British government proved to be reactive rather than proactive in the matter of service family welfare. Unlike the British government, the government of India had adopted a special category, 'missing believed prisoner of war', to deal with allowances for families of men missing from the Indian army.[127] In this way allotments could be continued at the equivalent of payments being made under the British Family Allowance system unless proof of death was furnished. There is no suggestion that the Treasury, or any of the Service Departments, ever proposed a similar category for British troops, despite a stated conviction that at least 80 per cent of those missing would eventually prove to have been taken prisoner. Had this been done it would have removed the necessity for continual reviews of payments under the 'missing' provision and greatly reduced the administrative costs involved. Instead the Treasury seems to have preferred to deploy resources in this way rather than run the risk of overpayment of allowances to families. Indeed, the first extension to allowances for the families of those still missing was agreed only 'in view of the strong political interest displayed at the present time regarding the position of Prisoners of War in the Far East'.[128] As had been the cases with increases to allowances, the government once again failed to take the initiative to provide for service families and had to be forced into action.

With the cessation of hostilities in the Far East in August 1945 and the release of prisoners, the conditions for extension of allowances ended. In November 1945, families of the 568 airmen still missing were given three months' notice that normal married allowance would cease and temporary allowances at pension rates would come into effect as it was 'practically certain' that news of any men missing but still alive would be received within a few weeks.[129] The air force felt that if news had not been received by that time there would, unfortunately, 'be little room for doubt' that the men were in fact dead.[130] The War Office issued similar notices although at this time 4,800 men of all ranks were still missing from the army.[131] Within the air force continuing efforts were made to trace the men still missing through search teams set up in Rangoon, Meiktila, Mandalay, Bangkok and Saigon to attempt to locate the wreckage of aircraft.[132] By May 1947, 62 wrecked aircraft had been located and the remains of 22 airmen recovered.[133] By October 1947 the search teams were beginning to be dismantled and, by January 1948, the operation was finally ended.[134] By then, of the 568 airmen still missing at the end of hostilities, 499 had been traced.[135]

At the beginning of this chapter we saw that it was indeed the intention of government that allowances should continue to be paid to families for time during which their menfolk were captive. Problems, however, began to arise whenever men were unaccounted for over an extended period of time as there was a lack of a coherent policy for periods when the actual status of a particular serviceman was unclear. Before December 1941, when dealing almost exclusively with those taken captive in Europe, the decision to adopt a 'wait and see' policy by extending allowances over short periods whilst awaiting official notification was not unreasonable. Both Germany and Italy were party to the 1929 Geneva Convention and, whilst communications were disrupted, notification through official channels was generally forthcoming. With the entry of Japan into the war and the huge losses sustained after the fall of Hong Kong and Singapore, however, the situation was radically altered.

Japan had not adopted the Geneva Convention and hence was not bound by its conditions regarding treatment of prisoners of war although, upon entry into the war, the Japanese Foreign Minister, Togo Shigenori, had agreed that the conditions of the Convention would be applied *mutatis mutandis*.[136] However, the Japanese Field Service Code of 1941 clearly sets out the prevailing Japanese attitude towards prisoners of war when it states that its own servicemen 'shall not undergo the shame of being taken alive'.[137] Given this underlying attitude it was inevitable that tensions would occur between cultural inclination and the treatment of prisoners of war prescribed not only by the Convention but also by the normal concerns of reciprocity of treatment. Although in December 1941 the Japanese created a Prisoner of War Information Bureau, its duty in relation to the dissemination of information regarding enemy prisoners was never adequately fulfilled. This is not to suggest that the Bureau deliberately set out to withhold information regarding Allied prisoners of war but rather that it did not see the importance to British families of such information. Its function of providing information regarding Japanese servicemen taken captive was similarly unfulfilled. A report on Bureau activities written in 1955 states that, when enquiries were received from next of kin, the Bureau 'replied appropriately in the light of Japanese traditional concepts'.[138] This suggests not only that notification to next of kin was not automatic but also that there was some reluctance to admit the shame of capture on the part of both government agencies and families alike.[139] Small wonder then that little priority was given to notification of prisoner of war status to other governments. It is, perhaps, more surprising that any notifications were received at all. However, for next of kin in Britain, and British government agencies, this resulted in extended periods of time, often from the moment of possible capture until liberation at the end of hostilities, when no definite news was received as to whether servicemen were dead, missing or actually prisoners of war. As a result, families remained in a state of limbo automatically eligible neither for full allowances nor for pensions.

This inevitably raises the question of why the government chose throughout the period from 1941 to 1945 to continue to extend 'missing' allowances on a short-term basis rather than agree a workable solution for the duration of hostilities. As we have already seen, the Indian government adopted a special category of 'believed prisoner of war' to circumvent the problem. Unfortunately the situation in India is a rare case where an actual comparison can be made. By and large the historiography of prisoners of war again concentrates on the living conditions and pay of the prisoners themselves, with little mention of their families. Even where fleeting mention of families is made there are no references to how allowances were administered to dependants while their menfolk were prisoner. As an example, Jonathan Vance in *Objects of Concern* mentions that Canadian prisoners enjoyed the 'benefit' of 'support for relatives'.[140] No mention is made of how this support was administered or of whether or not the actual status of the serviceman had to be confirmed as prisoner of war for this support to be forthcoming.[141] Although Fishman does consider in detail the administration of allowances to the families of French prisoners of war in Europe, this situation was rather different from that of prisoners of war in the Far East. With the collapse of the French army, huge numbers of soldiers were captured, but most families received notification by August 1940, or at the latest January 1941.[142] Whilst this wait of six months must have seemed interminable to the families concerned, in administrative terms the time scale, coupled with the fact that Germany was party to the Geneva Convention and thus bound to supply notifications, meant that it was feasible to wait and see if notification arrived before making any decisions regarding changes from allowances to pensions.

It is tempting to argue that the British decision, or rather non-decision, was economically driven. In earlier chapters we saw that, traditionally, pensions were paid at a lower rate than allowances, on the basis of the rationale that allowances were paid for the upkeep of the soldier's home for him to return to but that a widow might be expected to move to more modest accommodation. It might be argued, therefore, that keeping families on 'missing' allowances would prove the quickest and most convenient way, administratively, of transferring dependants from allowances to pensions. If families were transferred to a special 'missing believed prisoner of war' category this would then have necessitated more paperwork to alter them to pension status if notification that the man in question was dead were to be received. Figures for 1942, however, discount this argument as increases in both pensions and allowances of that year meant that, for other ranks, pension payments became higher than allowances. Table 3 gives the comparative figures proposed in a draft statement for increases in allowances and pensions dated February 1942.[143]

It seems, therefore, that there was no formal overall policy determined to deal with the situation where servicemen were classified as 'missing' for extended periods of time. The Foreign Office claimed to have found the Japanese 'not unreasonable' in other areas, although they did not specify precisely which areas, and perhaps continued to hope that the requisite information would

Table 3: Proposed increases in allowances and pensions 1942

Current rates		Category	Proposed rates	
Pensions	Family Allowance (inc. minimum allotment)		Pensions	Family Allowance (inc. minim alltoment)
22s 6d	25s 0d	Wife/widow (over 40 or with children)	25s 0d	25s 0d
31s 0d	32s 6d	Wife/widow + 1 child	34s 6d	33s 6d
37s 3d	38s 0d	Wife/widow + 2 children	41s 6d	40s 0d
42s 3d	42s 0d	Wife/widow + 3 children	47s 0d	45s 0d
15s 6d		Childless widow under 40	18s 6d	

Note: Figures taken from Proofs for Army Orders. Proof 3. 31 August 38. NA/AST11/122.

eventually be supplied regarding captured British servicemen for the administration of allowances to be adjusted accordingly. There is no evidence in the available sources to suggest that at any time the government discussed the possibility of finding a lasting solution to this problem based on the existing situation. Whatever the reason, the government, rather than taking the initiative, chose once again to act in a reactive rather than a pro active manner.

Notes

1 Minute Sheet Reg. No. 0103/2647 Ottley, Director of Finance, Treasury. 26 September 39 and agreed 05 October 39. NA/ WO32/9909.

2 Minute Sheet Reg. No. 0103/2647 Ottley, Director of Finance, Treasury. 26 September 39 and agreed 05 October 39. NA/ WO32/9909.

3 Brigadier Holland, War Office, speaking 07 April 43 at a meeting considering the raising of pay supplementation from two-sevenths salary to three-sevenths. NA/T162/792/E40219/2.

4 Letter R.F.L. Watkins, London SW16, to Iris Strange. 13 November 82. Box 43, Iris Strange Collection. University of Stafford, Special Collections.

5 Letter from Humphreys-Davies, Principal, War Office, to Crombie, Assistant Secretary, Treasury. 08 March 41. NA/T162/792/E40219/1.

See also ADM1/11909 and, for families who opted to remain at stations abroad, NA/T162/92/E40219/1.

6 Letter from Humphreys-Davies, Principal, War Office, to Crombie, Assistant Secretary, Treasury. 08 March 41. NA/T162/792/E40219/1.

7 Letter from Humphreys-Davies, Principal, War Office, to Crombie, Assistant Secretary, Treasury. 08 March 41. NA/T162/792/E40219/1. See also ADM1/11909 and, for families who opted to remain at stations abroad, NA/T162/92/E40219/1.

8 Letter from Humphreys-Davies, principal, War Office, to Crombie, Assistant Secretary, Treasury. 08 March 41. NA/T162/792/E40219/1.

9 From 31 December 41 the Treasury agreed that, following concessions granted to Civil Defence workers, allotments issued to families and dependants of deceased service personnel should continue at the actual rate in issue for the whole thirteen weeks rather than being reduced to compulsory rate. NA/T162/792/E40219/1.

10 Minute Sheet. 06 July 42. NA/ADM1/11909.

11 Minute Sheet. 06 July 42. NA/ADM1/11909.

12 Handwritten note, signature indecipherable. 08 July 42. NA/ADM1/11909.

13 Minute sheet. 06 July 42 and handwritten note Motterhead for Head of Navy. 08 July 42. NA/ADM1/11909.

14 Minute Sheet. 22 July 42. NA/ADM1/11909.

15 Comment by Skeat, Admiralty. 4th Meeting of Inter-departmental POW Co-ordinating Committee (Finance). 16 November 43. NA/WO163/639. Figures quoted by the Air Ministry at the same meeting for personnel missing in the Dutch East Indies were 80 per cent for officers and 69 per cent for other ranks.

16 Comment by Skeat, Admiralty. 4th Meeting of Inter-departmental Prisoner of War Co-ordinating Committee (Finance) 16 November 43. NA/WO163/639.

17 *Evening News*. 28 July 42, telegrams 30 July 42 and 31 July 42 and letter from Press Division, Admiralty, to *Evening News*. 02 August 42. NA/ADM1/11909.

18 Letter re Pension arrangements ref. CW. 18006/39. NA/T162/792/E40219/1.

19 Letter re Pension arrangements ref. CW. 18006/39. NA/T162/792/E40219/1.

20 Text of Broadcast by Sir Walter Monkton, KC, Director General of Ministry of Information, BBC Home Service, 25 April 41. Reports of the Permanent Committee Appointed by the Lord Mayor at the request of the Ministry of Information for the purpose of keeping up the morale of the Citizens and Disseminating News if Necessary. 13/05/41. Norfolk Record Office. N/LM1/34.

21 Text of Broadcast by Sir Walter Monkton, KC, Director General of Ministry of Information, BBC Home Service, 25 April 41. Reports of the Permanent Committee Appointed by the Lord Mayor at the request of the Ministry of Information for the purpose of keeping up the morale of the Citizens and Disseminating News if Necessary. 13/05/41. Norfolk Record Office. N/LM1/34.

22 Text of Broadcast by Sir Walter Monkton, KC, Director General of Ministry of Information, BBC Home Service, 25 April 41. Reports of the Permanent Committee Appointed by the Lord Mayor at the request of the Ministry of Information for the purpose of keeping up the morale of the Citizens and Disseminating News if Necessary. 13/05/41. Norfolk Record Office. N/LM1/34.

23 Letter ref. CW.18006/39 Admiralty to Secretary, Treasury. 09 December 39. NA/T162/792/E40219/1. The case of Helen Duncan continues to generate discussion up to the present day and a campaign to clear her name, aimed at proving that she was not fraudulent, is ongoing.

24 Letter ref. CW.18006/39 Admiralty to Secretary, Treasury. 09 December 39. NA/T162/792/E40219/1.

25 Letter re Pension arrangements ref. CW.18006/39. NA/T162/792/E40219/1.

26 Minutes of the 43rd meeting of the Co-ordinating (Inter-departmental) Committee on Dependants' Allowances. 20 April 42. NA/AST11/146.

27 Minutes of the 43rd meeting of the Co-ordinating (Inter-departmental) Committee on Dependants' Allowances. 20 April 42. NA/AST11/146.

28 Minutes of the 43rd meeting of the Co-ordinating (Inter-departmental) Committee on Dependants' Allowances. 20 April 42. NA/AST11/146.

29 Minutes of the 43rd meeting of the Co-ordinating (Inter-departmental) Committee on Dependants' Allowances. 20 April 42. NA/AST11/146.

30 Minutes of the 43rd meeting of the Co-ordinating (Inter-departmental) Committee on Dependants' Allowances. 20 April 42. NA/AST11/146.

31 Minutes of the 44th meeting of the Co-ordinating (Inter-departmental) Committee on Dependants' Allowances. 04 October 45. NA/AST11/146.

32 Minutes of the 44th meeting of the Co-ordinating (Inter-departmental) Committee on Dependants' Allowances. 04 October 45. NA/AST11/146.

33 Letter Moggeridge, Assistant Secretary, Admin. and Clerical Establishment, War Office, to Clough, Principal, Treasury. 04 December 43. NA/T162/792/40219/2.

34 Details of this case study can be found in: Letter Moggeridge, Assistant Secretary, Admin. and Clerical Establishment, War Office, to Clough, Principal, Treasury. 04 December 43. NA/

T162/792/40219/2 and Letter Clough, Principal, Treasury, to Moggerdige, Assistant Secretary, Admin. and Clerical Establishment, War Office. 08 December 43. NA/T162/792/40219/2.

35 Karlin, D. (ed.), *The Oxford Authors: Rudyard Kipling.* Oxford: Oxford University Press, 1999.

36 Minute Sheet 46/H/3951. 30 August 41. NA/WO32/9824.

37 Over issue of Family Allowances Resulting from Bigamy and Other Causes of Estrangement. 1941–1947. NA/WO32/9824.

38 Chatfield, V., *Theirs Not To Reason Why*, unpublished memoirs. IWM/P461. p. 23.

39 See for example Turner and Rennell, *When Daddy Came Home*, 'Don't Be Jealous'. pp. 109–140; Hartley (ed.), 'Love, Sex and Immorality', *Hearts Undefeated*. pp. 206–215.

40 Ferguson and Fitzgerald, *Studies in Social Services.* History of the Second World War Series, UK Civil Services. p. 98.

41 Survey published by Ferguson and Fitzgerald, HMSO, 1954, quoted in Lang, C., *Keep Smiling Through. Women in the Second World War.* Cambridge: Cambridge University Press, 1989. Central Statistical Office, *Statistical Digest of the War.* London: HMSO 1951. Table 4, quoted in Braybon and Summerfield, *Out of the Cage.* p. 214.

42 Letter Gardner, Principal, Admin. and Clerical Establishment, War Office, to Humphreys-Davies, Assistant Secretary, Treasury. 16 November 40 NA/T162/792/E40219/1.

43 Letter Gardner, Principal, Admin. and Clerical Establishment, War Office, to Humphreys-Davies, Assistant Secretary, Treasury. 16 November 40 NA/T162/792/E40219/1.

44 Letter War Office to Clough, Principal, Treasury. 13 March 44. NA/T162/792/E40219/3.

45 Letter War Office to Clough, Principal, Treasury. 13 March 44. NA/T162/792/E40219/3.

46 Letter War Office to Clough, Principal, Treasury. 13 March 44. NA/T162/792/E40219/3.

47 Letter War Office to Clough, Principal, Treasury. 13 March 44. NA/T162/792/E40219/3.

48 Letter War Office to Clough, Principal, Treasury. 13 March 44. NA/T162/792/E40219/3.

49 Letter War Office to Clough, Principal, Treasury. 13 March 44. NA/T162/792/E40219/3.

50 Letter War Office to Clough, Principal, Treasury. 13 March 44. NA/T162/792/E40219/3.

51 Letter ref. 48/Gen/745.(F.4) Lambert, Assistant Under-secretary of State, Central Branch, War Office, to Secretary, Treasury. 03 March 41. NA/T162/792/E40219/1.

52 Letter ref. 48/Gen/745.(F.4) Lambert, Assistant Under-secretary of State, Central Branch, War Office, to Secretary, Treasury. 03 March 41. NA/T162/792/E40219/1.

53 Letter ref. 48/Gen/745.(F.4) Lambert, Assistant Under-secretary of State, Central Branch, War Office, to Secretary, Treasury. 03 March 41. NA/T162/792/E40219/1.

54 Letter Humphreys-Davies, Under-secretary, Treasury to War Office c.c. Admiralty and Air Ministry. 07 March 40. NA/T162/792/E40219/1.

55 Letter ref. 0103/289/F.4.P.W. War Office to Treasury, signatures indecipherable, states that figures for these cases were between 40 and 50. 05 August 41. NA/T162/792/E40219/1. Minute Sheet Reg. No. 0103/2647. Signed Ottley Director of Finance, Treasury. 26 September 39 and agreed 05 October 39. NA/WO32/9909.

56 Notes of Inter-departmental Conference on Pay and Allowances. 11 March 40. NA/T162/792/E40219/1.

57 Record of the 17th Meeting of the Imperial Prisoner of War Committee, Sub-committee 'B'. 04 May 42. NA/WO163/589. The Phillimore Report estimates that, within the first few weeks of their entry into the war the Japanese had taken more than 120,000 British prisoners of war. Phillimore Report. p. 140. NA/WO366/26.

58 Letter ref. 0103/3706(F4) Lambert, Assistant Under-secretary of State, Central Branch, War Office, to Treasury. 26 February 42. NA/T162/792/E40219/1.

59 Letter Padmore, Assistant Secretary, Treasury, to Under-secretary of State, War Office. 11 March 42. NA/T162/792/E40219/1.

60 Letter Padmore, Assistant Secretary, Treasury, to Under-secretary of State, War Office. 11 March 42. NA/T162/792/E40219/1.

61 Letter Gardner, Principal Officer, Financial Staff, War Office, to Clough, Principal, Treasury. 31 October 42. NA/T162/792/E40219/1.

62 The Phillimore Report suggests that the lack of information regarding names of prisoners of war was due both to inefficiency in Tokyo and to the fact that Japanese military commanders were largely independent of central control and so did not transmit information to a central agency. Phillimore Report. p. 140. NA/WO366/26.

63 Letter Lambert, Assistant Under-secretary of State, Central Branch, War Office, to Secretary, Treasury. 27 March 42. NA/T162/792/E40219/1. This letter also calls for similar treatment to be accorded to families evacuated from the Netherlands East Indies, although numbers in this case are envisaged as being very small.

64 Letter Lambert, Assistant Under-secretary of State, Central Branch, War Office, to Secretary, Treasury. 27 March 42. NA/T162/792/E40219/1.

65 Letter Lambert, Assistant Under-secretary of State, Central Branch, War Office, to Secretary, Treasury. 27 March 42. NA/T162/792/E40219/1.

66 Letter Lambert, Assistant Under-secretary of State, Central Branch, War Office, to Secretary, Treasury. 27 March 42. NA/T162/792/E40219/1.

67 Letter Lambert, Assistant Under-secretary of State, Central Branch, War Office, to Secretary, Treasury. 27 March 42. NA/T162/792/E40219/1.

68 Handwritten, unsigned note to letter from Gardner, Principal Officer Financial Staff, War Office, to Clough, Principal, Treasury. 23 June 42. NA/T162/792/E40219/1.

69 Letter from Clough, Principal, Treasury, to War Office. 27 March 42. NA/T162/792/E40219/1.

70 Report from Clough, Principal, Treasury, on War Office letter. 27 March 42. NA/T162/792/E40219/1.

71 Letter Lambert, Assistant Under-secretary of State, Central Branch, War Office to Secretary, Treasury. 27 March 42. NA/T162/792/E40219/1.

72 Unsigned and undated letter War Office to Treasury. Probably early April 1942. NA/T162/792/E40219/1.

73 Letter Lambert, Assistant Under-secretary of State, Central Branch, War Office, to Secretary, Treasury. 27 March 42. NA/T162/792/E40219/1.

74 Letter Treasury to War Office. 22 April 42. NA/T162/792/E40219/1.

75 Letter Roseway, Director of Finance and Under-secretary of State, Finance Section, War Office, to Secretary of State, Treasury. 23 June 42. NA/T162/792/E40219/1.

76 Minutes of the Imperial Prisoner of War Committee, Sub-Committee 'A', meetings 7–14. NA/WO163/584.

77 Minutes of the Imperial Prisoner of War Committee, Sub-Committee 'A', meetings 7–14. NA/WO163/584.

78 Letter Roseway, Director of Finance and Under-secretary of State, War Office, to Secretary of State, Treasury. 23 June 42. NA/T162/792/E40219/1.

79 Letter Roseway, Director of Finance and Under-secretary of State, War Office, to Secretary of State, Treasury. 23 June 42. NA/T162/792/E40219/1.

80 Report, Clough, Principal, Treasury, on War Office, letter 23 June 42. 07 July 42. NA/T162/792/E40219/1.

81 Letter Lambert, Assistant Under-secretary of State, Central Branch, War Office, to Secretary, Treasury. 15 July 42. NA/T162/792/E40219/1.

82 Letter Lambert, Assistant Under-Secretary of State, Central branch, War Office to Secretary, Treasury. 15 July 42. NA/T162/792/E40219/1.
83 Letter War Office to Treasury. 15 July 42. NA/T162/792/E40219/1.
84 Letter War Office to Treasury. 15 July 42. NA/T162/792/E40219/1.
85 Letter War Office to Treasury. 15 July 42. NA/T162/792/E40219/1.
86 Letter War Office to Treasury. 15 July 42. NA/T162/792/E40219/1.
87 Letter War Office to Treasury. 07 December 42. NA/T162/792/E40219/1.
88 Letter War Office to Treasury. 07 December 42. NA/T162/792/E40219/1.
89 Letter from Treasury with copies to War Office, Air Ministry and Admiralty. 02 November 42. NA/T162/792/E40219/1.
90 Letter from Treasury with copies to War Office, Air Ministry and Admiralty. 02 November 42. NA/T162/792/E40219/1.
91 Letter from Treasury with copies to War Office, Air Ministry and Admiralty. 02 November 42. NA/T162/792/E40219/1.
92 Letter from Treasury with copies to War Office, Air Ministry and Admiralty. 02 November 42. NA/T162/792/E40219/1.
93 Details of this case study can be found in: Letter War Office to Mrs Hanks. 30 June 42, and Letter War Office to Treasury. 28 November 42. NA/T162/792/E40219/2.
94 Letter Medrow, Admiralty to Clough, Principal, Treasury. 03 April 42. NA/T162/792/E40219/1.
95 Letter Medrow, Admiralty to Clough, Principal, Treasury. 03 April 42. NA/T162/792/E40219/1.
96 The Imperial Prisoners of War Committee was established in November 1941, to 'secure co-ordination of the action of His Majesty's Governments in regard to matters relating to prisoners of war both in our own and enemy hands'. NA/WO163/152. Minutes of Imperial Prisoners of War Committee. June 1942. NA/T162/792/E40219/1.
97 Minutes of Imperial Prisoners of War Committee. June 1942. NA/T162/792/E40219/1.
98 Minutes of Imperial Prisoners of War Committee. June 1942. NA/T162/792/E40219/1.
99 It should be noted that officers of the Indian army could, in fact, make allotments through official channels, and in these cases the average allotment was 60 per cent of pay with some cases as high as 80 per cent. Minutes of the Imperial Prisoners of War Committee. 03 April 42. NA/T162/792/E40219/1. The question of naval allotments from pay rose again with the issue of ratings notified as missing

who had previously, under the navy system, been able to pay rent or other costs of housing by direct allotment. Indeed some of those ratings whose wives 'had a tendency to get into debt' were actually advised to pay housing costs by this means. In these cases where rent could clearly be seen as being part of a dependant's maintenance and a well-defined, discrete item, the Treasury raised no objections to the continuation of these allowances with the proviso that arrangements should be made for immediate stoppage if entitlement to allotment ended for any reason. Letter Treasury to Admiralty. 10 August 42. NA/T162/792/E40219/1.

100 Letter War Office to Treasury. 15 June 43. NA/T162/792/E4029/2.
101 Letter War Office to Treasury. 15 June 43. NA/T162/792/E4029/2.
102 Letter War Office to Treasury. 15 June 43. NA/T162/792/E4029/2.
103 Letter War Office to Treasury. 15 June 43. NA/T162/792/E4029/2.
104 Letter War Office to Treasury. 15 June 43. NA/T162/792/E4029/2.
105 Letter War Office to Treasury. 15 June 43. NA/T162/792/E4029/2.
106 Letter War Office to Treasury. 15 June 43. NA/T162/792/E4029/2.
107 Letter War Office to Treasury. 15 June 43. NA/T162/792/E4029/2.
108 Letter War Office to Treasury. 15 June 43. NA/T162/792/E4029/2.
109 Letter War Office to Treasury. 15 June 43. NA/T162/792/E4029/2.
110 Letter Treasury to War Office. 17 June 43 agrees to suggestions for the extension of allowances for the dependants of personnel missing in these areas. A further letter of 30 June 43 confirms the arrangements for the dependants of those declared missing in the more recent campaigns. NA/T162/792/E40219/3.
111 Letter Gardner, Principal, Financial Staff, War Office, to Clough, Principal, Treasury. 30 December 44. NA/T162/792/E40219/3.
112 Letter from Roseway, Director of Finance and Under-secretary of State, Financial Section, War Office, to Medrow, Admiralty. 10 August 42. NA/T162/792/E40219/1.
113 Letter Treasury to Medrow, Admiralty. 06 January 45. NA/T162/792/E40219/2.
114 Letter Treasury to Medrow, Admiralty. 06 January 45. NA/T162/792/E40219/2.
115 Letter Treasury to Medrow, Admiralty. 06 January 45. NA/T162/792/E40219/2.
116 Note of statement to the House of Commons by Sir John Grigg, Secretary of State for War. March 1945. NA/WO163/639.
117 Letter War Office to Treasury. 28 May 45. NA/T162/792/E40219/2.
118 Letter War Office to Treasury. 28 May 45. NA/T162/792/E40219/2.

119 Details of this case study can be found in: Letter Pensions Office, Norwich to Ministry of Pensions. 19 October 44. NA/PIN15/3339, and Letter Johnstone, Norcross Pensions Office, to Adams, Air Ministry. 11 November 44. NA/PIN15/3339.

120 Letter Johnstone, Norcross Pensions Office to Adams, Air Ministry. 11 November 44. NA/PIN15/3339.

121 Minutes of Imperial Prisoners of War Committee. 03 April 42. NA/T162/792/E40219/1.

122 Letter Gardner, Principal, Financial Section, War Office, to Clough, Treasury. 05 December 43. NA/T162/792/E40219/2.

123 Letter Gardner, Principal, Financial Section, War Office, to Clough, Treasury. 05 December 43. NA/T162/792/E40219/2.

124 Letter Gardner, Principal, Financial Section, War Office, to Clough, Treasury. 05 December 43. NA/T162/792/E40219/2.

125 Letter Gardner, Principal, Financial Section, War Office, to Clough, Treasury. 05 December 43. NA/T162/792/E40219/2.

126 Record of the 17th meeting of the Imperial Prisoner of War Committee Sub-committee B. 04 May 42 shows that the normal allotment in the Indian army could, in fact, be up to 80 per cent of pay and that it 'had been found necessary to give new officers general advice to avoid too high allotments'. NA/WO163/589.

127 Notes on 15th Meeting of the Imperial Prisoners of War Committee, Sub-committee B. 11 February 42. NA/AIR2/12305.

128 Letter Stedman, Treasury to Gardner, War Office. 17 December 43. NA/T162/792/E40219/2.

129 Revision of regulations for the Issue of Pay and Allowances of Missing Personnel. 27 October 45. NA/AIR2/6408.

130 Revision of regulations for the Issue of Pay and Allowances of Missing Personnel. 27 October 45. NA/AIR2/6408.

131 Figure noted in telegram from Secretary of State for India to War Department, Government of India. 07 June 45. NA/AIR2/6408.

132 Report of Missing Research Under AHQ Burma January 1946–May 1947. NA/AIR2/10199.

133 Report of Missing Research Under AHQ Burma January 1946–May 1947. NA/AIR2/10199.

134 Final Report of Missing Research Under AHQ. 01 January 48. NA/AIR2/10199[94A].

135 Handwritten note. October 1947. Signature indecipherable. NA/AIR/2/10199[91A].

136 Hata, Ikuhiko, 'Japanese Military and Popular Perceptions of POWs' in Moore and Fedorowich, *Prisoners of War and Their Captors*. p. 254.

137 Hata, 'Japanese Military and Popular Perceptions'. p. 255.

138 Hata, 'Japanese Military and Popular Perceptions'. p. 265.
139 Hata, 'Japanese Military and Popular Perceptions'. p. 265. See also Phillimore Report Part III, p. 140. NA/WO366/26.
140 Vance, J.F., *Objects of Concern. Canadian Prisoners of War Through the Twentieth Century.* Vancouver: University of British Columbia Press, 1994. p. 96.
141 Vance, *Objects of Concern.* p. 96.
142 Fishman, *We Will Wait.* p. 28.
143 Draft Statement on Revision of Pay and Allowances 1941–42. T162/646/E44411/1-2.

4

'The fortunes of war' – uncertainty and economic hardship

Sarah Fishman has identified that, for French prisoner of war wives during the Second World War, 'financial hardship was the rule'.[1] British prisoner of war wives often faced a similarly difficult financial situation and similar hardships. In addition to the delays to payment of allowances suffered by many service families, and the problems associated with ascertaining the true status of 'missing' servicemen, prisoner of war families often faced further delays to the payment of their allowances in relation to the physical arrangements for such payments.

In many instances these problems arose because the mechanisms for claiming allowances or altering the administration of existing allowances depended on the ability of servicemen to contact the administering agencies. As detailed in Chapter 1, claims by 'other ranks' for both Family and Dependants' Allowances generally had to be made by the servicemen themselves and processed through the Regimental Paymasters. Additionally, in the case of Dependants' Allowances, authority had to be provided by the serviceman for a stated allotment to be deducted from pay to trigger the payment of the allowance. This being so, any situation which resulted in difficulties in either ascertaining or confirming the wishes of the men involved necessarily led to problems of administration and the possible non-payment of allowances with all the inconvenience and deprivation that inevitably created.

For the families of men captured in Western Europe, the problems were not perceived as being insurmountable, although it was still appreciated that arrangements for the maintenance of families 'were apt to breakdown when they [the men] became prisoner of war or missing'.[2] Belligerent powers in this theatre of war had agreed to keep to the articles of the Geneva Convention, whereby prisoners of war were accorded facilities to transfer amounts of money 'to bank or private individuals in their country of origin'.[3]

Additionally communications with prisoners of war in Europe were a good deal more straightforward than those with men captured in the Far East, although 'straightforward' in this context is a relative term. Mail to and from British prisoners of war in Germany usually travelled by air to Lisbon and was then forwarded, usually by air but sometimes by rail or sea, to Rome, Switzerland or Stuttgart for onward transfer. Generally, where prisoners of war were stationary in one camp, mail took approximately three weeks to arrive.[4] As a result it was possible to ascertain if the men concerned wanted to make changes to allowances or allotments and to utilise normal written methods to obtain consent for any such changes.[5] Problems did, however, arise when prisoners were transferred from one camp to another as letters went astray or were not forwarded. This was a particular problem in 1943 when a total of almost seventy thousand men were transferred from camps in Italy to Germany and there were often delays in communication until the men were settled in camps in Germany. At one stage, all mail was frozen until new addresses had been received.[6]

Notes issued for the guidance of Camp Leaders in German prisoner of war camps set out the overall procedure for payment of allowances and reinforced the idea that major problems of communication with these men were not anticipated.[7] However, notes for the navy stated that, if new rates of pay came into force and it was necessary to increase the level of allotment from pay to continue to qualify for allowances, then the additional amount would automatically be deducted. New instructions regarding allotments, alterations or stoppages of allotments could then be notified by the men either 'writing direct to the Secretary of the Admiralty' or through a letter to a relative who would then send the letter on to the Admiralty.[8] Similarly for the army and air force, allowances continued to be issued as at time of capture with applications for changes to voluntary allotments being made in writing to the Regimental Paymaster or Senior Account Officer, War Casualties Non-Effective Accounts Depot respectively. Allowances for other ranks across the services were paid at local post offices by means of drafts from allowance books that were held by the wife or dependant, so most wives continued to draw their allowances in the same way that they had before their husbands were captured.

Officers' allowances, however, were paid direct into the officer's own bank account in the United Kingdom. Instructions for air force officers note that 'it is incumbent upon the officer to make suitable arrangements with his bank for providing his family and other dependants with funds' by sending a letter to Air Ministry Accounts for forwarding to the Manager of the branch in question.[9] Although it had been envisaged that such arrangements would be made before the officer was posted abroad, the assumption was made that no major problems would be encountered with prisoners of war communicating in writing with their families, their bankers or the service department concerned.

Only in the case of the air force had it been considered that possible cases of hardship might occur where arrangements had not already been made or where these arrangements had broken down. In these cases, the Air Council, alone of all the services, had the power to order that the whole or part of the officer's pay and allowances be paid to the wife or other dependant who could show that the officer concerned had previously contributed to their upkeep or that he would have contributed had he been aware of the circumstances.[10] In exercising this power every effort was made to 'interpret the officer's wishes from such evidence as is available' rather than to make provision based on the needs of the family.[11] The one major exception to this rule was the case of the families of merchant navy officers. Before June 1941 allowances for the wives and children of officers or ratings serving under naval discipline in Admiralty vessels who were taken captive were paid at the rates laid down by the War Office Pensions and Detention Allowances Mercantile Marine Scheme.[12] After this date a scheme came into operation whereby in excess of 75 per cent of net wages of prisoners of war, after deductions for camp pocket money (*Lagergeld*), income tax and Merchant Navy Officers Pension Fund, were paid direct to officers' dependants. This scheme provided directly for the needs of the families concerned and is in marked contrast to arrangements for other officers' families where the emphasis was placed on holding as much money as possible in the prisoner of war's personal account in Britain 'against the time when he came home'.[13]

In the light of these arrangements, it was not envisaged that serious problems would occur for the dependants of officers held captive in Europe as a result of an inability to draw on officers' bank accounts. However, this problem was exactly the one that arose for dependants of those captured in the Far East. Within the first few weeks of their entry into the war in 1941, Japanese forces had taken more than 120,000 British prisoners of war.[14] As the Japanese were not signatories to the Geneva Convention none of its guarantees applied, including the ability of prisoners to transfer money. In addition, although the treatment of enemy prisoners by other belligerents was often underpinned by considerations of possible reprisals against their own servicemen, this situation did not exist in the Japanese case. Not only did the Allies hold very few Japanese prisoners but, even where prisoners were held, the Japanese government was almost entirely indifferent to their fate. Any effort or expenditure on prisoners of war, including notification of captivity or mail services, was considered unnecessary and, although in 1943 a mail route was opened through Soviet Russia, letters were generally slow to arrive at their destinations, if they arrived at all.[15] Normal routes of communication could not, therefore, be relied on as a means for dealing with financial matters in these cases.

In fact, the Army Council already had powers, under Article 10C of the Royal Warrant 1940, to use the pay of missing officers or those taken prisoner of war for the benefit of their wives and dependants.[16] However, the regulations as they stood at that time were open to two possible interpretations. Under one interpretation, the Army Council could use all the pay owed to the officer when he was posted missing or captured, for the benefit of family and dependants irrespective of when these moneys were due to be paid. Alternatively, the Council could apply pay and allowances due only from the date the officer was posted missing or captured. Although originally it was proposed that the second alternative should be adopted, in fact in April 1942 the wider interpretation was accepted.[17] For either interpretation, it was agreed that, where the Paymaster in Manchester was satisfied that the officer was maintaining his wife to the amount claimed, an amount not exceeding the total of Family Lodging Allowance plus two-sevenths pay would be issued.[18] This amount could be increased where there was a larger balance standing to the officer's credit and the Army Council was satisfied that the officer had regularly contributed a larger amount. In seven cases payment was made to families resident in the UK in advance of the due date where hardship was claimed due to non-receipt of remittances from Hong Kong.[19] However, where pay and allowances were paid, on the officer's order, direct into a private banking account 'there would be nothing on which the Army Council could operate their special powers'.[20]

In cases where the wife did not have access to her husband's bank account, either through a letter of authorisation to withdraw funds or an arrangement to transfer money directly arranged by the officer before he was posted abroad, there was no way for her to obtain these funds. This was also the case where the account was held abroad and had become inaccessible owing to circumstances of war. To circumvent these problems it was suggested that, for prisoners of war, the Army Council could exercise its powers to divert pay and allowances before they were paid to the bank. In this way wives would get the allowances due to them before funds were transferred to the inaccessible account although any balance would 'continue to flow' in accordance with the officer's orders to his bank.[21] For dependants of other ranks, the problems of issue of allowances were not so great as Paymasters already had sufficient information regarding allotments to allow them to continue making appropriate payments to families, although the War Office envisaged that there would 'almost certainly be some unusual cases where some hitch will occur'.[22]

The navy considered that such a contingency as being taken prisoner ought to have been foreseen by the men concerned and claimed that their officers had been 'repeatedly urged to make provision for their families'.[23] In cases where families had been left stranded, departmental approval was originally granted for payments to be made to the family and charged against the officer's account.[24] However, the navy solicitor advised that such payments were outside the Admiralty's powers and, in the light of this, it was deemed necessary for all cases to be judged individually and payments made only where circumstances forced the issue rather than developing an overall policy for such cases.[25] The Commander in Chief in Ceylon who had already authorised such general payments was seen as having exceeded his authority as there was a 'considerable risk' of double payment occurring.[26] The equally 'considerable risk' of families not receiving any payment and facing financial hardship or destitution does not seem to have weighed in these considerations. In a similar move to that taken by the War Office, the Admiralty belatedly began to investigate the possibility of obtaining powers to issue allowances in these cases, powers that the Air Ministry already possessed for its officers held by enemy forces.[27]

With the fall of Singapore on 15 February 1942, the situation became even more complicated. In this instance the Paymaster, carrying some of the records, escaped to Australia and it was assumed that he would begin to function from there, paying allowances to the families concerned.[28] To avoid confusion, payments were made from this source to families who had escaped to, or were already in, Australia, but payment to families outside Australia were, from 14 February 1942, made from Manchester in the same way as those to families from Hong Kong.[29] For once, concern regarding the possibility of overpayments took second place to concern for families. Although it was appreciated that problems would arise if officers had themselves escaped to Australia and continued to draw pay there, it was felt to be in the best interests of the families to take this risk. The Paymaster was asked to report any payments made after the February date to officers whose families were not in Australia and, in this way, although there was some danger of families receiving double payment at least it was ensured that no family would be completely without funds.[30] However, problems continued to surface in this location up to January 1944 with regard to Royal Army officers who had been in the pay of the British Indian Army when they were taken prisoner.[31] In these cases, although payment of salary should have been taken over by the Manchester pay office, families would normally have continued to receive their allowances from local branches.[32] Generally the War Office felt that, as the most up-to-date information on pay increases and changes to allowances was held in the UK, it would be better to make the payments from Manchester to a local account which the wife could draw on.[33] In all cases, except that of merchant seamen outlined above, the prime considerations of the services and Treasury were to follow what they knew or perceived to be the wishes of the officer in question and to reduce the risk of overpayment. The actual level of need of the families concerned played no part in discussions on these issues. Instead, the War Office, in particular, was at some pains not to undermine the integrity of its officers by acknowledging the fact that many had left for service overseas without making adequate financial arrangements for their families.

In addition to the problems of payment of allowances associated with communication issues or lack of access to accounts, a number of other circumstances also gave rise to difficulties. Most commonly, these occurred where household income rose above the maximum limit for allowances to be applicable, or where the household income was already too high but the serviceman had made a voluntary contribution. But more immediate problems were caused for families where War Service Grants had been issued to meet pre-enlistment commitments or where a soldier continued to receive a 'balance of civil pay' (BCP) payment to make his army pay up to the level of civil pay he had received before enlistment. In both cases these allowances decreased as service pay increased as the man was expected to make up for the decrease in grant by increasing the amount he allotted to his family. However, whereas the BCP or War Service Grant had been paid direct to the family, increases in service pay went direct to the serviceman.[34] Effectively this meant that, when a serviceman's pay was increased, family income was immediately reduced until the serviceman could make arrangements to increase allotment, a situation obviously difficult for prisoners of war to expedite. In the case of War Service Grant, the situation was eased by the wife or dependants themselves writing direct to the Paymaster, who then referred the case to the War Office so that a diversion of additional allotment could be made to cover the reduction in income.[35] By April 1945 the number of cases of this class was 'considerable'. Cases involving changes to BCP were more difficult to estimate as Regimental Paymasters did not necessarily know when this was an issue, although, by November 1944, 3,478 BCP accounts were being maintained.[36] Of these cases, Family or Dependants' Allowances were issued on 2,006, with 1,360 cases being affected by a reduction due to payment of War Service Increment (WSI) or Japanese Campaign Pay (JCP) paid from 1 November 1944.[37]

The second major set of circumstances that gave rise to problems was associated with the payment of Dependants' Allowances where no direct instructions were available from the serviceman concerned, involving voluntary allotment to one member of a household who subsequently died. A War Office memo of 24 April 1945 stated that, where a soldier had been making a contribution in favour of one parent who then died, the Regimental Paymaster had the power to transfer this payment to the other parent as 'in all such cases it can be taken as conclusive that the soldier would have desired to continue such an allotment'.[38] Despite this, cases did occur where hardship was caused through misinterpretation or ignorance of the regulations. One such case was that of S/Sgt O'Toole of the Royal Electrical and Mechanical Engineers, a prisoner of war in Japanese hands.[39] S/Sgt O'Toole's wife was admitted to East Sussex Mental Hospital in October 1942 as 'a certified person of unsound mind' as a direct result of the experiences she had suffered during her evacuation from Hong Kong and during her subsequent return, via Australia, to England.[40] In February 1944 the County of Southampton Public Assistance Council enquired of the Regimental Paymaster in Leeds whether a Dependants' Allowance should be issued for Mrs O'Toole and if this could be paid direct to the County Council as a contribution towards the cost of her maintenance. Consideration was also given to whether or not a provisional issue of voluntary allotment could be made to Mrs O'Toole's parents, Mr and Mrs Fitton, whose only income was an Old Age and Supplementary Pension. Mr and Mrs Fitton were suffering hardship in trying to provide some extra comforts for their daughter. On Mrs O'Toole's admission to hospital it had been decided that conditions had not been met for continued payment of Family Allowance and this was suspended immediately. In December 1943 S/Sgt O'Toole's pay account held a balance of £299 6s 7½d.

A letter from the War Office to the Regimental Paymaster in Leeds dated 8 March 1944 confirmed payment of Family Allowance to the Public Assistance Committee in Southampton for Mrs O'Toole's maintenance. In addition, a deduction from his pay of 10s 6d per week was to be paid to Mr and Mrs Fitton 'in order that the parents may be able to procure some personal comforts for Mrs O'Toole'. Although this seemed a clear arrangement, confusion later arose as to whether the allowance had been granted for both Mr and Mrs Fitton or for Mrs Fitton only, as stated in a memo of 17 February 1944. In September 1943 this distinction became critical as Mrs Fitton died and, as the result of a misunderstanding about to the actual nature of the allowance, payments were suspended. In April 1944, Mr Fitton wrote to the War Office enquiring about the allowance. At the age of 73, his only income was Old Age and Supplementary Pension of £1 7s per week. He tried to visit his daughter once every two weeks but the fare was 4s and, as he had insufficient income to buy her comforts, he was obliged to take her some of his own rations. He requested the War Office 'for God sake do what you can too help me and oblige'. The War Office replied to the Regimental Paymaster that the difficulty with this case was 'not understood'. The diversion of 10s 6d per week from S/Sgt O'Toole's pay was quite clearly set out as being for Mrs O'Toole's *parents* and authority to pay the allowance to Mr Fitton was confirmed in July 1944. No further correspondence has come to light to show whether or not Mr Fitton was reimbursed for the period during which the allowances was suspended. If one assumes that the allowance ceased after Mrs Fitton's death in September 1943, and did not resume until July the next year this would mean that a deficit in payment of in the order of £22 had resulted – an enormous sum for a pensioner on an income of under £2 per week – purely as a result of administrative misinterpretation.

There appears to be no accurate way of estimating how many cases of hardship of this nature occurred. Although the O'Toole/Fitton case is the only one of its kind recorded in War Office or Treasury files, this does not necessarily mean that it is unique. It is possible that the correspondence regarding this case came to the notice of War Office officials because of its unusual combination of circumstances. If Mrs O'Toole had been well enough to remain in the care of her parents, Family Allowance would have continued to be paid to her and would have been at her family's disposal. If S/Sgt O'Toole had been serving in Europe, it would have been possible for Mr Fitton to write to his son-in-law and request extra funds which could have been provided from the £299 held in his pay account. The real problem, however, arose from the failure of the Paymaster concerned to read correctly the conditions of the diversion from pay. If Mr Fitton's plight had not been so extreme he might well not have written to the War Office direct and other families or relatives might well have suffered in silence without taking such direct action. Although this misreading may have been confined to one Paymaster, it seems unlikely that Mr Fitton was the only relative to suffer. Between 1942 and 1944 a total of 318 diversion orders were made – a figure small enough to suggest that many of them may have contained specific, individual instructions requiring careful perusal by Paymasters if they were to be administered correctly.[41] However, even if cases of this type were small in number, their existence suggests a lack of attention by those responsible for the payment of allowances to the details of their administration and an underlying attitude that afforded no importance to the needs of the service families relying on them.

In November 1944, a report was prepared by the Army Council summarising powers to order diversionary payments of this nature that clearly laid out the history, rationale and current position.[42] The Council's powers to order diversion from pay and allowances of an officer who was prisoner of war or missing in favour of a dependant was delegated, within certain limitations, to the Paymaster's Office in Manchester and local paymasters abroad. The rationale for this was that officers' arrangements for maintenance of families 'were apt to breakdown when they became POW or missing' and could cease altogether if no arrangements had previously been made with banks for funds to be drawn.[43] Problems were also recognised if payments were normally credited to banks abroad now in enemy territory. In addition, the report recognised that changing circumstances such as needs of education, cost of living rises or sickness sometimes resulted in the original provision becoming insufficient to meet needs.[44] Although diversions had originally operated only in cases where previous maintenance was provable, other cases had come to light where it was obvious that the officer would have wished to contribute if he had known of the circumstances and so powers were extended to cover these situations.[45] In addition to permanent diversion orders, interim orders could also be granted covering a period of two to six months to provide for immediate needs while enquiries into the officer's wishes were completed or where family circumstances were subject to continuing change and needed continual review.[46] Where a permanent order was made, this was normally reviewed only if the recipient applied for an increase or if there were new developments such as the return of a family from abroad.[47] All of these cases were ones that presented some form of difficulty and, as a result, they were forwarded to the War Office together with all the relevant information available. The applicant was also required to complete a pro-forma giving full details of the claim and certifying that these details were correct. Each case was then examined with reference to the officer's personal papers and confidential enquiries were made of his banker.[48] In some cases personal interviews with the applicant were requested but these were rare. Once a decision to order diversionary payments had been made, this fact was recorded in minutes in the officer's personal papers.[49] Straightforward cases were dealt with by the Paymaster without reference to the War Office.

The underpinning principle of any diversionary order was to attempt to carry out an officer's known or presumed wishes. To this end, provision previously made by the officer was used as a guideline to intentions but changes in family circumstances of which he could not be aware were also taken into consideration together with any improvements in his own financial situation.[50] In cases where the wife was demonstrably wholly maintained but not able to give the exact amount of maintenance, a maximum diversion of Family Lodging Allowance plus two-sevenths of pay applied although this maximum diversion was regarded as unusual and authorised only in exceptional circumstances. Orders for diversion were not made if it was thought that this would be against the officer's wishes or 'for the purpose of enforcing maintenance against an unwilling officer'.[51] Policy generally was, as has been seen earlier, to ensure that a reasonable balance remained in the officer's account against his return. Overall, the department attempted to maintain a balance between being placed in the position of trustee controlling a discretionary trust on behalf of the officers' families whilst at the same time working closely with bankers, trustees, relations and employers to 'ensure that officers' monies were properly applied'.[52]

No diversionary orders were granted on purely speculative grounds – that is, no orders were made purely on the basis that it would be the reasonable thing to do – if there was no evidence to support such a claim. At all times the War Office acted for the benefit of the serviceman concerned regardless of the possible hardship this might entail for families but, in reality, only a small number of applicants were refused diversion orders. Forty cases were refused because of a misunderstanding on the part of the wife who had not understood that the officer's original arrangements would be reverted to once the status of the officer was ascertained and normal pay and allowances resumed.[53] By and large, cases of deliberate misrepresentation of the facts to try to obtain diversionary orders were rare. In the majority of the other cases refused, it was clear that the officer in question had no intention of maintaining the applicant whether they had a moral claim to support or not and the War Office respected the officers' decisions.

For other ranks, the Council's powers to order allotments from pay of a soldier who was missing or a prisoner of war were again delegated to the Regimental Paymasters – provided they were straightforward. Generally these powers had been operative since

November 1943 as a result of the hardships some families had experienced when men who were missing or captive could not give instructions regarding allotments or changing family circumstances.[54] These changes most commonly included: the death or unemployment of the family breadwinner, usually the soldier's father; the illness of the applicant; the ending of some other form of income; increasing age or increases in the size of family all resulting in increased expenditure. In a number of other cases, parents or other relatives had become eligible for Dependants' Allowances while the men were missing or held captive but the allowance had not been issued as there had been no means of obtaining the necessary authority to make the required allotment from pay. Between December 1943 and July 1944, 230 orders of this nature were made, usually for an indefinite period as the soldier was missing or held captive in the Far East.[55] In addition, a small number of orders were made in respect of servicemen captive in Europe until instructions from the serviceman were received.[56] The amounts involved ranged from 5s 7d per day down to 3d, with the smaller amounts generally being to supplement an allotment previously authorised by the soldier to qualify the recipients for Dependants' Allowance which they had become entitled to in the soldier's absence.[57] In the case of Dependants' Allowances the amount of the order was fixed at contributory allotment level and, in cases where the allowance was transferred to another dependant on the death of the recipient, the allotment continued at the level already operative. In cases where the order was required to meet a loss of income, logically, this was at the required level to meet the shortfall.

Again, cases requiring further investigation came to the War Office through Regimental Paymasters together with details of pay, date of casualty, details of past and current allotments and next of kin. The Assistance Boards normally arranged investigation of these cases, with SSAFA becoming involved in interviews and making confidential reports.[58] In urgent cases an interim allotment could be made pending investigation and payments were generally made from the date of application although in certain cases, where the soldier's intentions could be precisely established, orders could be given for retrospective payment.[59]

For the families of both officers and other ranks, steps were taken to ensure that those who needed to know that such provision could be made did know, although it was seen as undesirable to publicise the matter too highly for fear of 'inviting a mass of undesirable applications'.[60] Although the War Office believed that few dependants remained unaware of the existence of these diversionary powers, thanks to the work of the various agencies such as Welfare Officers and SSAFA in addition to the Paymaster, they also commented that 'it was remarkable how very few cases have come in relation to the number of our prisoners of war'.[61] Rather than considering the possibility that these low numbers resulted from a lack of efficient communications however, they regarded them as a comment on how well the army administrative arrangements for paying families were working.

By December 1944 the War Office, presumably with a view to large numbers of prisoners of war being released in the foreseeable future, was giving consideration to ways in which these diversionary orders could be stopped in cases where officers 'became effective again'.[62] Again it appears that its priority was to ensure against the possibility of unnecessary extra provision for families who could once again access funds direct from the servicemen concerned. For officers it was envisaged that the order would become invalid as soon as he was once again 'operative'.[63] Payments would be stopped and the officer issued with a statement of all payments made plus a reminder that he should now make his own arrangements for maintenance of his family and dependants. Originally, other ranks were to be informed of the issue of allotments under diversion and given a limited period, fourteen days, to apply for continuation of the allowance. This was later changed so that the allotment would remain in place unless the soldier indicated his wishes otherwise.[64]

Just as there had been many exceptions to the regulations governing the issue of general service allowances following the introduction of conscription, so a myriad of special cases and financial problems arose in connection with the families of those taken captive. In the case of families of officers evacuated from Hong Kong and Singapore to Australia, many arrived destitute.[65] For example, the wives of junior officers faced 'extreme difficulty' in trying to meet mess charges out of the proposed two-sevenths of pay and it was agreed to waive these charges for the families of junior officers only.[66] For families in Britain, changing family needs during long periods when menfolk were still posted as 'missing' for extended periods caused many problems. Mrs May Sawford of

Swansea wrote to the War Office in June 1943 enquiring about the possibility of an Education Grant for her two eldest sons aged 6 and 8 to go to the Bible College School.[67] If her husband had been officially declared dead she would have been able to apply for this grant as a matter of course but, as he was still officially 'missing', she thought this was not permissible. In fact an Education Grant could be allowed in this type of case but, as a letter from the Pensions Office in Blackpool to the Ministry of Pensions in August of the same year suggests, the difficulty was that the War Office did not want the fact that it could grant these allowances to be 'too widely advertised'.[68]

Problems with the payment of allowances to the families of those taken captive were not, however, the sole prerogative of the families of British prisoners of war. Similar problems existed for captives of other nationalities held by British and Dominion agencies. For example, in March 1943 Italian prisoners of war held by British forces expressed concern that they were unable to remit money to their families in Ethiopia, which was no longer occupied by British forces.[69] The Foreign Office suggested that it might be possible to send money to these families if the consent of the Emperor was obtained on the basis that this would mean that the Ethiopian government would then have to provide less support itself for these families.[70] In the event, it transpired that the Italian prisoners of war in question were being held in India and that the majority of Italian civilians had been removed from Ethiopia. In November 1943, the War Office wrote to the Foreign Office stating that 'We should certainly not allow Italian prisoners in India or anywhere else to send money to their families in Italy'.[71] Instead a scheme was proposed whereby prisoners of war could transfer part of their credit balances of pay at home to their families. However, the conditions imposed on such a scheme by the Italian government, and the rate of inflation in Italy at the time, were such as to make the amounts involved 'too trivial to be worth the trouble'.[72] In fact the amount which would have eventually been remitted to the family was in the region of 12s (50 lire) per month. Once again the driving force behind the decision seems to have been the scale of the administrative burden caused by the implementation of such a system rather than the needs of the families concerned.

Obviously then, significant problems existed for some families of those taken captive in relation to the actual mechanisms for the transfer of monies. As has already been seen, for the families of other ranks this problem was often circumvented as the wives and dependants involved were issued with books of drafts, which could be drawn at a designated post office. Additionally the amount that the serviceman normally allotted from his pay was known to the Paymasters involved, and allotment at this level could be continued despite loss of contact with the serviceman himself. Although problems did arise when changing family circumstances might have warranted an increase in this allotment, by and large allowances continued as normal for the families and dependants of other ranks. For the families of officers, however, the situation was very different. In these cases Family Allowance was paid direct to the bank account of the officer himself who then transferred funds to family and dependants. Although Paymasters knew the amount of allowance, the actual amount transferred to wives and other dependants remained a matter of conscience for the officer himself. In cases where the officer had not made arrangements for his wife and dependants to draw funds direct from his bank, these became completely inaccessible when the officer was taken captive.

However, problems of this nature had not been entirely unforeseen. A draft letter of October 1939 from an Under-secretary of State at the Foreign Office had suggested that:

> In the absence of machinery for the transmission of money from POWs to their relatives in the country to which they belong, the provisions of Article 23, if carried out, would involve considerable hardship to the dependants of officers who were captured.[73]

The same letter continues with the assertion that, although discussions had taken place with the Red Cross regarding mechanisms for sending parcels, food and 'comforts' to prisoners of war themselves, 'no mention is made of how money will be got to their families'.[74]

For the families of those officers captive in Europe it was possible that, with the co-operation of their captors, correspondence could be sent to banks in England to expedite this situation.[75] However, for the families of those taken captive in the Far East, the situation did indeed become desperate. The attitude that it was a matter of personal responsibility for the officer himself to have made arrangements with his bank for his wife or other dependants to be able to draw funds from his account was common in all three services. As already detailed, only the air force had in place a contingency scheme whereby pay and allowances could be transferred direct to families if proof of earlier financial provision could be produced. Although it may not seem unreasonable to expect an officer to take this responsibility, this assumption needs to be set against the prevailing service and government attitude towards the whole question of prisoners of war. We have already seen the Treasury regarding it as 'unnecessary and undesirable' to shape policy for this eventuality. Within the services themselves there was precious little encouragement for men to consider the possibility of a time when, in the words of A.J. Barker, they might be 'no longer effective in the business of war' and a 'liability to friend and foe alike'.[76] Given this general attitude, it seems unrealistic then to have expected officers, additionally charged with the responsibility for the upkeep of their men's morale, to dwell on such a possibility. There was, therefore, an inherent tension in governmental thinking between the attitude they took towards preparing men for the possibility of being captured and the responsibility they expected the men to undertake towards providing for their families in such an eventuality. The possibility that these conflicting attitudes might lead to financial hardship for the families of those concerned was not a consideration in the development of policy on these issues.

Notes

1 Fishman, *We Will Wait*. p57.
2 Report on exercise of powers to order diversionary payments from Pay and Allowances of officers and soldiers for the support of their dependants, delegated by the Army Council to AG3(d). 15 November 44. NA/T162/792/E40219/1.
3 Pay for Missing Personnel and Prisoners of War. 26 September 39. NA/WO32/9909. See also Minutes of the 1st Meeting of the Imperial POW Co-ordinating Committee (Finance). 13 August 43. NA/WO163/639.
4 Phillimore Report. Part II. NA/WO366/26.
5 Foreign Office File FO916/256 contains a wide range of memos, letters and requests both to and from prisoners of war in Germany regarding financial payments in respect of alterations in payments to dependants and families in addition to requests for 'discreet' enquiries to be made regarding the fidelity of wives.

6 Phillimore Report. p. 56. NA/WO366/26.

7 Phillimore Report. pp. 277–287. NA/WO366/26.

8 Phillimore Report. 'Notes for the Guidance of Camp Leaders' p. 284. NA/WO366/26.

9 Phillimore Report p. 56. For army officers the situation was substantially the same although in this case instructions were to be sent directly to the banks concerned. NA/WO366/26.

10 Revision of Regulations for the issue of Pay and Allowances of Missing Personnel. 27 October 45. NA/AIR2/6408.

11 Phillimore Report. p. 56. NA/WO366/26.

12 Notes on Mercantile Marine officers and ratings serving under naval discipline (T.124 ratings). 18 March 40. NA/WO32/9909.

13 Phillimore Report. p. 102. NA/WO366/26.

14 For comparison, the Phillimore Report estimates that in May 1945 a total of approximately 170,000 Commonwealth prisoners of war were in German hands. Phillimore Report. p. 56. NA/WO366/26.

15 Notification of prisoners of war in the Far East. Imperial Prisoners of War Committee, Sub-committee A. 02 June 43. NA/WO163/586.

16 Article 10C Royal Warrant 1940 states that: 'Army Councils, or officers authorised by them, may order an allotment of pay from a soldier officially declared prisoner of war or missing to any one person provided that: a) the person is one to whom the soldier would be permitted to make an allotment of voluntary payment. b) the authorities were satisfied that the soldier, under normal circumstances, would have contributed to the support of the person in question. c) any allotment made was subject to the regulations pertaining to allotments from pay and regarded as having been authorised by the soldier.' NA/T162/792/E40219/2.

17 Reg. No. 46/GEN/1591, Minute sheet 1. 30 March 42. NA/WO32/10715.

18 Family Lodging Allowance was paid to officers living off base and included payments for light, heat and other utilities which would have normally been provided free of charge in army accommodation. Reg. No. 46/GEN/1591, Minute sheet 1. 30 March 42. NA/WO32/10715.

19 Reg. No. 46/GEN/1591, Minute sheet 1. 30 March 42. NA/WO32/10715.

20 Reg. No. 46/GEN/1591, Minute sheet 1. 30 March 42. NA/WO32/10715.

21 Reg. No. 46/GEN/1591, Minute sheet 1. 30 March 42. NA/WO32/10715.

22 Reg. No. 46/GEN/1591, Minute sheet 1. 30 March 42. NA/WO32/10715.

23 Note, Meadrow, Admiralty. 28 August 42. NA/ADM1/11909.
24 Note, Meadrow, Admiralty. 28 August 42. NA/ADM1/11909.
25 Note, Meadrow, Admiralty. 28 August 42. NA/ADM1/11909.
26 Note, Meadrow, Admiralty. 28 August 42. NA/ADM1/11909.
27 Note, Meadrow, Admiralty. 28 August 42. NA/ADM1/11909.
28 Statement regarding officers and men missing from Hong Kong and Singapore. 17 April 42. WO32/10715.
29 Statement regarding officers and men missing from Hong Kong and Singapore. 17 April 42. WO32/10715.
30 Statement regarding officers and men missing from Hong Kong and Singapore. 17 April 42. WO32/10715.
31 Draft memo. To Regimental Paymasters regarding applications for dependants' allowances and allotments received from relatives. 07 July 44. WO32/10715.
32 For an example of this type of case see correspondence from November 1943 relating to Major G.H. Garlick, RAMC, whose family were resident in India and paid from the Meerut pay office. NA/WO32/10715.
33 Statement regarding officers and men missing from Hong Kong and Singapore. 17 April 42. WO32/10715.
34 Improvements in War Service Grants. 27 May 42. T213/3/DP43/05.
35 Improvements in War Service Grants. 27 May 42. T213/3/DP43/05.
36 Memo regarding further delegation to the Regimental Paymaster of diversionary powers under Article 10C of Royal Warrant for Pay 1940 in respect of other ranks prisoners of war. 24 April 45. NA/WO32/10715[72A].
37 Memo regarding further delegation to the Regimental Paymaster of diversionary powers under Article 10C of Royal Warrant for Pay 1940 in respect of other ranks prisoners of war. 24 April 45. NA/WO32/10715[72A].
38 Memo regarding further delegation to the Regimental Paymaster of diversionary powers under Article 10C of Royal Warrant for Pay 1940 in respect of other ranks prisoners of war. 24 April 45. NA/WO32/10715[72A].
39 Details of this case study can be found in: Letter, Howell (Major) for Regimental Paymaster, Leeds, to Inspector Pay Services, War Office, London 21 January 44 [1A]; Copy letter Howell (Major) for regimental Paymaster, Leeds, to Inspector, Pay Services, War Office, London 21 January 44 [F4B]; Letter Paymaster, Leeds, to War Office, 22 February 44 [F9B]; Letter Relief Office, Aldershot, unsigned, to Regimental Paymaster, Leeds 08 February 44 [F9B]; Letter Regimental Paymaster, Leeds, to War Office 22 February 44 [6A]; Memo War Office to Regimental Paymaster, Leeds 29 February 44 [7A]; Memo

War Office to Regimental Paymaster, Leeds, 08 March 44 [10A]; Note Regimental Paymaster, Leeds, to Paymaster in Chief, War Office, London 17 March 44; Loose Minute Howell (Capt.) 28 March 44; Form Letter, War Office to Regimental Paymaster, Leeds, 31 March 44; Letter Mr C. Fitton to War Office 10 April 44; Form Letter War Office to Regimental Paymaster, Leeds, 08 April 44 [12A]; Letter War Office to Regimental Paymaster, Leeds, 24 April 44 [12B]; Letter Regimental Paymaster, Leeds, to War Office 27 April 44 [13A]; Letters C.V. Rooker, War Office, to Regimental Paymaster, Leeds, 02 February 44; Note Regimental Paymaster, Leeds, to Under-secretary of State, War Office 12 February 44; Note Regimental Paymaster, Leeds, to Under-Secretary of State, War Office 08 June 44 [15A]; Handwritten note Regimental Paymaster, Leeds, to Under-secretary of State, War Office 21 July 44 [18A]; Note Regimental Paymaster, Leeds, to Under-secretary of State, War Office 02 August 44 [19A]; Schedule of Allotments, signed Lucas-Tooth, War Office 17 July 44 [16]. NA/WO32/10715 [15A]; Handwritten note Regimental Paymaster, Leeds, to Under-secretary of State, War Office 21 July 44 [18A]; Note Regimental Paymaster, Leeds, to Under-secretary of State, War Office 02 August 44 [19A]; Schedule of Allotments, signed Lucas-Tooth, War Office 17 July 44 [16]. NA/WO32/10715.

40 Family Allowance for Wife (without children) in Rate Aided Institution sets out the general conditions governing payments of Family Allowance in such cases. NA/WO32/10449.

41 Draft memo regarding the further delegation to Regimental Paymasters of diversionary powers under Article 10C of the Royal Warrant for pay 1940 in respect of prisoners of war. March 1945. NA/WO32/10715.

42 Report on exercise of powers to order diversionary payments from the pay and allowances of officers and soldiers for the support of their dependants delegated by the Army Council to AG3(d). 15 November 44. NA/WO32/10715.

43 Report on exercise of powers to order diversionary payments from the pay and allowances of officers and soldiers for the support of their dependants delegated by the Army Council to AG3(d). 15 November 44. NA/WO32/10715.

44 Report on exercise of powers to order diversionary payments from the pay and allowances of officers and soldiers for the support of their dependants delegated by the Army Council to AG3(d). 15 November 44. NA/WO32/10715.

45 Report on exercise of powers to order diversionary payments from the pay and allowances of officers and soldiers for the support of their

dependants delegated by the Army Council to AG3(d). 15 November 44. NA/WO32/10715.

46 Report on exercise of powers to order diversionary payments from the pay and allowances of officers and soldiers for the support of their dependants delegated by the Army Council to AG3(d). 15 November 44. NA/WO32/10715.

47 Report on exercise of powers to order diversionary payments from the pay and allowances of officers and soldiers for the support of their dependants delegated by the Army Council to AG3(d). 15 November 44. NA/WO32/10715.

48 Report on exercise of powers to order diversionary payments from the pay and allowances of officers and soldiers for the support of their dependants delegated by the Army Council to AG3(d). 15 November 44. NA/WO32/10715.

49 Report on exercise of powers to order diversionary payments from the pay and allowances of officers and soldiers for the support of their dependants delegated by the Army Council to AG3(d). 15 November 44. NA/WO32/10715.

50 Report on exercise of powers to order diversionary payments from the pay and allowances of officers and soldiers for the support of their dependants delegated by the Army Council to AG3(d). 15 November 44. NA/WO32/10715.

51 Report on exercise of powers to order diversionary payments from the pay and allowances of officers and soldiers for the support of their dependants delegated by the Army Council to AG3(d). 15 November 44. NA/WO32/10715.

52 Report on exercise of powers to order diversionary payments from the pay and allowances of officers and soldiers for the support of their dependants delegated by the Army Council to AG3(d). 15 November 44. NA/WO32/10715.

53 Report on exercise of powers to order diversionary payments from the pay and allowances of officers and soldiers for the support of their dependants delegated by the Army Council to AG3(d). 15 November 44. NA/WO32/10715.

54 1st Meeting of Inter-departmental POW Co-ordinating Committee (Finance). 13 August 43. NA/WO163/639.

55 Report on exercise of powers to order diversionary payments from the pay and allowances of officers and soldiers for the support of their dependants delegated by the Army Council to AG3(d). 15 November 44. NA/WO32/10715.

56 Report on exercise of powers to order diversionary payments from the pay and allowances of officers and soldiers for the support of their

dependants delegated by the Army Council to AG3(d). 15 November 44. NA/WO32/10715.

57 Report on exercise of powers to order diversionary payments from the pay and allowances of officers and soldiers for the support of their dependants delegated by the Army Council to AG3(d). 15 November 44. NA/WO32/10715.

58 'History of SSAFA'.

59 Report on exercise of powers to order diversionary payments from the pay and allowances of officers and soldiers for the support of their dependants delegated by the Army Council to AG3(d). 15 November 44. NA/WO32/10715.

60 Letter, Pensions Office, Blackpool, to Raffill, Ministry of Pensions. 27 August 43. NA/PIN15/2635.

61 Notes on service pay and allowances: comparison with Assistance Board Allowances. 26 May 43. NA/AST11/155.

62 Note War Office. 27 December 44. NA/WO32/10715.

63 Note War Office. 27 December 44. NA/WO32/10715.

64 Letters Feehally (Col.), War Office, to Army Pay Office Manchester and all Regimental Paymasters. 12 and 14 September 45 respectively. NA/WO32/10715.

65 Notes on payment of allowances to families of officers evacuated to Australia. Undated but probably early 1942. NA/T162/792/E40219/2.

66 The cut-off point for this waiving of charges was at the rank of Lieutenant-Colonel. Letter from War Office to Treasury. NA/T162/792/E40219/2.

67 Details of this case study can be found in: letters Mrs May to War Office. 22 June 43, and Pensions Office, Blackpool, to Raffill, Ministry of Pensions. 27 August 43. NA/PIN15/2635.

68 Letter Pensions Office, Blackpool, to Raffill, Ministry of Pensions. 27 August 43. NA/PIN15/2635.

69 Unsigned copy letter to Treasury. 24 March 43. NA/FO916/671.

70 Unsigned copy letter Treasury to War Office. March 43. NA/FO916/671.

71 Letter 18 November 43 War Office to Roberts, Foreign Office. NA/FO916/671.

72 Unsigned letter War Office to Roberts, Foreign Office. 18 November 43. NA/FO916/671.

73 Draft letter, Under-secretary of State, Foreign Office (signature indecipherable). October 1939. NA/WO32/9909.

74 Draft letter, Under-secretary of State, Foreign Office (signature indecipherable). October 1939. NA/WO32/9909.

75 Under the terms of the Geneva Convention junior officers were allowed to send up to four letters home per month in addition to four postcards whilst senior officers, padres and medical officers could send up to six letters plus four postcards. Other ranks were allowed two letters and four postcards. Gilbert, A., *POW. Allied Prisoners in Europe 1939–1945*. London: John Murray, 2006. p188.

76 Barker, *Behind Barbed Wire*. Caption to photo 3 and p. 52 respectively.

5

'Nobody would tell you anything' – official secrets and bureaucratic misinformation

To suggest that fiscal worries were the sole, or even prime, concern of service families in general and prisoner of war families in particular would be misleading. For many, and not just those in Britain, lack of information about missing husbands, fathers, sons and brothers was arguably an even more pressing concern than a lack of finances. Sarah Fishman, in her study of the everyday life of French prisoner of war wives, reports 'lack of news' as one of the main causes of emotional difficulties experienced by such women.[1] In Britain Mrs Buswell, whose husband, a gunner in RAF 99 Squadron, was shot down over Germany in late 1944, spoke for many when she claimed 'You were so helpless. You couldn't do anything and you couldn't find out anything. Nobody would tell you anything.'[2] Clearly, then, the manner in and extent to which news and information about loved ones taken captive was communicated to the families in question played an important part in maintaining their emotional if not physical well-being.

By the war's end, a total of 192,335 British service personnel had been in held in enemy captivity for some period of time. Of these personnel, the great majority left behind wives or other dependants. Yet even though the government recognised that the treatment of prisoners of war was 'always likely to assume political importance', no clear strategies for collating and disseminating information were developed before 1939.[3] Even though experiences during the First World War had suggested that there was a necessity for clearly designated areas of responsibility within government departments for prisoner of war matters, the potential problems were again severely underestimated.[4]

In that conflict, the War Office had established a Prisoner of War Directorate and a Government Committee on the Treatment by the

Enemy of British prisoners of war,[5] whilst information about prisoners was largely collected from escaped or repatriated British
prisoners and then collated by the Prisoner of War Department at
the Foreign Office.[6] Given these arrangements it was almost inevitable that disagreements would arise between the various departments as to just who was ultimately responsible for prisoner of war
matters. As we have seen in earlier chapters, a predisposition existed
within the War Office to regard its claims in such matters as para-
mount because of the greater numbers of army personnel involved.
In an attempt to settle these disagreements, an inter-departmental
committee was established in February 1916 under the chairmanship of Lord Newton, Under-secretary of State for Foreign Affairs,
to co-ordinate the work of all government departments concerned
with prisoner of war matters. Initially consisting of representatives
from the Foreign Office, War Office, Home Office, India Office,
Colonial Office, Admiralty, Air Ministry, Board of Trade and
Ministry of Shipping, by the latter stages of the war the committee
had expanded to include representatives of the Dominions.[7]
However, as this committee was not given any real authority over
the departments involved, internal disagreements continued.

Matters came to a head in October 1916 when the Foreign Office
refused to have any further dealings with prisoner of war matters
and the War Committee of the Cabinet established an independent
Prisoners of War Department to deal with this work.[8] However,
once again, no clear authority was established and matters of disagreement over policy continued to be referred back to the War
Committee. Confusion was heightened by the establishment of
three further bodies dealing specifically with prisoner of war
matters: the Prisoners of War Information Bureau, the Central
Prisoners of War Committee of the Red Cross Society and the
Order of St John of Jerusalem, and the Government Committee on
the Treatment by the Enemy of British Prisoners of War.[9] Although
the existence of separate committees may have been intended to
facilitate access to information, in fact it led to much confusion in
the minds of those families seeking information about missing servicemen. This confusion was further reinforced by the fact that all
committees, no doubt with the best of motives, were prepared to
answer general queries regarding prisoner of war matters without
necessarily referring the enquirer to the responsible government
department.[10]

The so-called Belfield Report, 'Work in Connection with Prisoners of War from August 1914 to January 1919', outlines six major areas of public dissatisfaction with the manner in which matters relating to prisoners of war were treated by the government.[11] Amongst these, a lack of information, together with a lack of awareness as to which authority was ultimately responsible for prisoners, features highly. Nevertheless, as we shall see in the course of this chapter, the same areas of dissatisfaction again became evident in public perception of the government treatment of prisoners of war and their families during the Second World War. Despite the fact that most government departments had established permanent public relations or press departments during the interwar years, no co-ordinated policy for the dissemination of information to the general public had been devised.[12] Similarly, no clear-cut policy had been developed between the various departments involved for the dissemination of information to the families of those taken captive.

In 1939, the government gave general responsibility for prisoner of war matters into the hands of the War Office 'because the majority of [. . .] prisoners in enemy hands come from the army'.[13] In fact, during the period of the 'phoney war' so few servicemen fell into enemy hands that the subject was not one of immediate concern. Additionally, while the war remained an exclusively European one, the issue of prisoners was not regarded as one of pressing urgency. All parties involved were signatories of the Geneva Convention of 1929 and, as such, had agreed to abide by common regulations both for the treatment of prisoners themselves and for notification of their status to national governments.

However, when 44,000 men from the British Expeditionary Force fell into German hands in June 1940, prisoners of war matters attained a much higher profile, and the inadequacies of the existing arrangements were recognised by the War Office.[14] Consequently, a separate Directorate of Prisoners of War (DPW) was established. Sir Harold Satow and Mrs M.J. Sée, in what is otherwise a largely uncritical review of the work of the Foreign Office's Prisoner of War Department during the Second World War, claim that there was 'no excuse' for not having seen before this time that such a department would be needed.[15] They then go on to suggest that the whole task of dealing with these matters would have been made a great deal easier if both the War Office and Foreign Office had realised at an earlier stage that concerns relating to prisoners of war would 'require continuous effort'.[16] Indeed the issue of government policy towards prisoner of war families only being developed reactively in response to problems rather than as a coherent policy is one that forms a recurring theme throughout the period of the Second World War.

By late 1941 the scale of prisoner of war matters had resulted in the Directorate increasing in size to include three official branches, although it unofficially operated six.[17] For the purposes of this book the most important branches were: PW2 dealing with the interpretation of the Geneva Convention; PW3 concerned with the welfare of British prisoners in enemy hands; and PW4 dealing with censorship and correspondence. Overseeing the Directorate as a whole were a Director, initially Major-General E.C. Gepp, CB, DSO, a Deputy-Director, Major-General V. Bloomfield, CB, DSO, and two Assistant Adjutant Generals.[18] By March 1945 the Directorate had further increased to consist of 36 military officers, nine junior civil servants and 78 clerks – indicating the scale to which prisoner of war matters had expanded.[19] However, not all prisoner of war issues came under the jurisdiction of the DPW. Both the Foreign Office and other branches of the War Office themselves retained an interest, together with the navy and the air force as it was recognised that none of the services could or should be 'relieved of their immediate responsibility to the next-of-kin of their own personnel nor [sic] for the immediate problems of those personnel'.[20] Consequently, from the outset, relatives were faced with a bewildering array of departments when trying to obtain information on missing servicemen. They were, however, assured by newspaper articles that 'without any application on their part' strenuous efforts were being made to trace all missing personnel, and a leaflet was prepared by the War Office detailing the procedure for notifying relatives of servicemen missing or taken prisoner.[21] To some extent this confusion was ameliorated in October 1940 when all work on lists of British prisoners of war was transferred to the DPW but, not surprisingly given the circumstances, news often came to relatives more quickly through unofficial channels than through official channels.[22] For example, David Rolf quotes the case of Private Bowers, captured in Belgium in the summer of 1940, who managed to pass hand written messages to Red Cross nurses. These messages were then forwarded to his

mother long before she received official notification that he was
missing, let alone a prisoner of war.[23]

Information about prisoners received from enemy governments,
with the exception of propaganda broadcasts, was regarded as
'official' and most commonly took the form of lists sent to the
Prisoner of War Information Bureau of the Foreign Office in the
relevant country.[24] These bureaux were established as a requirement of the Geneva Convention Article 77 which stated that

> a belligerent power is bound to set up an Information Bureau for the
> purpose of furnishing as soon as possible information as to the cap-
> tures of prisoners of war, with particulars of identity, to enable the
> families to be quickly notified, and official addresses to which letters
> to the prisoners may be sent by their families.[25]

The bureaux were required to forward this information through
two channels – the International Committee of the Red Cross in
Geneva and the relevant protecting power.[26] For British prisoners
of war the protecting power was initially the United States, but after
its entry into the war in December 1941 the Swiss government took
over this role.[27]

Despite the fact that one of the main functions of these bureaux
was 'to enable the families concerned to be quickly notified', many
families were dissatisfied with the service.[28] With increasing delays
in 'official' information it became inevitable that many relatives,
unable to obtain information in any other way, turned to 'unofficial' sources. Figure 1 gives an overview of both official and unofficial sources of information. These included lists prepared by
British legations and neutral sources, lists based on escapees' stories,
lists based on enemy propaganda broadcasts and lists broadcast by
the Vatican – regarded by some as 'very amateurish'.[29] All 'unofficial' lists received in London were analysed and then either
recorded as 'acceptable' so raising their status to that of official
lists, or 'unconfirmed' which gave no guarantee of their accuracy.[30]
Not surprisingly, in the light of long delays in 'official' notification,
unofficial broadcasts acquired a large following and it became
common practice for those who heard the broadcasts to pass the
information on to the families of those mentioned in case they,
themselves, had not been listening.[31] A miscellaneous file at the
Imperial War Museum contains 26 letters and cards expressing
thanks to those who had passed on information from a single

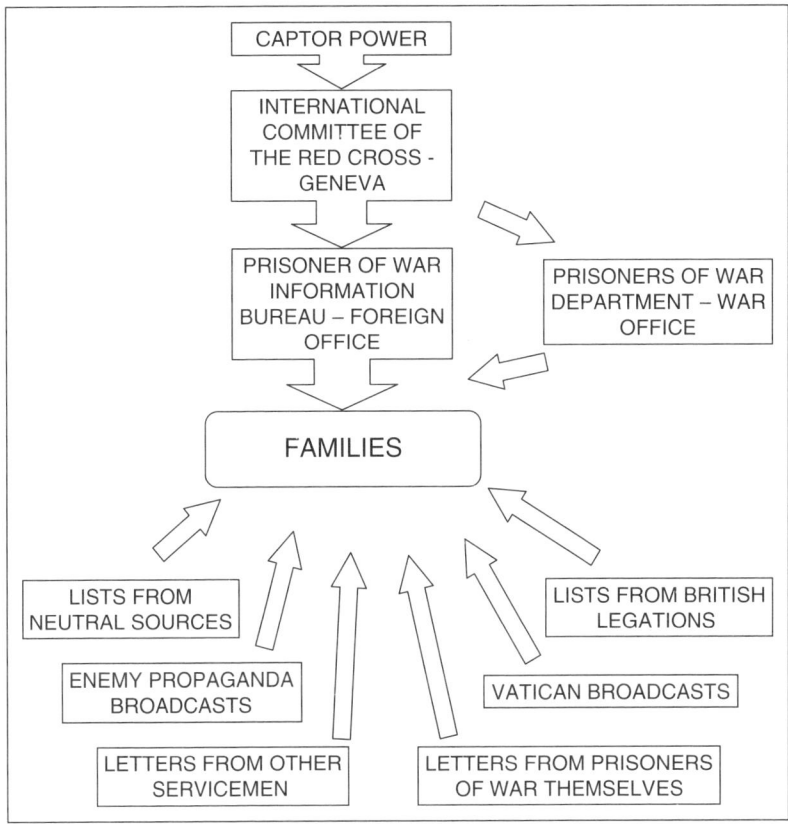

Figure 1: Possible sources of information for prisoner of war families
Source: Compiled from information contained in Imperial Prisoner
of War Committee Minutes (NA/WO163/582), SHAEF tables of the
organisation of the Prisoner of War Executive (NA/WO219/1402) and
Satow and Sée *The Work of the Prisoners of War Department
during the Second World War* (Foreign Office, 1950).

broadcast in November 1944.[32] Mrs Ginnard of London E1 received
23 letters from strangers who had heard her husband's name mentioned. Mr and Mrs Owen of Salford, whose only son had been
taken prisoner at Anzio, 'didn't realise that anyone could be so
good' when they received numerous letters following the broadcast
of his name.[33] Mrs Heath of Colchester, however, first heard that
her husband, who had been missing since May 1940, had been

taken prisoner from a rather different 'unofficial' source when a fireman from the pit where he had worked heard his name mentioned in a nightly broadcast by Lord Haw-Haw.[34]

As we have already seen in the case of Private Bowers, some families had direct communications from prisoners themselves before receiving official notification of their captive status. In these cases the War Office asked the relatives to keep them informed.[35] In fact, although such communications were not regarded as sufficiently reliable to act as confirmation of status, the BBC still forwarded transcripts of these broadcasts to the relevant service department to be checked against their missing lists.[36] An example of the time lapsed between unofficial and official notification being received by families is provided by the case of Captain G.W. Smith, reported missing on 30 September 1944 and believed to have been taken captive in Germany.[37] Correspondence received by his parents from the War Office suggested that it 'may be some time before an official notification to that effect is received' and asked that, if any unofficial confirmation was received, they would 'kindly notify this office'. On 6 December, Captain Smith's parents received a further communication from the War Office telling them that a broadcast on the German European Service had contained a message, believed to be from their son, saying that he was in good health and would write as soon as possible. However, this broadcast could not be regarded as 'official' and their son was still to be officially regarded as 'missing'. By the time Captain Smith was 'officially' confirmed as a prisoner in Oflag 79, some five months later, his parents had already heard from him direct and from the 'padre' of his regiment.

Public perception, not unnaturally, was that for families to hear direct from their relatives before receiving official notification indicated that there was 'something wrong with the machinery'.[38] The Imperial Prisoners of War Committee, however, determinedly chose to see this in a positive light, suggesting instead that it showed that arrangements in the enemy country for forwarding mail were working 'satisfactorily'.[39]

However, despite the caution on the part of the War Office to ensure official notification of captive status before informing families, rare occasions of official notification still proving to have been premature did exist. The mother of Private Thompson, of the Royal Army Medical Corps, was somewhat surprised to receive official notification that he had been taken prisoner in July 1940. At the time in question, he was on honeymoon in Leeds. At a similar time, Mrs J.S. Walker of Pudsey, in Leeds, was equally confused to receive official notification that her husband, a Lance-Corporal driver in the RASC, had also been taken prisoner when his regiment had not left England.[40]

Additional confusion resulted from the fact that, although the DPW was meant to be dealing with the ICRC and the protecting power solely through the Prisoner of War Department at the Foreign Office, the War Office had established its own contacts in both London and Geneva, enabling it to receive notification lists direct. Despite these actions on its part, however, it still viewed independent action by others unfavourably. The wives of the British Ambassadors in Lisbon and Turkey were both reprimanded for forming private organisations to provide parcels and comforts to British prisoners of war.[41] This type of action was seen as being in direct contravention of government policy formulated in the wake of similar action during the First World War.[42] At that time the government had felt that such initiatives were detrimental to morale, as they were unable to provide comforts for all prisoners and argued that those not receiving comforts would be in danger of becoming demoralised by their perceived neglect. To some extent these fears were justified, as was demonstrated by a similar situation in July 1942 when a number of prisoners received large amounts of mail from unknown well-wishers in response to newspaper advertisements and appeals although such appeals had also been made in earlier years.[43] As early as June 1940 the *Yorkshire Evening News* ran an article entitled 'Drop the Boys a Line' in which readers were assured that 'a letter, even from a casual acquaintance, would do a world of good'.[44] In addition to being 'detrimental to the morale of less fortunate prisoners', such initiatives also had the effect of delaying 'legitimate' mail, and the Imperial Prisoners of War Committee officially condemned all letters written by strangers in response to such appeals.[45]

On arrival at a permanent prisoner of war camp, all prisoners were issued with a postcard on which to inform their next of kin of this fact and to provide a mailing address. Many of these cards were pre-printed with little space for personal comments, a system employed in both European and the Far Eastern theatres of war, as is shown by a later card received by Mrs M.S. Rookwood from her husband, Acting Bombadier John Rookwood, in Borneo.[46] Acting Bombadier Rookwood only signed the card without completing any of the suggested phrases, so its formulaic nature can be clearly seen:

Dear ....

Have received letters/no letters.
My health is ....
Hope everything is well with you, and you are receiving your allotment.
Please remember me to ....[47]

Even within Europe, there were numerous failures of this system, with specific examples quoted by the War Office at Stalags XVIIIA and XVIID in Germany and at Capua in Italy.[48] In the Far East, despite continual attempts by both the British government and charitable organisations to improve the situation, communication with those taken captive remained problematic throughout the war. Mr and Mrs J. Bannister of Bicester, Oxfordshire, were so relieved when they finally heard from their son in Taiwan in July 1943 that they published the letter in the *Bicester Advertiser*.[49]

Even in the best of circumstances the route for mail from the Far East was convoluted. Letters and cards from Singapore, for example, were first sent, by sea, to Tokyo and then, by sea again, to Raslin in Korea. From Korea, mail travelled overland to Mukden, across Siberia to Moscow and then on to Istanbul, Trieste, Geneva and Lisbon before finally being forwarded by air to London (Figure 2).[50] Further constraints also existed in that all letters sent to prisoners of war in the Far East had to be typewritten, or block printed, and, from October 1943, limited to a maximum of 25 words.[51] These strictures were claimed to make censoring faster but, as Vivienne Chatfield noted, 'It was no easy matter to make an interesting note in only twenty-five words'.[52] After the surrender of Japan it became clear however that, even where letters complied with these conditions, precious few ever reached their intended destination or recipients.

In general, three main factors affected the length of time taken for official notification that a man had become prisoner to be confirmed, although this was inevitably affected by particular circumstances in each theatre of war.[53] Firstly, the number of prisoners

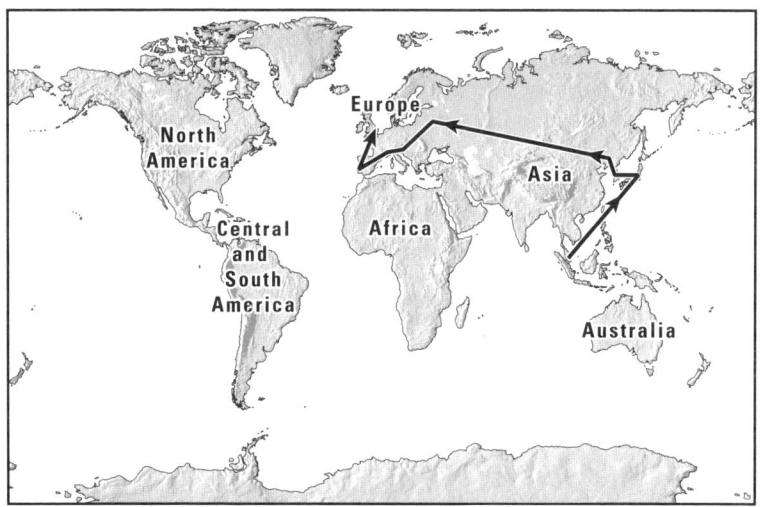

Figure 2: Map of approximate route of POW mail from the Far East
(compiled using information taken from NA/WO165/59)

captured at any one time could affect the period taken for notification to be received. Where comparatively small numbers of men
were captured, as in the Libyan campaign, notification was normally received within four to five weeks, but after the siege of
Tobruk in June 1942, where 33,000 men were reported missing,
delays were much longer.[54] In fact, by the end of the seventeen-week
period during which 'missing' allowances were paid to the families
of these men, 25 per cent still remained unaccounted for.[55]

Secondly, the medical condition of the man himself at time of
capture could also affect the speed of notification. In general,
arrangements for obtaining information about men held in hospitals were not good. Additionally, many of the seriously wounded
were too ill either to provide identification or to be moved from
Field Hospitals to camps where notification could be more speedily
effected. In the event of prisoners dying in captivity, a reciprocal
arrangement existed with the German government that photo-
graphs of the grave, taken by the Red Cross, should be sent to the
home government.[56] Although photos of German graves were forwarded in this way, no photos of British graves, with the exception
of a small number of air force graves, were received from Germany.
In November 1942 the Japanese government proposed that the

ashes of deceased British prisoners in the Far East should be returned on exchange boats.[57] Although the British government was keen to show that a prisoner of war was not 'regarded as a dishonoured man', they were equally wary of any attempt to play Dominion governments off against one another or any possible reciprocal demands.[58] The matter was, therefore, referred to the Imperial Prisoner of War Committee, Sub-Committee A, whose terms of reference included the co-ordination of policy with regard to prisoners of war concerning more than one government within the Empire 'with a view to avoiding undesirable differences of treatment'.[59] The Committee noted that it was agreed policy of all the Dominion governments that the bodies of their nationals should not be sent home for burial while hostilities continued. Requests by families for the return of bodies or ashes from France, the Middle East and other theatres of war had all been 'consistently refused'.[60] In keeping with this policy a reply was sent to the Japanese government requesting that all prisoners of war dying in captivity should, with the exception of Sikhs and Hindus, be buried locally with appropriate rites. Hindus and Sikhs were, where possible, to be cremated and their ashes scattered into a river or into the sea.[61]

Finally, the locality of the actual capture itself often affected the speed of notification. Germany did not forward notification of prisoner of war status until prisoners actually reached a camp within the Greater Reich, and in some cases this caused serious delay.[62] For example, the families of those servicemen taken prisoner during hostilities in Crete did not receive notification for almost six months. Mrs Parkes, who claimed that her husband was taken prisoner in Germany in January 1941 and then transferred to Italy, received no notification of his official status for three months. Her comment that 'really the first joy was when we got a letter ourselves, yer know, from him' must have been echoed by many.[63] Although Mrs Parkes's comments regarding delay in notification remain valid, it seems likely that she has reversed the locations here and that her husband was in fact taken captive in Italy and later transferred to Germany.

For families whose menfolk were taken prisoner in the Far East, long delays in notification became almost inevitable given the locality of capture. Indeed the Japanese themselves invoked this argument in attempting to explain the delay in notification of the men taken prisoner during the three Burma campaigns.[64] However, even before the introduction of particular problems related to prisoners in the Far East, the whole question of possible delays in notification had clearly become a matter for concern and confusion for the families involved. The Foreign Office considered that what constituted an 'undue delay' could be decided only when all the circumstances of capture were taken into consideration as different circumstances would inevitably result in different time scales being regarded as acceptable.[65] In addition, to accept any form of 'unofficial' notification was seen as weakening the case for insisting on speedy 'official' notification.[66] Although this argument was, no doubt, true, it can have been of little comfort to families anxiously awaiting news of any kind. The whole concept of different time scales for different circumstances of capture must also have caused confusion for relatives not conversant with all the military ramifications of different campaigns.

In the case of navy personnel, as we have already seen, there was often a 'deliberate delay' between the date a seaman was known by the Admiralty to be missing and the date at which this information was forwarded to the next of kin. However, even when a delay had been declared unacceptable, it was still no easy task, even within Europe, for the Foreign Office to decide the appropriate channel for complaint.[67] In cases where delay resulted as a matter of policy, the protecting power was deemed the appropriate channel, whereas, if delay was due to inefficient administrative procedures, complaint could most effectively be made to the Prisoner of War Bureau concerned. In many cases representation to belligerent powers proved effective only when some degree of reciprocity could be enforced or a 'threat made in relation to traffic in the opposite direction'.[68] In this respect the work of the Imperial Prisoners of War Committee in establishing a common policy aimed to be effective in ensuring that one Dominion government could not be played off against another.[69] A similar policy was extended to the American government where separate but parallel approaches were favoured emphasising the solidarity of all governments in the matter.[70] However, in the matter of Japanese civilians interned in the United States, Washington had not supplied lists to the Japanese government and so their claims for reciprocal treatment were open to question, a factor that the British Foreign Office regarded as 'exceedingly tiresome'.[71]

Indeed, with the entry of Japan into the war, the problems of notification had become even more acute. By May 1942, fewer than 0.1 per cent of the captives claimed by the Japanese government had been officially notified to the Prisoner of War Information Bureau at the British Foreign Office,[72] and Sub-committee A of the Imperial Prisoner of War Committee noted that there were a number of 'unsatisfactory' features with regard to prisoners in the Far East.[73] These included the general lack of information regarding numbers and locations of captives in Japanese hands, the lack of information regarding deaths in captivity and the lack of information about subsequent transfers of prisoners of war. Vivienne Chatfield, whose husband was taken prisoner in 1942, believed that he was held for the whole period of his captivity in Java where he had been captured. In fact, on his liberation in September 1945, she learnt that he had been transferred four times, ending up in Singapore, by way of Batavia.[74] For the British government the problem was often one of how to explain such delays to the families concerned without increasing worries about ill-treatment or public dissatisfaction with the way the government was handling the situation.

Almost inevitably, with the lack of official notification, unofficial and sometimes politically dangerous sources came into play. In March 1944 the Swiss Consul in Bangkok received secretly the names of six thousand British prisoners being held in Siam.[75] The onward transmission of this list proved problematic, as to transmit in cipher might render the names inaccurate for identification purposes and it was feared that such a long transmission would attract Japanese attention. The Swiss themselves expressed a preference for sending the list, by courier, to Shanghai and then, by mail, to Siberia for onward transmission to Tehran. From here the list could be sent either to the British Embassy in Tehran or to Berne. The War Office considered that the best course would be to enlist Russian help but in the end the decision was left with the Swiss. In the event, the list was eventually taken to Tokyo personally by a member of staff from the Swiss Consulate who requested that the Soviet Ambassador should transmit it to the British Embassy in Moscow. The urgency of this information to the families, or government, seemed not to be appreciated by the Swiss diplomats as by February 1945 the list had still not been transmitted. At this time it was viewed as probably being out of date and less politically sensitive and could be sent 'by the hands of any diplomatic colleague who would consent to take it'.[76] As, in the meantime, Turkey, Brazil, Egypt, Romania and 'the rest' had declared war on Japan, it was envisaged that a 'flock of diplomats' would now be coming home any of whom could bring the list with them.[77] Although the matter remains unresolved in the archival sources, it is indicative of the convoluted attempts made to obtain official information from this difficult area.

By September 1943 delays in notification from the Far East were such that the International Red Cross negotiated a radio message scheme through Radio Suisse.[78] Under this scheme prisoners of war who had been out of contact with their next of kin for a specified period, usually three months, were allowed to exchange radio messages limited strictly to family news. The messages were grouped to save on transmission along the lines of 'Prisoners of War X, Y and Z all in good health and ask news of their relatives'.[79] The success of this scheme was, however, tempered by the fact that what purported to be personal messages from the Far East were inevitably mixed with propaganda and spoken in a clearly Japanese voice.[80]

Other radio links, however, proved rather more successful. In January 1941, Australia Radio accepted an invitation from the Japanese-controlled Radio Batavia to begin a system of exchanging broadcast messages.[81] Although the system did not finally come into operation until August 1944, once begun it continued to broadcast messages at the rate of three hundred per week, despite the fact that the Japanese ended their co-operation.[82] Originally intended only for the next of kin of Australian prisoners of war and civilian internees, the scheme was widely used by the next of kin of all British Commonwealth prisoners of war and internees who were resident in Australia. However, despite continual attempts on the part of the government and charitable organisations to secure channels of communication, problems remained throughout the war for the families of those taken captive in the Far East. Iris Strange spoke for many when she recorded many years later, 'For me, as with so many others, there was no news once Singapore fell to the Japanese, except of terrible atrocities in the camps.'[83]

Once information was received in London, the process of notifying the families concerned was still 'by no means a simple clerical task'.[84] Difficulties ensued for a variety of reasons such as the omission of nationality by the enemy Prisoner of War Information

Bureau which made it difficult to differentiate British from Dominion servicemen, the abbreviation or 'mutilation' of names, and from insufficient detail being included that would have aided positive identification, such as regimental numbers.[85] If all details were decipherable, notification was normally distributed to other government and service departments within 24 hours for onward distribution to next of kin. Problems associated with notifications from the Far East proved to be so acute that a campaign began for a specific department to be established to deal with information from this area. Anthony Eden, Secretary of State for Foreign Affairs, received a deputation of MPs and relatives of British prisoners of war in the Far East, all of whom wanted a 'single channel of communication' between the government and the public to deal with enquiries concerning both prisoners of war and civilian internees in this location.[86] The deputation expressed concern that a number of enquiries had been passed from one department to another without relatives receiving any satisfactory answers and expressed the need for 'somewhere where the public could go or write to and be sure of a reply'.[87] That this concern was strongly felt is clear from a petition, presented in February 1944, from relatives of men missing in Singapore and Malaya:

> We, the undersigned, must bring to your notice the fact that the fate of our men in Singapore and Malaya is, to date, unknown.
>
> Most of us, wives, mothers, sisters, have waited with almost inexhaustible patience to learn the fate of those dear to us. The time has arrived when we feel something definite must be done. We have made allowances for the disinclination of our enemies, the Japanese, to forward the names through the usual channels, but we feel that the British Government are strong enough in 1943 to force the issue in this direction.
>
> We have all waited since the capitulation in 1942, and have no evidence of the safe landing of our men on the island of Singapore or the peninsula of Malaya, such were the conditions.
>
> This business may, in the eyes of the world, seem a military catastrophe, with the details of which we are not concerned, but the fate and treatment of these thousands of our men is very much our concern, and we insist that the attention of the Government is given immediately to this, and that a responsible Committee be formed to watch the interests of these prisoners and their next-of-kin; also that some arrangements are entered into whereby these names can be sent through with the shortest possible delay.[88]

In its last paragraph this petition hints at a public perception that the official attitude to the fall of Singapore and Hong Kong was seen solely as a military catastrophe. To the families concerned it appeared that there had been no consideration given to the effect the events might have had on their emotions and day-to-day lives.

In response to these increasing concerns from the next of kin of those missing in the Far East, and supported by an increasing number of MPs, the Prisoner of War Far East Enquiry Centre was established as an extension of the War Office Enquiry Centre.[89] Not all government departments were in favour of this development. Neither the Air Ministry nor the Ministry of War Transport (who dealt with enquiries concerning merchant seamen) was keen to hand over enquiries to a central bureau, and the Colonial Office felt that the Centre had been established 'as a political sop' to prevent further campaigning for a separate Ministry to deal with prisoner of war matters.[90] However, all departments concerned ultimately co-operated to provide information from their own sources in order for the Centre to be able to respond to as many enquiries as possible, although personnel for interviewing and clerical duties were drawn from experienced staff at the War Office Casualty (Prisoner of War) Branch.[91] In addition, a special set of instructions was issued to staff outlining a variety of methods for dealing with enquiries. Personal or telephone enquiries were dealt with by the liaison officer from the service concerned, whilst written enquiries were transferred to the department concerned.[92] In these cases the enquirer was to be informed 'by means of a non-stereotyped letter' of this action.[93]

To the general public, however, it must have appeared that some queries were dealt with preferentially by the centre while others, apparently at random, were forwarded to the various service departments. Colonel Phillimore wrote to the War Office at the time, arguing that any suggestion of enquirers being passed from one agency to another would be seen as a red rag by MPs.[94] Correspondence from the Air Ministry indicates that it also felt that this procedure would lead only to further confusion for relatives.[95] Agreement was finally reached that all general enquiries regarding policy, plus all cases where the enquirer did not know the correct department to contact, would be dealt with by the Enquiry Centre.[96] Specific enquiries regarding individual prisoners would be directed to the various Service Departments. There remains some doubt,

however, as to whether the details of these procedures were communicated to the relatives concerned.

There is evidence too that the tone of replies to enquiries from
next of kin was initially less than sympathetic. An undated War
Office circular suggests that replies to enquiries had sometimes been
'couched in rather curt official language' which might be either
'unintelligible to the recipient' or 'unnecessarily unsympathetic'.[97]
The circular continued: 'It must be remembered that many letters
received in the Record Office are written by people with little
understanding of official "jargon" and however trivial the matter
appears officially, it is usually one of vital importance to them'[98]
and went on to suggest that replies should be 'couched in simple
straightforward language so that the recipient may clearly understand that their queries have not been treated casually but have
received proper consideration.[99] Not only is this unusually humane
circular undated but its author remains unaccredited and the conditions surrounding its production unknown. The number of enquiries received by the Centre nevertheless more than justified its
existence. In June 1944 alone the Centre dealt with 376 personal
callers, 27 telephone enquiries and 922 enquiries by letter.[100]

The Enquiry Centre also published a handbook for relatives
setting out the problems of obtaining information from the Far East
and explaining how the situation there differed from that in
Europe.[101] Although sources from the Red Cross and the War Office
do not make the point explicit, this handbook, together with the
one for relatives of those held captive in Europe, was not necessarily
provided free to the families concerned. The cover of the handbooks
show them as having a cost of 2d although it is not clear whether
this charge was applied only to members of the public wanting to
obtain a copy rather than to prisoner of war families.[102]

The authorities were keen for the public in general, and relatives
in particular, to understand that they 'had no power until victory
is won to actually compel the Japanese authorities to do anything
to which they are ill-disposed'.[103] The whole question of reciprocity,
regarded as so important in ensuring fair treatment of prisoners of
war in Europe, possessed no leverage in the Far East. However,
even given these limitations, the whole picture of how much of the
information held by the government was actually released to
the relatives of those taken captive in the Far East remains
incomplete.

Throughout 1942 information regarding the treatment of prisoners in the Far East was heavily censored.[104] This was, in part at least, to prevent the general public, whom the authorities regarded as unable to appreciate the difficulties and possible repercussions of publicising the conditions in the camps, from concluding that the government was not doing everything possible to expedite the situation. The Phillimore Report of 1949 suggested that reports regarding the ill treatment of prisoners of war aroused

> bitter resentment which can have serious repercussions on a government which cannot show that it has done all within its power to avert such action, mitigate its effect and generally improve the welfare of our own men in the hands of the enemy.[105]

Although, as early as February 1942, the Imperial Prisoners of War Committee was reporting in its 'Summary of Action' that reports were being received of atrocities in Japanese camps,[106] many of the reports at this time were conflicting so that no pattern of treatment across the area could be established. For example, in April 1942, one report from Macao on Stanley Camp in Hong Kong described the conditions as 'inhuman' whilst another of the same time asserted that prisoners there were 'receiving sufficient food'.[107] By 1943 the War Office had positive evidence of appalling treatment and deaths of prisoners of war working on the Burma–Siam railway.[108] However, they expressed a fear that if this information, together with evidence of atrocities in other camps across the region, leaked out, it would be 'very difficult' to justify their earlier silence to the public.[109] In fact the information did indeed 'leak out' when, in December 1942, the *Sunday Graphic* carried a report in their Stop Press section entitled 'War Prisoners Die of Starvation' based on the testimony of three British sailors who had escaped to Chungking from a Japanese transport.[110]

As a result the War Office received hundreds of enquiries from relatives concerned about the discrepancy between official reports and this eyewitness account.[111] The Ministry of Information prepared a statement for broadcast stating that the government,

> knowing the great distress caused to the families of British POWs and internees in the Far East from lack of news, wished to take this opportunity of telling them what had been done and the reasons why up till then they had received so little information.[112]

In the event, the promised broadcast was not made until August 1943 as the government deemed it necessary to co-ordinate a simultaneous release with the Dominions and India, and wanted to allow for sufficient advance publicity so that the broadcast would attract the maximum number of listeners.[113] The numbers of enquiries received by the War Office and Far East Enquiry Bureau from worried relatives was not apparently considered sufficient evidence of interest in the subject to save next of kin from a further eight months of worry over these conflicting reports. When the broadcast was finally made, on 16 August 1943, the Foreign Office suggested that the success of the broadcast, in terms of listening figures, proved that propaganda, if handled correctly, was an effective weapon.[114] As we saw earlier in the cases of families receiving communications direct from captured relatives before receiving official notification, the government once again determinedly attempted to put a positive gloss on the situation. The fact that, at this time, there were estimated to be in the region of 50,000 to 55,000 British servicemen in Japanese hands would seem to suggest that there was little chance of such a broadcast failing to accrue high listening figures.[115]

The War Office enforced similar news censorship on the 'Avant Project' in 1943, dealing with the proposed exchange of prisoners with the Axis powers.[116] To prevent 'false optimism' on the part of the next of kin, censorship was applied so completely that many relatives had no knowledge of the proposed exchanges until October 1943 when 'they suddenly discovered a missing husband, brother or son at their front door'.[117] Small wonder, then, that many families became so suspicious of both the quality and level of information they received from official sources that they turned for support and information to local and charitable groups.

By 1944 the government had modified its whole stance on the withholding of information regarding conditions in the Far East. Whereas earlier the release of such information had been viewed as likely to cause friction with the Japanese authorities resulting in still worse treatment of prisoners, this was now seen as having potential to aid efforts to achieve better conditions.[118] The 34th meeting of the Imperial Prisoners of War Committee, Sub-committee A, in April 1944 noted that there had been a 'violent' Japanese reaction to publicity regarding the conditions in the camps and saw this as indicating a 'sensitiveness' to world opinion.[119] For example, the

Committee suggested that Japanese military pride could be stung by hinting that the Tokyo government was unable to control the military, who had direct charge of prisoners. The meeting also suggested that campaigns highlighting these issues would 'bring home the facts' to the British public.[120] This was a strange *volte face* considering that, until 1942, it was considered necessary to keep these details from the public for fear of political repercussions.

As has already been seen, the families of those who were officially notified as having been taken captive were keen not only to receive all possible information but also to do everything possible to ease the plight of captivity for their loved ones. Earlier chapters have dealt with the topic of personal parcels delivered through the Red Cross and the difficulty of providing clothing and personal items in these parcels. For the families of servicemen who had been officially notified as having been taken captive another possible method of easing the difficult and expensive matter of replacing clothing also existed through the disposal or recovery of personal effects. For many prisoners of war, at least in Europe, their effects often contained items such as extra clothing and blankets that could be forwarded to them.[121] The extent of financial saving possible by recovery of this kit is shown in an extract from the journal of an escaped prisoner which states that his next of kin had not been notified of the whereabouts of his kit and so did not know how to claim it. As a result, the serviceman had to purchase new kit himself on his arrival home at a cost of £70.[122]

Until 1941 pay books, effects and the wills of soldiers reported missing were generally sent in the first instance to the Paymaster in Liverpool.[123] However, by late 1941 'numerous complaints' had been received from the next of kin of both officers and other ranks taken prisoner that they had not been allowed access to their relatives' kit.[124] The question raised in reality was whether or not it was lawful for the War Office to authorise the handing over of a soldier's or officer's property without his prior consent. Although it was recognised that in some cases soldiers might not wish all their effects to be forwarded to their relatives, the more practical question of shortage of clothing for those taken captive also came to bear on this issue.[125] Effects for both officers and other ranks included letters, documents, personal papers and articles of sentimental or intrinsic value. Kit was defined, for officers, as uniform clothing, camp kit and saddlery.[126] Other ranks were presumed to have no kit other than 'effects' as all other belongings consisted of government property, which had been issued to them. In practice, however, it was agreed that 'every soldier accumulates a stock of articles such as woollen garments, which are neither effects nor army property' and these articles were, therefore, also classed as 'kit'.[127]

In June 1942 the War Office suggested a compromise whereby personal effects would not be released but kit could be, provided an indemnity was obtained from those removing items of kit preventing any future claims against the War Office by the serviceman for this action.[128] The final agreed procedure for officers' kit was laid out in 'Personal Property (Kits. etc.) of British Army Officers who are Prisoners of War'.[129] Under this procedure the kit of an officer who was taken prisoner was to be sent to the UK for storage following a minimum retention period of one month in the theatre of war in which the officer was captured. A personal representative of the officer, who could produce evidence that they had the authority to act on behalf of that officer, might then claim the kit. If no prior authority existed, the kit could be released to that representative provided an indemnity signed by the officer was produced to indemnify the department against any subsequent claims for the kit. Alternatively kit could be claimed where the War Office received direct instructions from the officer that the kit was to be disposed of in this way. Although the procedure appeared tedious it was nevertheless possible, given time, for the families of those taken prisoner in Europe to obtain such instructions. Personal effects of both men and officers still could not be claimed.

To facilitate the claims procedure, Messrs Cox and King in Liverpool who, under contract to the War Office, undertook the storage of both kit and effects, agreed to sort the items they received into 'kit' and 'effects'.[130] The War Office undertook to pay Messrs Cox and King 6d for opening a parcel for the purposes of identification and a further 5s for sorting, making an inventory and re-securing the parcel[131] although, in reality, kit and personal effects were already parcelled separately by Cox and King so there should have been no immediate problem with this arrangement.[132] However, with the opening of the Far East Enquiry Centre it became clear that there were a large number of 'retrospective' cases needing to be dealt with.[133] The Director of Freight Movement felt that the delay was due to the fact that Messrs Cox and King were not carrying out notifications properly although he saw no merit in changing the system as, in fact, very few applications to claim kit had been received.[134] A letter of January 1944 from the officer in charge of the Infantry Records Office, Exeter, to the War Office states that, to 230 letters sent to next of kin regarding the procedure for claiming kit, only 53 replies were received.[135] Of these, 28 said that, since the fall of Italy, they had no address for the serviceman to obtain authority for release of kit, ten demanded its release simply on the grounds that they were next of kin and fifteen others also expressed this demand, saying that, although they had written for authority, no reply was likely to be forthcoming within four to six months. The letter goes on to state that 'In most cases the writers express feelings varying from distress to indignation and a combination of both that this baggage is not being forwarded to them'.[136] In fact the kit of the particular battalion in question, the South Wales Borderers, presented particular problems: as their normal peacetime station was in India, some of the baggage had been packed away some 25 months earlier in November 1941.[137] The Officer in Charge felt that 'it was more than probable that it would be advantageous to the contents to be taken out and exposed to the air or otherwise dealt with, though possibly in the case of clothing it may already be too late after two years in a hot climate'.[138] Further problems arose with other battalions also based overseas before the outbreak of war as, in setting up homes in these areas, a number of men had accumulated many bulky possessions.[139] In August 1943 the Officer in Charge, Infantry and AEC Record Office in York, wrote to the Under-secretary of State at the War Office regarding the problem of the 'great quantity' of heavy kit weighing 'approximately two tons' which had already been received and the amount of this type of kit which it was anticipated would arrive in the near future.[140] Even if enough manpower had been available to sort these items, many of the trunks were 'locked and roped' making them virtually impossible to open.[141] Although the Officer in Charge requested permission to despatch these items direct to the next of kin, there is no record of any suggested solution from the War Office.[142]

Whilst the primary concerns of the War Office in this matter were to protect the interests of the men and their own actions against possible future repercussions, there is some evidence that they were not totally without concern for the families involved. Mrs

Chippendale of Westminster, who had enquired into the whereabouts of her son's effects, received a reply from the Director of
Organisation himself, in December 1943, apologising for an initial
reply she had received whose curt tone he considered was 'not one
which was approved by the War Office'.[143] She was then assured
that her particular enquiry was being taken up with the Record
Office concerned.[144] However, cases still arose where communications between families and the War Office broke down. In May
1942 Mr Burn, the father of Captain Michael Burn (KRR) No. 2
Commando who was held captive in Germany following the St
Nazaire raid, rang Messrs Cox and King requesting that his son's
kit should be forwarded direct to him as next of kin.[145] Mr Burn
wanted to send items of clothing from this kit to his son in Germany.
When it was explained that this could not be done without authority from his son Mr Burn was 'extremely rude' in his remarks and
inferred that this action was 'causing the very gravest of hardship'.[146] Mr Burn continued shouting 'in a loud voice' about red
tape and finally closed the conversation by slamming down the
phone. He then sent a letter to the War Office saying that it
appeared 'disgraceful and unnecessary that additional unhappiness,
worry and expense should be caused to relatives' because of some
legal principle and expressing his disbelief that such a 'wooden
principle' could not be broadened.[147] For Mr Burns, the immediate
problem lay in the fact that relatives were allowed only to send one
personal parcel to prisoners per quarter and he believed that, if the
kit were not released immediately, he would not be able to send
additional clothing from the kit to his son in time for Christmas.
The War Office, adhering to its affirmed policy of treating enquiries
with 'proper consideration', replied that 'some concession to meet
the special circumstances could doubtless be arranged'.[148] In fact,
given that, at this time, correspondence with those held captive in
Germany was taking approximately six weeks to arrive, Mr Burn
could probably have written to his son to arrange the necessary
permission in sufficient time to allow the parcel to be forwarded
before Christmas. The actual resolution of the problem in this case
and any compromise reached are not recorded.

Throughout this chapter clear parallels have been shown between
the government attitude towards developing a coherent policy for
the administration of service allowances and for administering the
dissemination of information to families. In both cases, despite clear

warnings from SSAFA in relation to allowances, and from the Belfield Report in relation to prisoners of war, no adequate preparations were made before the event and government responses remained reactive rather than proactive – a situation that continued even after the scale of the problem had been realised. In fact, on the question of dissemination of information, government strategy to the general public as a whole, not just to prisoner of war families, can be seen to have been indecisive at best. Under government circular 2269 of 1942, it had been planned to centralise information available to the public in local enquiry centres providing the public with one central agency to which they could apply for advice on a wide range of topics.[149] The Sheffield Information Centre, for example, located in the Town Hall, dealt with requests ranging from details of accommodation addresses for wives visiting their husbands stationed in the area, to an enquiry on how to make up rabbit skins.[150] However, despite the success of this scheme, it was then suggested that information should be made available in more diverse locations, such as local Post Offices.[151] In the matter of information for the next of kin of prisoners of war such inconsistencies led to a general lack of confidence in the information and advice available from government agencies. The Belfield Report had been explicit in its recommendation that, in the event of a future war, 'the most practical course of action would be to establish at once an interdepartmental committee' to deal with prisoner of war matters.[152] This advice was ignored and, from the outset, the fact that responsibility for prisoner of war matters cut across departmental boundaries caused confusion for the families concerned, if not for the departments themselves.

There can be no doubt that many problems were caused by lack of experience in the departments concerned in dealing with the general public. Traditionally, service dependants were regarded as secondary to the men concerned. The responsibility of the War Office was towards the soldiers under their care, and the welfare of the families involved concerned them only in so far as it might affect the well-being or effectiveness of the men concerned. The Army Morale Report for the period November 1943 to January 1944 makes this position abundantly clear, stating that when a soldier's family are happy 'he has something to fight for: if his family is in distress he cannot give his whole mind and heart to his soldiering'.[153] Nevertheless, once the soldiers had been taken captive, the War Office was then faced with the task of dealing direct with the families concerned and, very often, with families in a distressed state. As we have seen, after a somewhat shaky start, the War Office did begin to tackle this problem by attempting to ensure that enquiries received intelligible and considerate replies. However, in addition to the issue of communication, more fundamental issues appear to stem from the whole attitude of the armed services to the question of prisoners of war in general.

David Rolf suggests that the 'tardy realisation of new realities' that faced the government when large numbers of servicemen were taken prisoner, precluded the formulation of a coherent policy.[154] Despite this, there must remain some question as to whether or not this lack of foresight was the sole reason for the lack of a coherent policy. There can be no doubt that a reluctance existed on the part of the armed services to foster what could be seen as a defeatist attitudes amongst servicemen by encouraging them to consider the possibilities of capture. As we have already seen, the Treasury expressed itself as reluctant to formulate policy on the 'assumption that the British Army habitually throws away its arms' and, by implication, is taken prisoner.[155] Additionally, in the Far East, the likelihood of the Japanese attempting to take Singapore had been seen as a remote possibility at best. Both Winston Churchill and Leslie Hore-Belisha had dismissed the idea, deeming the Japanese to be too 'sensible' and 'prudent' to risk such a venture.[156] Similarly, servicemen themselves were not encouraged to consider the realities of being taken prisoner or to prepare for this eventuality. Jonathan Vance, in his study of Canadian prisoners of war during the twentieth century, refers to a small amount of training provided for Canadian servicemen in Britain on how to avoid capture, conduct in captivity and techniques of escape.[157] However, those involved in the training recollect little time being spent on these issues and reported that most servicemen 'never contemplated that they might fall into enemy hands'.[158]

In addition, although the British government professed itself to be keen to demonstrate to the Japanese in particular that British prisoners of war were not 'dishonoured men', some actions speak to the contrary. Alice Truman, the wife of a submariner taken prisoner after the loss of HMS *Seal* in 1940, apparently received a letter from the local authority in Gosport where she was resident stating, 'We understand that your husband is in a prisoner of war camp and he is of no further use to the country for the war effort so we are going to requisition your house'.[159] Mrs Truman's testimony is taken from a taped interview held at the Imperial War Museum Sound Archive, consequently it has not been possible to check whether or not this is an accurate quotation from the letter. But, whatever the actual wording, the impression she received from the letter was only too clear. If, as this account suggests, contradictions existed within government circles in attitudes towards the whole question of prisoners of war, it is not surprising that these tensions prevented the formulation of a coherent overall policy towards their families.

The Phillimore Report, one of a series of works compiled on the authority of the Army Council, concluded that the problems experienced during the First World War were not repeated because of the 'close and excellent understanding' that existed between the War and Foreign Offices.[160] However, the reliability of this particular report remains open to question and there can be little doubt that the proliferation of responsibility for prisoner of war matters across a wide range of departments did cause serious confusion for the families of those taken captive.[161] In addition the report claimed that, wherever possible, the public received the fullest information from the War Office but, as we have seen in the case of information regarding conditions in the Far East, this was demonstrably untrue. The fact that a newspaper article finally forced a government statement is conveniently overlooked.

Similarly, the sheer proliferation of local and 'self-help' prisoner of war committees, detailed in the next chapter, cannot be attributed solely to the desire of families to try to participate actively in helping their menfolk. The need for these committees and associations to exist as centres for the dissemination of information and to provide practical help to families argues all too clearly for a lack of information from, and a lack of confidence in, government sources. So does the evidence from those families who took comfort from 'unofficial' sources of information when 'official' sources failed them. For many, the lack of a coherent policy in the dissemination of information to next of kin and handling of enquiries led to a feeling of isolation and frustration. Many, as in the case of Mrs Buswell, mentioned above, 'just stayed at home and lived in the hope that he [her husband] would come back.'[162]

Notes

1 Fishman, *We Will Wait*. p. 66.
2 Buswell, IWM Sound Archive 7276/3.
3 Minutes of the 1st Meeting of the Imperial Prisoners of War Committee. 05 November 41. NA/WO163/152.
4 See Belfield Report 'Work in Connection with Prisoners of War from August 1914–January 1919'. NA/FO916/14/32749.
5 Belfield Report. NA/FO916/14.
6 Belfield Report. p. 2. NA/FO916/14.
7 Belfield Report. p. 2. NA/FO916/14.
8 Belfield Report. p. 2. NA/FO916/14.
9 Belfield Report. p. 3. NA/FO916/14.
10 Belfield Report. pp. 4–5. NA/FO916/14.
11 Belfield Report. p. 5. NA/FO916/14.
12 For further discussion of the dissemination of information and the role of the Ministry of Information see, for example: Grant, M., *Propaganda and the Role of the State in Inter-war Britain*. Oxford: Clarendon Press, 1994; MacKay, R., *The Test of War. Inside Britain 1939–45*. London: UCL Press, 1999; McLaine, I., *Ministry of Morale. Home Front Morale and the Ministry of Information in World War II*. London: George Allen and Unwin Ltd, 1979; and Balfour, M., *Propaganda in War 1939–1945. Organisations, Policies and Publics in Britain and Germany*. London: Routledge and Kegan Paul Ltd, 1979.
13 Foreign Office to Prisoner of War Relatives Association. 29 March 43. FO916/562.
14 Satow and Sée. *The Work of the Prisoners of War Department*. p. 5.
15 Satow and Sée. *The Work of the Prisoners of War Department*. p. 5.
16 Satow and Sée. *The Work of the Prisoners of War Department*. p. 5.
17 Phillimore Report. Part 1, Chapter 1. NA/WO366/26 and FO916/230.
18 Phillimore Report. Part 1, Chapter 1. NA/WO366/26 and FO916/230.
19 Phillimore Report. Part 1, Chapter 1. NA/WO366/26 and FO916/230.
20 Phillimore Report. Chapter II, pp. 15–16. NA/FO916/230.
21 *Henley Standard*. 23 August 40. Centre for Oxfordshire Studies.
22 Rolf, 'Blind Bureaucracy', p. 49.
23 Rolf, 'Blind Bureaucracy', p. 50.
24 Imperial Prisoner of War Committee. Notification of Capture and Subsequent Moves of British Prisoners of War in Enemy Hands. 03 November 41. NA/WO163/582.
25 Imperial Prisoner of War Committee. Notification of Capture and Subsequent Moves of British Prisoners of War in Enemy Hands. 03 November 41. NA/WO163/582.

26 Prisoners of War Information Bureau: Functions. NA/FO916/230.

27 Rolf, 'Blind Bureaucracy'. p. 55.

28 Article 77 Prisoner of War Convention 1929. NA/FO916/230.

29 Satow and Sée, *The Work of the Prisoners of War Department*. p. 73.

30 Imperial Prisoners of War Committee. Notification of Capture and Subsequent Moves of British Prisoners of War in Enemy Hands. 03 November 41. NA/WO163/582.

31 IWM Dept of Documents. Misc. 94, Item 1434.

32 IWM Dept of Documents. Misc. 94, Item 1434.

33 IWM Dept of Documents. Misc. 94, Item 1434.

34 IWM Sound Archive. 128/66.

35 Imperial Prisoners of War Committee, Progress Reports August 1941–December 1943. NA/WO163/582.

36 'Tracing Prisoners of War', *Henley Standard*. 23 August 40. Centre for Oxfordshire Studies.

37 Details of this case study can be found in: Telegrams and Letters dated 30 September 44, 14 November 44, 06 December 44, 21 February 45 and 07 January 45. IWM/95/30/1.

38 Imperial Prisoners of War Committee Report. 03 November 41. WO163/582.

39 Imperial Prisoners of War Committee Report. 03 November 41. WO163/582.

40 *Yorkshire Evening News*. 26 July 40. Leeds City Library, Local Studies Archive.

41 Prisoner of War Information Bureau: Functions. NA/FO916/230.

42 Belfield Report. p. 4. NA/FO916/14.

43 Imperial Prisoners of War Committee; minutes, summaries of action and Progress reports. August 41–December 43. Report of July 42. NA/WO163/582.

44 'Drop the Boys a Line'. *Yorkshire Evening News*. 07 June 40. Leeds City Library, Local Studies Archive.

45 Although attention is often focused on the delay of mail both to and from prisoners, a small number of prisoners never received or sent mail at all. Where such a situation was noted, the names of these prisoners were reported by their Camp Leader and enquiries made via the British Red Cross encouraging their next of kin to write. Presumably for some families and prisoners the problem was one of functional illiteracy although the issue does not appear to have been raised as such. Phillimore Report, Part II, Section 'Mail' NA/FO366/26 and Imperial Prisoner of War Committee, Summary of Action, July 1942. NA/WO163/582.

46 Department of Documents, IWM/88/5/1. Acting Bombadier Rookwood subsequently died in Borneo on 27 February 1945.

47 Department of Documents. IWM/88/5/1.
48 Unsigned memo War Office to Foreign Office. 03 November 41. NA/FO916/2.
49 Graham, M. *Oxfordshire at War*. Stroud: Alan Sutton Publishing Ltd, 1994. p. 76.
50 Even then accidents occurred. In August 1943 a large amount of mail from prisoners in the Far East was destroyed in the final stages of its journey when the transport from Lisbon to London caught fire. Out of 33,000 items of mail only 11,000 were salvaged and many of these were damaged beyond the point of legibility. DPW Summary of Action 1941–47. Notes for August 1943. NA/WO165/59.
51 Minutes of the 24th Meeting of the Imperial POW Committee, Sub-committee A. 28 August 43. NA/WO163/586.
52 Chatfield, V., 'Theirs Not to Reason Why'. Unpublished memoir. Department of Documents. IWM/P461.
53 Foreign office draft of paper for circulation to Imperial Prisoner of War Committee. 17 October 42. NA/FO916/230.
54 Letter Gardner, Principal, Financial Section, War Office, to Clough, Principal, Treasury. 31 October 42. NA/T162/792/E40219/1, and Dear, I.C.B. (ed.), *The Oxford Companion to the Second World War*. Oxford: Oxford University Press, 1995. p. 1140.
55 Letter 31 October 42. T162/792/E40219/1.
56 Burial arrangements for deceased prisoners of war. 22 September 44. NA/FO916/876.
57 Minutes of the 16th Meeting of the Imperial Prisoners of War Committee, Sub-committee A. 21 December 42. NA/WO163/585.
58 Extraordinary Meeting of the Imperial Prisoners of War Committee, Sub-committee A. 23 November 42. NA/WO163/585.
59 Minutes of the Imperial Prisoners of War Committee, Sub-committee A, June 1941–April 1942. NA/WO163/583.
60 Minutes of the 16th Meeting of the Imperial Prisoners of War Committee, Sub-committee A. 21 December 42. NA/WO163/585.
61 Minutes of the 16th Meeting of the Imperial Prisoners of War Committee, Sub-committee A. 21 December 42. NA/WO163/585.
62 Draft paper for circulation to the Imperial Prisoners of War Committee. 17 October 42. NA/FO916/230.
63 Sound Archive, IWM/12864/1.
64 Telegram, Foreign Office to Protecting Power, Berne. 04 January 45. NA/FO916/1358.
65 Draft paper for circulation to the Imperial Prisoners of War Committee. 17 October 42. NA/FO916/230.
66 Draft paper for circulation to the Imperial Prisoners of War Committee. 17 October 42. NA/FO916/230.

67 Comments on Draft Paper for circulation to the Imperial Prisoners of War Committee. 17 October 42. NA/FO916/1056.

68 Comments on Draft Paper for circulation to the Imperial Prisoners of War Committee. 17 October 42. NA/FO916/1056.

69 Minutes of the 1st Meeting of the Imperial Prisoners of War Committee. 05 November 41. NA/WO163/152.

70 Foreign Office telegram. 06 January 44. NA/FO916/1056.

71 Cipher Washington to Foreign Office. 14 January 44, and Foreign Office comments on telegram from Washington. 24 January 44. NA/FO916/1056.

72 Percentage calculated from the figures available in NA/WO32/9906.

73 Minutes of the Imperial Prisoners of War Committee, Sub-committee A. 02 June 43. NA/WO163/586.

74 Chatfield, 'Theirs Not to Reason Why'.

75 The progress of this list has been traced through the following files: Cipher Berne to Foreign Office 26 January 44; Letter Prisoner of War Dept, Foreign Office, to Earl of Iddesleigh, DPW, War Office 28 February 45; Letter War Office, signature indecipherable, to Prisoner of War Dept, Foreign Office 05 March 45. NA/FO916/1358.

76 Letter War Office to Whitteridge, Prisoner of War Dept, Foreign Office. 05 March 43. NA/FO916/1358.

77 Letter War Office to Whitteridge, Prisoner of War Dept, Foreign Office. 05 March 43. NA/FO916/1358.

78 Notes on the International Red Cross Committee Radio Message Scheme. 03 September 43. NA/WO163/586.

79 Letter War Office to Whitteridge, Prisoner of War Dept, Foreign Office. 05 March 43. NA/FO916/1358.

80 Notes on the International Red Cross Committee Radio Message Scheme. 03 September 43. NA/WO163/586.

81 Paper on broadcasting of messages to prisoners of war and civilian internees in Japanese hands. 04 May 45. NA/WO163/588.

82 Imperial POW Committee, Sub-committee A. Meetings 41–52. NA/WO163/588.

83 Letters Iris to Robert Strange, 1941–42. The Iris Strange Collection. University of Stafford.

84 Comments on draft paper for circulation to the Imperial Prisoners of War Committee. NA/FO916/230.

85 Draft paper for circulation to the Imperial Prisoners of War Committee. 17 October 42. NA/FO916/230.

86 Letter Colonial Office to various Service Departments. 10 February 44. NA/WO32/11118[5A, B, C, D and E].

87 Letter Colonial Office to various Service Departments. 10 February 44. NA/WO32/11118[5A, B, C, D and E].

88 Copy, without signatures, of petition 'Men Missing – Singapore and Malaya' presented to the Secretary of State for War by a deputation of MPs and relatives. 10 February 44. NA/WO32/11118[1B].

89 Prisoners of War Central Enquiry Bureau – formation and functions. NA/WO32/11118.

90 Note Colonel S.J. Cole, Temporary Administrative Assistant, Colonial Office. 17 March 44. NA/CO980/205.

91 Prisoners of War Central Enquiry Bureau – formation and functions. NA/WO32/11118.

92 Draft Handbook for staff. Prisoner of War Central Enquiry Bureau. NA/WO32/11118.

93 Draft Handbook for staff. Prisoner of War Central Enquiry Bureau. NA/WO32/11118.

94 Letter Phillimore to Gardner, Principal, Admin. and Clerical Section, War Office. 09 May 44. NA/WO32/11118.

95 Letter Sir Arthur Street, KCB, KBE, CMG, CIE, MC. Permanent Under-secretary of State, Air Ministry, to Elves, War Office. 13 April 44. NA/WO32/11118.

96 Prisoners of War Central Enquiry Bureau – formation and functions. NA/WO32/11118.

97 Circular Instruction 2/210. Undated. NA/WO32/10798.

98 Circular Instruction 2/210. Undated. NA/WO32/10798.

99 Circular Instruction 2/210. Undated. NA/WO32/10798.

100 Notes on the first month's working of the Far East Enquiry Centre. 01 July 44. NA/CO980/205.

101 A copy of this handbook 'A Handbook for the Information of Relatives and Friends of Prisoners of War and Civilians in Japanese or Japanese-occupied territory' together with a copy of 'A Handbook for the Information of Relatives and Friends of Prisoners of War', intended for the families of those held captive in Europe, can be found in NA/CO980/205. A draft copy also exists in NA/WO32/11118.

102 Prisoners of War and Civil Internees Publicity: Prisoners of War (Far East) Enquiry Centre. NA/CO980/205.

103 Draft Handbook. Prisoners of War Central Enquiry Bureau – formation and functions. NA/WO32/11118.

104 Draft Handbook. Prisoners of War Central Enquiry Bureau – formation and functions. NA/WO32/11118.

105 Phillimore Report. Part 1, Chapter 1. NA/WO366/26.

106 Imperial Prisoners of War Committee, Summary of Action. March 42. NA/WO163/582.

107 Imperial Prisoner of War Committee Report. April 1942. NA/WO163/582.

108 Imperial Prisoners of War Committee August 1941–December 1943: minutes, summaries of action and Progress reports. NA/WO163/582.

109 Imperial Prisoners of War Committee August 1941–December 1943: minutes, summaries of action and Progress reports. NA/WO163/582.

110 *Sunday Graphic*. 27 December 42. NA/WO32/9906.

111 Draft of Announcement by Ministry of Information. August 1943. NA/WO32/9906[226B].

112 Draft of Announcement by the Ministry of Information, August 1943. NA/WO32/9906[226B].

113 Note, Under-secretary of State, Foreign Office. 31 July 43. NA/WO32/9906[208A].

114 Letter Prisoner of War Dept, Foreign Office, to Elwes, War Office. 27 August 43. NA/WO32/9906[227A].

115 Figures taken from NA/FO916/7782.

116 Rolf, 'Blind Bureaucracy'. p. 61.

117 NA/WO32/11136. Quoted in Rolf, 'Blind Bureaucracy'. p. 61.

118 34th Meeting of the Imperial Prisoners of War Committee, Sub-committee A. 26 April 44. NA/WO163/587.

119 34th Meeting of the Imperial Prisoners of War Committee, Sub-committee A. 26 April 44. NA/WO163/587.

120 34th Meeting of the Imperial Prisoners of War Committee, Sub-committee A. 26 April 44. NA/WO163/587.

121 Minute Sheet 1. 01 June 42. NA/WO32/10798.

122 Extracts from Journal of Escaped Prisoner of War. Journal undated but escaped on 09 September 43. NA/WO32/10798.

123 Minute Sheet 5. 01 June 42. NA/WO32/10798.

124 Minute Sheet 5. 01 June 42. NA/WO32/10798.

125 Minute Sheet 5. 01 June 42. NA/WO32/10798.

126 Minute Sheet 5. 01 June 42. NA/WO32/10798.

127 Minute Sheet 5. 01 June 42. NA/WO32/10798.

128 Personal Property (Kits etc.) of British Army Officers Who Are Prisoners of War. Minute Sheet 7A. NA/WO32/10798.

129 Personal Property (Kits etc.) of British Army Officers Who Are Prisoners of War. Minute Sheet 7A. NA/WO32/10798.

130 Minute Sheet 45/General/5631. 31 August 42. NA/WO32/10798.

131 Minute Sheet 45/General/5631. 31 August 42. NA/WO32/10798.

132 Minute Sheet 45/General/5631. 31 August 42. NA/WO32/10798.

133 Note, Director of Freight Movement, War Office. 19 June 44. NA/WO32/10798.

134 Note, Director of Freight Movement, War Office. 29 June 44. NA/WO32/10798.

135 Letter Office in Charge Infantry Records Office, Exeter, to Under-secretary of State, War Office. 28 January 44. NA/WO32/10798.

136 Letter Office in Charge Infantry Records Office, Exeter, to Under-secretary of State, War Office. 28 January 44. NA/WO32/10798.

137 Letter Office in Charge Infantry Records Office, Exeter, to Under-secretary of State, War Office. 28 January 44. NA/WO32/10798.

138 Letter Office in Charge Infantry Records Office, Exeter, to Under-secretary of State, War Office. 28 January 44. NA/WO32/10798.

139 Note Officer in Charge, Infantry and AEC Record Office, York, to Under-secretary of State, War Office. 28 August 43. NA/WO32/10798.

140 Note Officer in Charge, Infantry and AEC Record Office, York, to Under-secretary of State, War Office. 28 August 43. NA/WO32/10798.

141 Note Officer in Charge, Infantry and AEC Record Office, York, to Under-secretary of State, War Office. 28 August 43. NA/WO32/10798.

142 Note Officer in Charge, Infantry and AEC Record Office, York, to Under-secretary of State, War Office. 28 August 43. NA/WO32/10798.

143 Letter Bear, Director of Organisation, War Office, to Mrs Chippendale, Westminster. 02 December 43, commenting on a letter she had received from the Records Office 31 March 43. NA/WO32/10798.

144 Letter Bear, Director of Organisation, War Office, to Mrs Chippendale, Westminster 02 December 43. NA/WO32/10798.

145 Details of this case study can be found in: Unsigned note of phone call 14 May 42, Letter Burn, Duchy of Cornwall, to Weston, War Office. 14 May 42, and Letter War Office to Burn, Duchy of Cornwall, 14 May 42. NA/WO32/10798. Although the initial phone call and letter may well have been from the same date, it seems likely that the War Office reply is misdated.

146 Unsigned note of phone call Burn to War Office. 14 June 42. NA/WO32/10798.

147 Letter Burn, Duchy of Cornwall, to War Office. 14 June 42. NA/WO32/10798.

148 Letter War Office to Burn, Duchy of Cornwall. 14 June 42. NA/WO32/10798.

149 Letter Information Officer, Sheffield to Town Clerk, Sheffield. 15 October 42. Sheffield Information Committee 1941–1944. CA43/1. Sheffield Archives.

150 Letters 14 October 44 and 18 February 44 respectively. Sheffield Archives CA43/1. The Committee did, however, draw the line at E. France of Maltravers Road, Sheffield, whose request to be put in touch with a girl he could marry was deemed not to be 'within the province of the information bureau'.

151 Letter Information Officer, Sheffield, to Town Clerk, Sheffield. 15 October 42. Sheffield Information Committee 1941–1944. CA43/1. Sheffield Archives.

152 Belfield Report. Item 16, p. 6. NA/FO916/14/32749.

153 Report of Morale in Army. NA/WO32/15772[50A].

154 Rolf, 'Blind Bureaucracy'. p. 47.

155 Letter Humphreys-Davies, Treasury, to War Office 07 March 40. NA/T162/792/E40219/1.

156 Memo Rt Hon. W. Churchill to Chamberlain, Prime Minister. 27 March 39, and Memo Hore-Belisha, Financial Secretary, Treasury, to Admiralty. 21 November 39 respectively. Churchill Archive, HOBE 5/55/55 and 5/89/59.

157 Vance, *Objects of Concern*. p. 100.

158 Elliot, Maj. S.R., *Scarlet to Green*. Toronto: Canadian Security and Intelligence Association, 1989. p. 399. Quoted in Vance. *Objects of Concern*. p. 101.

159 IWM Sound Archive, 12365/2.

160 Phillimore Report. p. 20. NA/WO366/26.

161 Phillimore Report. p. 19. WO366/26.

162 IWM Sound Archive, 7276/3.

6

'By ourselves, for ourselves' – unofficial information, self-help and charities

Not surprisingly, in the light of the shortcomings of official systems of notification detailed in the previous chapter, large numbers of prisoner of war families turned to charitable and 'self–help' groups for information and support. In general, all war charities were governed by the regulations laid down in the War Charities Act of 1916.[1] However, although the Charity Commissioners also showed interest in other classes of charities such as societies incorporated under the Companies Act or by Royal Charter such as the Royal Patriotic Fund in the First World War, by and large local war charities were left to their own devices.[2] In December 1938 a Standing Conference of Voluntary Organisation in Time of War was established to facilitate communications between voluntary organisations and the statutory authorities.[3] This Conference, incorporating 94 voluntary organisations concerned with a range of wartime voluntary efforts, also originally included the Soldiers, Sailors and Air Force Families Association (SSAFA), but in February 1941 the Charities Commissioners made the decision that SSAFA need not register under the War Charities Act as it was 'deemed not to be a war charity'.[4] Presumably the decision was made in the light of the fact that SSAFA continued its work in both peacetime and war.

Of these national organisations, those concerned with prisoners of war focused their efforts almost exclusively on the needs of the captives themselves rather than on those of the families concerned. For example the Young Men's Christian Association (YMCA), which undertook a great deal of work in providing educational and recreational materials for prisoners, appears to have had little or no direct contact with their families.[5] Some national agencies found that, although they were open to queries of all types, service families made little use of their facilities. Most preferred to address their queries to specific agencies. In Norwich, for example, the Citizens' Advice Bureau (CAB), which opened in July 1943, reported that, although the public generally came to regard it as 'a place where every question however serious or however trivial, may first be asked', few specific queries relating to prisoner of war allowances came its way.[6] The CAB itself saw this small number of queries as due to the fact that there were 'organisations in the city to deal with these specific problems'.[7] However, two major national charities did become involved with the needs of these families as well as those of the prisoners.

SSAFA had been closely involved with service family welfare since its inception in 1885. The Association continued to work at full stretch throughout the Second World War and beyond when, once again, its work proved to be vital to the well–being, if not the actual survival, of families.[8] Many testimonies exist to this effect from families and servicemen alike. For example, an aircraftman serving in the Outer Hebrides in 1942 wrote to the Association expressing his gratitude for the help and advice his family had received and saying that it had been 'a great relief to me to know that my family has someone to go to'.[9] The Association also saw its work of giving advice and support as being as important as providing actual financial relief.[10] Considering that the overarching aim of the Association was, and still is, to look after the families of all service personnel, it is perhaps not surprising that its archives show little provision of assistance specifically related to prisoner of war families. These families were visited in the normal course of events, as were all other service families in need of assistance. Those to whom assistance was given were dealt with strictly on the basis of need, regardless of the status of the serviceman involved. In this way the case of the wife of a serviceman taken captive at Singapore, who arrived in England with three children, having lost all her possessions, was dealt with in the same way as any other destitute service family.[11]

However, SSAFA was able to provide special assistance to prisoner of war families in one particular respect. The Chief Censor of the Prisoner of War Department of Postal and Telegraph Censorship called on the services of SSAFA to assist in dealing with mail which, for one reason or another, was classified as 'undeliverable'.[12] As has been shown in the previous chapter, many problems were associated with the delivery of mail from enemy territories and these problems did not end once the mail reached British soil. Not only were Prisoners of War themselves moved from one location to another but, with the increasing frequency of bombing raids on major British cities, many families were either evacuated or forced to move when their homes were destroyed. In fact, between 1939 and 1945, the Post Office recorded 60 million changes of address in a total population of 40 million.[13] By late 1941 the Chief Censor had handed to SSAFA 2,200 letters which the Post Office regarded as undeliverable as the addressees had moved as a result of evacuation or bombing.[14] All such letters were carefully sorted by SSAFA and, where possible, then sent on to local representatives for delivery. However, in many cases the original address had become indecipherable because of subsequent re–directions, crossings out and various other marks and stamps. Using the services of a Mr Guerin, a well–known handwriting expert, the Association was able to employ infrared and other photographic techniques to expose the original address so that work on tracing the families concerned could begin from their last known address.[15] In all, during the period of the war SSAFA handled 5,500 such letters, of which they managed successfully to deliver 3,300.[16]

Although the SSAFA archives provide little detail of work directly concerned with prisoner of war families as distinct from service families in general, this is not to suggest that they were not involved in providing support for these families. In December 1944 a letter to Major–General the Viscount Bridgeman in connection with visits to next of kin to offer advice on receiving homecoming prisoners of war makes this very clear.[17] The War Office had suggested that these families should be visited only once in this connection and that the British Red Cross (BRC) should make this visit. SSAFA felt that this would threaten links it had already established where it had 'given considerable help to the families of prisoners of war, both in regard to their financial troubles and their private and domestic problems'.[18] A draft reply from the War Office stated that it was sure that the BRC would 'take into account any ties between particular families and the SSAFA'.[19] It is clear, however, that the War Office did not intend to intervene. This does, however, raise the question of possible tensions between various charitable organisations each of which laid claim to being *the* organisation primarily concerned with the welfare of prisoner of war families. The War Office, however, appeared to be impartial in the matter, favouring no one organisation above another as it turned to SSAFA rather than the BRC to obtain information regarding the family circumstances of dependants of soldiers missing in the Far East in 1943.[20] At the time they had assured SSAFA that the numbers of families involved would be 'extremely small' – a serious miscalculation.[21]

Other correspondence within the SSAFA archive also indicates this possible tension between charitable organisations concerned with service family welfare in general, and prisoner of war families in particular. In May 1940 SSAFA had sent a resolution to the British Legion Whit Conference saying that it 'felt obliged to register strong protest' that the Legion was widening its scope to include the dependants of servicemen and so causing an overlap of interests.[22] The Legion appear to have ignored this protest as SSAFA Council Minutes for the following month note that, at the Conference, the Legion had decided to include dependants in its field of interest. The Council noted that all branches were to be instructed that they 'must continue to co–operate' with the Legion.[23] Similarly, SSAFA Council minutes in March 1941 note that the Women's Voluntary Service was also 'overlapping' in the area of clothing distribution.[24] However, SSAFA itself was not averse to promoting its own interests as the major provider of services to the families of those taken captive. Its services in tracing the next of kin of prisoners of war who had changed addresses, reported in SSAFA archives as the sole prerogative of SSAFA, were in fact also carried out by the BRC. The Second Annual Report of the BRC War Organisation notes that it had been asked, by the Prisoner of War Department at the War Office, to assist in tracing the whereabouts of next of kin who had failed to notify change of address and 'through the help of liaison officers, this information was invariably obtained'.[25] As we shall see later in this chapter, this tension between organisations was not limited to Britain. In Canada too, various charitable organisations continually jostled for primacy in the field of prisoner of war family welfare.

In terms of general involvement with prisoner of war families, such as dissemination of information and advice on sending parcels, the BRC was traditionally rather more intimately involved. At the beginning of the First World War no overall organisation had existed to oversee the sending of food, clothing and 'comforts' to British prisoners although a number of unofficial local and regimental committees were engaged in this work.[26] This lack of overall organisation was perceived as creating inequalities whereby some prisoners received an abundance of parcels while others received none. To counteract this situation a Central Prisoner of War Committee was established in the autumn of 1916 under the direction of the BRC to impose some degree of coherence.[27] Initially the decision to leave such work to charitable institutions was based on a fear that captors would confiscate parcels if they were seen as originating from home governments.[28] Supplies from charitable organisations were regarded as being more likely to reach their intended destinations. In the light of this, the Belfield Report recommended that the Hague Convention of 1907 should be revised so that official consignments to prisoners of war would be protected from confiscation.[29] Although the Report also suggested that there had been some public dissatisfaction with the handling of parcels for prisoners of war, the work received 'almost universal praise'.[30] With the commencement of the Second World War and in the initial stages of the 'phoney war' in 1939, most of the immediate tasks relating to the welfare of British prisoners of war were again left to the Red Cross. This despite the fact that the Belfield Report had claimed that there could be 'little doubt' that these responsibilities should have been undertaken by a government department, rather than being left to charitable organisations[31] – and despite the fact that no efforts had been made to establish whether or not the organisation could actually fulfil these responsibilities.[32] As we have already seen in the previous chapter, with the loss of large numbers of men from the BEF in May 1940 the need for a separate Directorate of Prisoners of War was recognised. However, the continuing involvement of the BRC had the unfortunate corollary of providing the government with a convenient scapegoat for some of its own shortcomings.

During the Second World War, every prisoner in Europe was entitled to receive an initial parcel when first captured; three food parcels per fortnight; medical comforts and one personal parcel, later known as next of kin parcels, every three months.[33] Initially prisoners also received a bread parcel although this practice was discontinued after May 1940.[34] By the autumn of 1940, with large numbers of British prisoners in camps in Germany and relief routes through France and Belgium often closed, the situation regarding parcels became critical.[35] The *Sunday Express*, in conjunction with

Mrs Winifred Coombe Tennant, whose own son was held prisoner in Oflag VIB, led a campaign which was highly critical of the work of the Red Cross in managing the forwarding of parcels.[36] In fact, the Post Office, not the BRC, was largely responsible for the transmission of these parcels but it proved more convenient for the government to allow the BRC to shoulder the lion's share of the blame.[37] A subsequent enquiry, ordered by Sir Stafford Cripps, the Lord Privy Seal, under the chairmanship of the Solicitor General, Sir William Jowitt, was designed to forestall any further public discussion of the matter.[38] Although Irene Ward, MP for Wallsend, a consistent critic of the government, was promised that the results of the enquiry would be forwarded to the Secretary of State for War, the report, which was highly critical of the government's role in the matter, was largely suppressed. The then newly formed Prisoner of War Relatives Association (POWRA), however, continued to pursue the matter, causing Field Marshal Sir Philip Chetwode, Chairman of the BRC, to comment on the foolishness of its work – an attitude which characterised the relationship between the two organisations for the duration of the war.[39] A note in Irene Ward's private papers, initialled W.C.T. and probably from Winifred Coombe Tennant, hints at governmental manoeuvrings to prevent collaboration between the two organisations and prevent the truth being exposed before 'I.W. [Irene Ward] touched off the dynamite'.[40] However, the persistent, and erroneous, view held by the general public that the BRC was to blame for these problems continued to serve the government well by deflecting criticism from its own ill–thought–out provision. As the note to Irene Ward suggests, 'the P.M. would not hesitate to throw anybody to the wolves, . . . , as he was not in a position to face further unpopularity'.[41] The BRC Annual Report of 1939–40 notes that the BRC War Organisation

> allowed itself to be regarded by the public as being responsible for features of the service which were the responsibility of others who, not unnaturally, since they saw the Prisoners of War Department fighting their battles, did not themselves come forward at the time to declare their own accountability.[42]

Indeed, the misapprehension was allowed to persist until July 1941 when it was finally admitted in the House that despatch of these parcels was outside the control of the BRC.[43] As this admission was never made as an official public announcement, it may be assumed that large sectors of the British public continued to believe that the BRC was to blame.

The question of next of kin parcels posed problems for many families as well as for the Red Cross. From October 1940 the War Organisation of the BRC had established a next of kin section at St James's Palace. Here a card index was established bearing the name, camp address and Red Cross registration number of each prisoner of war, together with the name and address of their next of kin.[44] As each registration was made, a next of kin label, two invoice sheets, an acknowledgement card and instructions were mailed to the relatives of the prisoner.[45] This paperwork initiated the process for sending parcels as the label entitled the next of kin to send their parcel to a packing centre while the invoice sheets were used for listing the contents of these parcels. From the beginning, strict censorship was exercised over the contents, partly for security reasons but also as enemy authorities prohibited a range of items as diverse as nail files, glass mirrors and toilet paper.[46] Despite this, the BRC Second Annual Report of 1940–41 noted that its War Organisation had recorded that 10 per cent of all articles included in next of kin parcels had had to be removed as they fell into the range of prohibited items.[47] Initially all parcels were forwarded to a central depot but, by 1941, local packing centres were established in many areas and members of local Prisoner of War Committees often spent time working voluntarily in these centres.[48]

Although the parcels were regarded as of prime importance, as, through them, prisoners would 'keep in touch with home and would not feel that they had been forgotten', their compilation caused serious financial worries for families of many allied prisoners of war.[49] With the introduction of clothing rationing, next of kin were obliged to buy clothing for prisoners of war using their own coupons that were subsequently refunded.[50] For many the initial outlay of coupons caused considerable hardship, as they were then unable to purchase clothing for themselves or other family members. To offset this in Britain, the Prisoner of War Directorate at the War Office issued 40 extra clothing coupons to next of kin.[51] These coupons were sent in advance to allow purchases to be made in time to be included in parcels. In this respect the relatives of British prisoners of war fared better than their counterparts in

France. There the Vichy government consistently refused to issue wives with additional textile points so that they could purchase clothing to send to their husbands.[52] For many wives of French prisoners of war the choice had to be made between clothing for themselves and their children or clothing for their husbands. In 1943 one woman wrote that she was still wearing her 'old, shabby clothes from before the war' whilst another recorded that she had 'cut up a bed sheet to make blouses and dresses'.[53]

From early 1942, with the rationing of soap and chocolate in Britain, these items were held at parcel packing depots and added to parcels by the BRC if money was sent to cover the costs.[54] At a later date chocolate was added as a gift of the Red Cross War Organisation.[55] In France too, many wives, despite being given an extra 2 francs per day from May 1941 to pay for such items to be included in parcels, were forced to rely on the charity of the Red Cross.[56] Fishman records that pressure was brought to bear, not only on wives but also on children, to make 'loving self–sacrifices' to compile personal parcels by contributing their own chocolates or sweets, although this was not always done without resentment.[57] However, as the official Red Cross historians suggest, for many families 'the cost of the articles in a parcel, if it were to be worth sending, was beyond their means'.[58] In this context local Prisoner of War Committees throughout Britain also stepped in to try to ensure that all families in their areas were able to provide their relatives with worthwhile next of kin parcels. For those prisoners whose records showed that they had not received any next of kin parcels, for whatever reason, the BRC either provided for them to be 'adopted' by local Prisoner of War Committees or to be sent 'gift' parcels provided by the Central Packing Depot or a BRC County Committee.[59]

Normally, the time from the receipt of a parcel at the depot to the despatch of new labels and coupons to the next of kin for their next parcels was two days.[60] The only exceptions to this were particularly busy periods, such as early 1943, when an average of 1,300 next of kin parcels were received per day at the Central Packing Depot.[61] By keeping within these limits it was hoped to ensure that relatives had sufficient time to make their purchases before the next parcel was due to be sent.[62]

In 1942, in conjunction with the Foreign Office, the BRC established a special Correspondence and Enquiry Section for the families of servicemen held prisoner.[63] When a serviceman was officially notified to his family as being in enemy hands, a file was opened in which all contacts with both the prisoner of war himself and his next of kin were recorded together with the relevant addresses.[64] These files were kept up to date where possible, but with prisoners being moved from camp to camp and families being frequently relocated owing to evacuation, war damage and the demands of a war economy, this proved to be a major undertaking. Through the Section, next of kin were provided with information on how to communicate with prisoners of war and on how to send parcels.[65] In addition relatives were able to visit the Enquiry Section in person, a facility not readily provided by the Foreign Office. For many families, correspondence with the Enquiry Section lasted throughout the war from initial notification of prisoner of war status to repatriation at the end of hostilities.[66]

Following the fall of Singapore, a similar Far East Correspondence and Enquiry Section was opened to compile similar files on the next of kin for prisoners in this theatre of war.[67] Although the Section began with just six names, by September 1944 files were held on 47,000 captive servicemen.[68] This Section found information especially difficult to obtain and used such diverse sources as the International Red Cross, unofficial broadcasts and letters from prisoners written direct to the Section or to relatives in an attempt to keep the files up to date.[69] In August 1943 alone the Section received more than 220 personal callers. In September of the same year seven thousand enquiries were received by mail.[70] Small wonder then that, for many families, it was commonly assumed that the best way to obtain information was to 'ask the Red Cross about it'.[71] Similarly, many prisoners themselves contacted the Society expressing concerns for the safety of their families during intensive bombing campaigns on British cities. In all cases replies from the Society were 'as from one friend to another', in marked contrast to the official, if not officious, replies often received from government agencies.[72] The official history of the BRC considered that these replies served to form a link between the prisoner and his next of kin 'devoid of official prejudices'.[73]

Tensions between the various agencies involved with prisoner of war family welfare were also manifest in other spheres, with each regarding itself as the prime agency concerned. Following the intensive bombing of major British cities, Colonel Lord Nathan, Eastern

Command Welfare Officer, was appointed to organise an enquiry bureau for all three services so that servicemen could obtain information regarding the safety of their families in Britain.[74] SSAFA archives suggest that SSAFA itself, rather than the BRC, was involved in this facility, opening a special office to deal with these enquiries with financial support from the Treasury. The SSAFA Overseas Department opened in May 1941 and by November was dealing with one thousand cases per month.[75] There is no doubt that both the BRC and SSAFA were involved, but their individual records give no clue that other organisations were involved.[76] Rather they suggest that each organisation was the sole agency responsible. As with government agencies, this apparent lack of communication between charitable agencies involved in the welfare of prisoners of war and their families led to confusion and a less efficient service for families than would have been possible if all agencies had co–operated.

In May 1942 a more immediate channel for maintaining contact between next of kin and those taken prisoner in Europe was established when the Prisoner of War Department of the BRC released the first issue of the periodical *The Prisoner of War*.[77] This first issue contained an open letter from the Queen asserting that the next of kin of prisoners of war, especially mothers, wives and sisters, were often in her thoughts, plus the first instalment of an article by Winston Churchill entitled 'I Was a Prisoner Once' relating his experiences during the Boer War.[78] The purpose of the magazine was 'the enlightenment and guidance of next–of–kin' and a typical issue contained extracts from prisoners of war's letters, photos from camps in Europe and summaries of reports on camps and camp conditions by the protecting power or the War Office.[79] The magazine also returned to suggestions as to what should and should not be included in letters. News to be omitted included the loss of ration books, news of having been ill and of bombing 'near misses'.[80] Suggestions of news that should be sent included news of how money had been saved, of things children had learnt and of films seen.[81] An article entitled 'When You Write to Him', as has already been mentioned, also contained the suggestion that wives should tell their husbands whom they had been to see the film with.[82]

In addition to being sent to all next of kin, the periodical was also circulated to public libraries, to any MPs who requested it in order to answer queries from their constituents, and to Red Cross Societies in the Dominions for circulation to next of kin in their localities.[83] As a condition of its licence, the magazine was not allowed to carry any advertising, nor was it to be offered for sale.[84] Although the magazine deliberately included the 'unsatisfactory' side of camp life so that it could not be accused of only showing the brighter aspects, all such reports carried the note that, where poor conditions had been found, the protecting power had been called in to make representations to the authorities.[85] In early 1941 the USA, as the then protecting power for British interests, made 44 protests of this nature to the German government.[86] However, like the government, it also came in for adverse criticism when information was delayed or incomplete. In July 1941 the Rochdale and District Prisoner of War Committee learnt that British prisoners of war were being forced to work in salt mines and coal mines in Germany.[87] In response they demanded that German prisoners should be made to carry out similar work in Britain, disregarding or being unaware that complaints had already been made in respect of this ill–treatment.[88] For the editors of *The Prisoner of War*, and later particularly for those involved in the production of *Far East*, it would always prove to be a difficult balancing act between being accused of not presenting a true picture of camp life and being accused of causing unnecessary distress to relatives.

In 1943 discussions took place between relevant government departments and the BRC as to whether or not this periodical should also be issued to the relatives of prisoners in the Far East.[89] The Prisoner of War Department of the BRC expressed some concern that relatives might not fully appreciate the obstacles to its work in this area and so might feel that captives in the Far East were receiving less support, especially from the Red Cross, than those in Europe.[90] However, a letter in *The Times*, complaining that *The Prisoner of War* was not available to the relatives of those held captive in the Far East, was perceived as indicative of public feeling on the subject.[91] As a result from February 1944 these relatives were instead issued with their own magazine entitled *Far East*.[92] Issued initially at irregular intervals, *Far East* later became a monthly publication and, in the light of the particular problems surrounding the whole issue of notification from this area, was also issued to the next of kin of those men posted 'missing'.[93]

Cambray and Briggs claim that this journal was able to alleviate some of the anxieties of the families of those held captive in this area by providing them with details of camp life and information about what the Red Cross was doing for prisoners in this location.[94] Given the overall problems of communication in this area, the initial reservations of the Red Cross about how its work in the Far East would be viewed and the need to strike a balance between providing accurate information and causing undue worry, the quality and quantity of information released to families must be open to question. The first edition of *Far East*, in February 1944, contained a warning that 'we know nothing reliable about the camps'.[95] The May 1944 issue, whilst containing an article 'Life in a Japanese Prison Camp' based on a broadcast made by Lieutenant J. Lambert, an artillery officer held captive in Java, carried the reminder that 'it should be borne in mind that the script of the broadcast was censored by the Japanese authorities'.[96] For the families, however, any news was better than no information at all. The editorial of the final issue, in December 1945, suggested that, although hard news had been sparse, letters from relatives had made it clear that 'anything was better than silence'.[97]

In addition to the Enquiry Centres and the two periodicals, the Red Cross also released a number of films to help inform families, and the general public, about conditions for prisoners of war. *In Enemy Hands* was released for theatrical distribution in 1942, and the short silent films *Until the Day* and *A Bit of Home* shown in non–theatrical locations in 1942 and 1943 respectively.[98] In 1945 British Gaumont made the film *Prisoner of War* which it then presented to the War Organisation for general release.[99]

On a local level BRC County Committees organised meetings for relatives in their areas to allow for the exchange of information between relatives and to help explain regulations and legal matters.[100] The work of these committees had begun in the winter of 1939 as a result of the necessity to supplement official issues of hospital supplies during an outbreak of flu.[101] Although initially their only duty was to 'meet reasonable requests' for supplies for soldiers in inadequately equipped hospitals, they were later utilised for a wide variety of administrative tasks.[102] The annual reports of three committees quoted in Cambray and Briggs show the diversity of their work.[103] In addition to hospital and medical services they were also involved in next of kin parcel packing centres, next of kin clubs, postal messages schemes, library services, cinema collections and flag days.

The Legal Department, however, often proved itself to be more of a 'friend' to prisoners of war themselves than to their families. By and large the Department refused to serve legal documents, usually divorce papers, on men held captive, although they did undertake investigations on prisoners' wives.[104] In 1942 one prisoner of war received information that his wife had gone off with another man taking the former's small daughter with her.[105] He expressed concern for the welfare of the child and asked the Legal Section of the War Office to assist him in tracing his wife and instigating divorce proceedings. Although the War Office was unable to trace the wife, the Red Cross Legal Department, acting on a 'slender clue', was able to help.[106] They then obtained proof of misconduct in the form of a birth certificate for a (later) illegitimate child and not only assisted in the divorce proceedings but also arranged to visit the wife and reported back to the husband that the daughter was well.[107] In other cases such investigations had a happier outcome. Again in 1942 a prisoner received news, from his family, that his wife was behaving improperly and his child was being neglected and the Legal Department undertook to make investigations on the prisoner's behalf.[108] In this case, however, the reports were unfounded. Investigations showed that the wife did not get on well with her husband's family and the information had been malicious. In fact the child was well looked after and there was no real reason to suspect the wife's behaviour.[109]

County Committees also organised 'prisoners' friends' who maintained contact directly with relatives through 'friendly calls', 'homely gatherings' and 'informing talks'.[110] From 1941 onwards more general personal contact was established with next of kin when local parcel packing centres began to be established around the country. Although a range of volunteers often staffed many centres, including members of local prisoner of war committees, all worked in close association with the national BRC. To aid the compiling of next of kin parcels the Board of Customs and Excise agreed that these centres should be provided with clothing and toilet articles free of purchase tax provided that they were not taken home by relatives but made up into parcels at the local packing centre.[111]

In an effort to supplement the information provided through both the Enquiry Centres and journals, meetings organised by the BRC were held at a variety of locations across the country where relatives could pool information and ask questions.[112] Although the actual number of such meetings is not recorded, Mr S.G. King, Controller of the Far East Section, personally addressed more than 150 where audiences varied between thirty and three thousand.[113] One regular feature of these meetings was an open question and answer session where speakers attempted to cover a wide variety of issues, many of them of a critical nature. In this way the BRC War Organisation hoped to ease 'what might have developed into a difficult situation between the Government and relatives of prisoners' concerning lack of information and government action regarding conditions for those held captive in the Far East.[114]

Between 1 and 20 May 1944 the BRC, in conjunction with the *Daily Telegraph*, held an exhibition in the grounds of Clarence House in London, purporting to show the day–to–day life of prisoners of war.[115] The Red Cross felt this type of exhibition to be necessary to give prisoners of war's relatives, as well as the general public, 'a closer insight into the lives of officers and other ranks held in German captivity'.[116] The exhibition was laid out in a number of 'huts' showing typical living quarters, examples of possible works of art or crafts undertaken, recreation, education, food, medical services and religious facilities. The 6d booklet which accompanied the exhibition also contained maps of all prisoner of war and civilian internment camps. In his introduction to the booklet, Field Marshal Sir Philip Chetwode, Chairman of the Joint War Executive Committee, expressed his belief that 'no subject has been of greater interest to the public or evoked more sympathy than the situation of British officers and men of all services in enemy hands'.[117] However, although many people may have attended the exhibition, it remained located in London and so inaccessible for the great majority of prisoner of war relatives spread around the country. Similarly, although Sir Philip considered that captives in 'enemy hands', rather than just in German hands, were of great concern and interest to the public, no similar exhibition was suggested showing the daily lives of those held captive by the Japanese.[118] Although it is possible that insufficient information was available, it seems more likely that the government felt it wiser not to draw any further attention to conditions in the Far East in case this further raised public discontent with the amount being done for these prisoners. Whereas the 'German' exhibition could be utilised to show prisoners of war maintaining their morale through sport and education and being gainfully employed in recreational activities, the same possibilities did not exist for an exhibition portraying conditions in Japanese captivity.

Overall, the work of the BRC in connection with prisoners of war's families remains difficult to quantify. Although Cambray and Briggs record that 'pages could be filled' with 'expressions of gratitude' received from relatives, they also admit that 'what the correspondence section did for next–of–kin and other relatives, and for the prisoners themselves, cannot be assessed in precise terms'.[119] No indication is given in their official history of the BRC during the war of numbers of relatives visited or of the scale of locally based activities. Similarly, the annual reports of the BRC War Organisation, although they do record the amount of correspondence received at certain times by the central offices, give no indication of numbers of families visited. As we shall see later in this chapter, local prisoner of war committees also instigated similar activities, and their existence must suggest that the cover provided by BRC schemes was patchy at best.

As has already been shown, relations between the BRC and the War and Foreign Offices were by no means straightforward. Whilst in some instances the relationship was essentially a symbiotic one with all those involved gaining some benefit, other examples have shown how government departments were not above letting the Red Cross take the blame for actions which would have brought them into conflict with public opinion. At the same time, however, these same departments proved to be protective of the Red Cross when it was attacked by others – a case in point being the criticisms mounted by the Prisoner of War Relatives Association (POWRA), the only relatives, group to operate on a national level.

Details of exactly when and how the POWRA was founded have proved difficult to establish. Cambray and Briggs note that the War Organisation of the BRC had assisted it financially to become established and provided it with office space in the belief that the Association might prove a valuable link between the War Organisation and relatives of prisoners of war.[120] A POWRA news sheet of March 1943 makes it clear that the Association had been in existence at least since 1941.[121] The Phillimore Report, however, refers to it having been established 'at a comparatively late stage in the war' and as a direct result of some of its members, supported by some Members of Parliament, disapproving of the BRC.[122] The Association appears to have operated in two almost completely separate spheres. On a local level, many branches came into being largely, as the Foreign Office dismissively commented, 'presided over by ladies who are relatives of prisoners of war'.[123] Reports appear from a number of sources of representatives from these branches speaking at local meetings of prisoner of war committees. For example, in 1942 Mrs Stewart, the Organising Secretary of the Association, and a Mr Thorne from the Edinburgh Branch spoke to the Huddersfield Prisoner of War Committee.[124] A note from the Colonial Office recorded that Mrs Stewart regularly toured the country 'from Scotland to Cornwall', speaking to well–attended gatherings.[125] Although the content of these talks is rarely made explicit, the Colonial Office described some of her opinions as being 'wildly inaccurate' and it determined to 'keep in touch' to correct these ideas.[126]

The Head Office of the Association, described by the Foreign Office as being 'inferior to its branch organisation' had, however, rather more specific interests.[127] Throughout the course of the war, it campaigned continually at ministerial level and through its spokesperson in the House of Commons, Miss Irene Ward, for the introduction of a single body to be responsible for all prisoner of war matters.[128]

Although the Belfield Report following the First World War had been explicit in its recommendation that, in the case of a future war, 'the most practical course would be to establish at once an interdepartmental committee', as we have already seen in the previous chapter, this advice was disregarded.[129] A letter of October 1940 from the Foreign Office to the Earl of Galloway, apparently in response to an enquiry by him on this matter, stated that 'it had not been found necessary' to set up such an independent department.[130] In January 1942 the matter was again raised by the Walsall and District Co–operative Society in a letter to William Adamson, the Labour MP for Cannock, which was subsequently passed first to the Foreign Secretary and then to the Prime Minister.[131] The letter urged the government to take action 'for the welfare of British Prisoners of War' by setting up an interdepartmental committee. Eden replied, somewhat tersely, to the effect that, although this suggestion had been considered by the government, it was not prepared to adopt it and that he did not feel that he could add anything further on the matter.[132]

Robert, Lord Vansittart, who had become temporary President of POWRA from 1942 following the resignation of Lord Ebbisham, instigated much of the discussion around this issue.[133] However, even at this early stage, the Association appears to have been making enemies within government circles. Sir George Warner of Sutton Courtney House, Oxfordshire, who was being touted as the next president, was advised by Sir Harold Satow at the Foreign Office to 'steer clear of the association'.[134] Sir George was advised that 'while their intentions are no doubt excellent they have fallen foul of the War Office and were aggressively inclined towards the Foreign Office'.[135] Sir Harold followed up these remarks with a later letter in which he suggested that 'whilst it [POWRA] is a reputable body it does not seem to be run by people of weight'.[136] However, whilst the Foreign Office might be dismissive of the ladies who presided over the branches of POWRA, it was rather more difficult for them to dismiss Robert, Lord Vansittart. In addition to having been a member of the Prisoner of War Department during the First World War, Vansittart had also been personal secretary to both Stanley Baldwin and Ramsay Macdonald and, from 1930 to 1938, Permanent Under–secretary of State at the Foreign Office.[137] Throughout the course of the war, while he continued to act as the main POWRA correspondent with the War and Foreign Offices, the matter of a single inter–departmental committee could not be dismissed out of hand.

In May 1943 Eden again found it necessary to reply to enquiries from Vansittart regarding the possibility of the appointment of a Parliamentary Under–secretary of State to oversee prisoner of war matters.[138] This time the reply was rather more conciliatory in tone, Sir Anthony suggesting that he would 'prefer to keep this very important subject under my own eye . . . and to answer myself in Parliament for its [Prisoner of War Department] work' and hoping that Lord Vansittart and his 'friends' would not press their idea.[139] Vansittart replied that he felt Sir Anthony's letter might satisfy the 'strong desire for a whole–time Parliamentary Under–secretary'.[140] However, his optimism appears to have been misplaced, as the matter still remained unresolved in November of that year, when a deputation met with Rt Hon. Richard K. Law, Minister of State at the Foreign Office.[141]

POWRA's requests that a single organisation should be established to oversee prisoner of war matters were generally dealt with by the Foreign Office. By and large, the requests were dismissed with the suggestion that POWRA 'either did not know or preferred to ignore that there was in fact a committee known as the Imperial Prisoners of War Committee which plays the part which they would wish to be played by the Interdepartmental Committee which they advocate'.[142] This type of reply took no account of the fact that the Imperial Prisoners of War Committee concerned itself with the welfare of prisoners of war themselves and not with their next of kin and relatives in Britain. The Foreign Office also correctly suggested that the Newton Committee, which had operated during the First World War, had not solved inter–departmental problems, as it had had no authority over the various departments involved.[143] Again, however, this suggestion is beside the point as POWRA was not suggesting such a committee. Rather it favoured a 'proper Prisoner of War Department' such as, it claimed, had been established during the First World War and of which Lord Vansittart had, for a short time, been head.[144] However, the veracity of these recollections must be open to some doubts as the letter in which these comments were made also goes on to suggest that this Department had been under the auspices of the Foreign Office. As we have seen in the previous chapter, and as a pencil marginal note to this letter confirms, the Foreign Office had, in fact, disowned the Prisoner of War Department in 1916 and refused to accept any further responsibility for prisoners of war.[145]

The actual recommendations made by POWRA are also rather confused. Although its major campaign suggests that the focus of their attention was a separate department to oversee all prisoner of war matters, other letters make reference to a desire for an inter–departmental committee, to include representatives of various charitable organisations and voluntary bodies interested in prisoner of war matters.[146] In fact, the suggestion of a separate Minister overseeing all matters relating to prisoners of war was debated in the House of Commons in November 1944 and was rejected by the government spokesman, Clement Attlee, then Lord President of the Council.[147]

Whilst the Foreign Office considered that 'better results were obtained by encouraging them [POWRA] along lines which agree with official policy rather than by snubbing them', by June 1943 the War Office had ceased to be in any way sympathetic.[148] To a large extent this hostility was attributed to what was seen as POWRA's 'constant and unfair' criticism of the BRC and a feeling that encouraging them would result in 'real damage to the BRC's work and in diminished contributions to their funds'.[149] Cambray and Briggs note that this criticism of the BRC actually took place whilst POWRA was benefiting from the use of its accommodation.[150] In a letter to MPs in March 1942 the Association voiced a lack of confidence in the BRC's POW Department and pressed for MPs' support in appointing a 'first class' businessman as managing director.[151] This managing director was to be supported by a small committee of businessmen plus representatives of POWRA to look after the interests of next of kin.[152]

This championing of the BRC may seem rather inconsistent on the part of the War Office, considering the way in which it had allowed the BRC to take the blame for problems in distribution of parcels. In fact the Prisoner of War Department of the BRC was rather more stoical on the matter, seeing POWRA as 'too unimportant to be able to do any harm',[153] a view echoed in the Phillimore Report, which concluded that the 'absence of any solid ground for this criticism' led to the Association soon ceasing 'to be of serious importance'.[154]

One government department did, however, manage to retain the semblance of a cordial relationship with POWRA. From 1943 until the winding up of the Association in December 1945, a correspondence between the Organising Secretaries and Colonel S.J. Cole at the Colonial Office ensured a channel through which POWRA could be monitored.[155] Starting from the standpoint that 'the public must not be allowed to suffer through any internecine misunderstandings between those who have the duty, or have voluntarily undertaken a duty, of serving them',[156] the Colonial Office maintained a watching brief on the activities of the Association by giving its speakers material to use on their tours and providing its own representatives to speak at POWRA meetings. Both Colonel Cole and Lord Vansittart spoke at a meeting at Caxton Hall in January 1944 for relatives and repatriated men.[157] However, Colonial Office correspondence suggests that the relationship, on its side at least, was opportune rather than truly warm. Letters from 1943 and 1944 warn of 'having to be careful in dealing with her [Mrs Stewart]' and of the Association trying to involve the Colonial Office in 'jealousies' between themselves and the BRC.[158] Nevertheless, when Mrs Stewart retired in May 1945, Colonel Cole wrote her a personal letter to which she sent a handwritten reply saying how pleased she was that her 'puny efforts had been of some material assistance'.[159] Similarly with the winding up of POWRA in December 1945, W. Laing, Mrs Stewart's successor as Organising Secretary, wrote to Colonel Cole expressing thanks for the 'courtesy' which the Colonial Office had always shown the Association. Colonel Cole replied saying, 'We have been helped and encouraged in our work by the ready and cordial co–operation which we have always met from the POWRA collectively and from each of you individually. You have done grand work.'[160]

Although it is not clear that there were any direct links between prisoner of war relatives associations in various countries, it is interesting to note that POWRA in Canada proved to be a similar thorn in the flesh of government agencies. In Britain the Colonial Office noted that 'any slip on the part of the BRC is like pennies from Heaven for Mrs Stewart'.[161] Similarly, Jonathan Vance records that the Canadian POWRA also came to 'resent the privileged status of the Red Cross'.[162] This is not to suggest that all prisoner of war relatives associations were waging an orchestrated campaign against the Red Cross in various Dominion countries, rather that national associations and committees run by relatives of prisoners of war often felt themselves best able to represent their own interests; a fact which is perhaps unsurprising given the lack of coherent governmental policy. In Britain POWRA was keen to stress that the constitution of the BRC provided for the assistance of prisoners whereas their organisation existed to help relatives to help prisoners.[163] However, although the Canadian government's provision for dealing with prisoner of war matters appears to have been as poorly organised and ill thought–out as that of the British government, the Canadian POWRA did not campaign to improve this. Instead it concentrated its efforts on establishing its claim to be the 'only registered war charity whose sole purpose was the welfare of Canadian POWs' and their ascendancy over the Canadian Red Cross in these matters.[164]

In Britain POWRA was not the only body to express dissatisfaction with the way that the government was handling prisoner of war matters. A letter from the Westminster Co–operative Party to

Richard Law also expressed unease and requested information as
to whether or not responsibility for these matters might be concentrated in the hands of one minister.[165] Law replied expressing regret
that there was still 'uneasiness' regarding the existing ministerial
and administrative arrangements for handling these matters. His
letter concluded,

> It is necessary to remember that His Majesty's government, in endea-
> vouring to secure proper treatment for our prisoners, have to sur-
> mount great difficulties arising out of the policy and mentality both
> of the Nazi regime in Germany and of those now in control of affairs
> in Japan. I can assure you that we are doing our utmost to overcome
> these difficulties.[166]

Although there were undoubtedly 'difficulties' of this nature, the
question remains, however, as to how many of the obstacles for
relatives, at least, would have been circumvented if a coherent
policy towards prisoners of war and their families had been formulated at an earlier stage. Law's reply appears to miss the point of
the Co–operative Party's query, which did not relate to the level of
effort being expended by the government on prisoner of war matters
but rather to the way in which this effort was administered and
organised. David Rolf suggests that the 'tardy realisation' by the
government of the 'new realities' it faced when large numbers of
its servicemen fell into enemy hands largely precluded any genuine
thought as to how a coherent policy might be developed.[167] Echoes
can be heard here of the same complacent attitude that had been
shown by the service departments in the 1930s to the suggestion to
formulate a coherent policy for allowances.

In many areas of Britain the work of national organisations was
supplemented by the formation of local prisoner of war committees
and support groups. Often these committees were established in
response to local need and as a direct result of local men having
been taken prisoner. For many next of kin, lack of news of loved
ones and a feeling of isolation led to a desire to pool such information as was available and to meet with others in a similar situation
in an attempt to provide mutual comfort and support. In France
too Sarah Fishman records that many wives 'agreed that loneliness
was "the hardest thing"'.[168] In contrast to the actions of the British
government, Vichy responded by establishing the Fédération des
Associations de Femmes de Prisonniers in Lyons and the Femmes

d'Absents in Paris to provide support to prisoner of war's wives.[169] This action, however, should not be viewed as wholly altruistic. Under French law, prisoners of war's wives were not able to establish themselves as heads of families when their menfolk were absent, and the two organisations served the dual purpose of supporting prisoners of war's wives and ensuring that the role of the absent husband or father was not usurped.

In Britain such groups tended to operate on very local levels, from the homes of their organisers or from local community centres. Consequently, although there is a great deal of circumstantial evidence for their existence, and many references to them in other archival sources such as local newspapers, little direct material has survived. Evidence from the Barnsley Prisoner of War Fund suggests that some such committees may have been continuations or reformations of committees established during the First World War, but again there is little concrete evidence to substantiate this. Fishman reports a similar situation in France where, although such groups had proved invaluable in 'raising the consciousness' of prisoner of war wives, after the war they disappeared without trace.[170] As already recorded at the beginning of this chapter, the Norwich branch of the CAB referred to 'organisations within the city' dealing specifically with prisoner of war matters.[171] However, no mention is made of what these organisations were and no further reference to them appears to exist in the Norwich archives. Often references to such committees occur in the pages of local newspapers, reporting fundraising events and activities. For example, throughout the war the *Henley Standard* contained small news items on the work of the Prisoner of War Fund, Henley and District Committee.[172]

This committee was founded in August 1940 with the stated aims of: raising funds for parcels and comforts; forming a register of all prisoners of war's families in the district; ascertaining the interests of prisoners so that each prisoner could be supplied 'with matter to keep his mind occupied' and finally of furthering the interests of the prisoners of war on their release, especially in terms of employment.[173] The average cost of a next of kin parcel was in the region of 16s, well beyond the means of some families. Consequently, the suggestion was made that groups of people should join together and 'adopt' a local prisoner of war to ensure that all the men from the area received personal parcels.[174] Later reports suggest that this suggestion met with some success as, in July 1943, the Marsh

Gibbon Women's Institute meeting included the reading of two letters from 'adopted' prisoners of war.[175] By mid–September the Committee's fund had grown to £606 5s 5d although, in the later months of the year, fundraising for the cause was overshadowed by the local Spitfire Fund which raised a staggering £4,915 5s 5d in four months.[176] The Committee also widened their remit to include providing information to relatives, as the Red Cross was 'under great pressure', and sending a letter of appreciation for 'gallant conduct' to all local men taken captive.[177] In order to collate information regarding each prisoner, local groups were set up in the surrounding district, a practice that also seems to have been common in other areas of the country.[178]

On 12 June 1941 the *Yorkshire Evening News* reported that an informal meeting of wives and mothers of Leeds men who had been taken prisoner had been held at the Briggate offices of the newspaper. At the meeting it was resolved to 'form a Leeds POW Club, under the auspices of the newspaper'.[179] All Leeds women whose husbands or sons had been taken captive were to be invited to join, and it was hoped to hold 'social gatherings' every month.[180] From this beginning the idea spread throughout the area, with branches of the Club being opened in Harrogate, Featherstone, Aireborough, Horsforth, Cleckheaton and Wakefield by early 1942.[181] In July 1942 the Club took the innovative step of inaugurating the first 'packing centre on wheels' to make the sending of Red Cross next of kin parcels easier for those who could not get to packing centres sited in the main towns.[182] On its inaugural journey the mobile centre visited the headquarters of the Spen Valley Club at Cleckheaton.[183] Reports of the various branches of the Club continued to appear in the 'It Happened in Yorkshire' section of the newspaper throughout the period but it has not proved possible to locate any further archival information even when the location of the meetings is known. For example the Wakefield branch is known to have met every Wednesday at the Bull Hotel in Wakefield but its records seem to have disappeared without trace.[184]

The Barnsley Prisoner of War Fund also provides a good example of this type of local committee. This Fund was originally founded in 1918 to provide for British prisoners of war from the Barnsley area in enemy countries.[185] Following the First World War, a trust was established to administer the letting of four houses to repatriated prisoners of war and their dependants resident in the area, and to other ex–servicemen.[186] However, the resources of the trust proved inadequate to maintain the houses, which were then sold and the income generated from the sale made available for grants or loans to former prisoners of war and their dependants resident in the Barnsley area.[187] The trust continues to meet twice yearly to the present day.[188] However, although the necessity for the keeping of minute books and books of accounts was formally laid down in the Trust Deed of 1918, no records survive from the period of the Second World War.

One rare example of a largely intact archive from a Committee of this nature does, however, exist. On 18 May 1940 the *Huddersfield Weekly Examiner* contained a report headed 'Huddersfield Men in Norway Fight' which gave the names of ten local men who had been taken prisoner in Norway.[189] Amongst these men was 2nd Lt R.B. Smailes of the King's Own Yorkshire Light Infantry, whose mother was instrumental in forming the Huddersfield Prisoner of War Committee. The first meeting of the Committee was held in June 1940, when it was decided to hold regular meetings on the third Wednesday of every month.[190] By August, 25 local men had been taken captive, all of whom had already contacted their relatives.[191] By October, 72 families had been visited by members of the committee, all of whom were 'very grateful and cheerful'.[192] At Christmas of the same year a party was held for wives, mothers and children of prisoners of war with 99 people being entertained by a conjurer and films.[193] All children attending the party were given a cash gift of 1s. This party became an annual event continuing up to December 1944, by which time it had become so large that numbers from 'large' families were limited and two sittings were necessary for the food.[194]

In the summer of 1941 a second annual event was added in the form of a Garden Party to which 'sweethearts' were invited in addition to wives, mothers and children.[195] The original event, which 103 people attended, was held in the garden of a committee member but, by 1943, upwards of three hundred people were attending and the event had to be moved first to Ravensknowle Park and then, in 1944, to Greenhead School.[196] A third annual event was also added in October 1942 – a church service which was 'greatly appreciated and very well attended'.[197]

After September 1942 the number of prisoners of war from the Huddersfield area had risen to 210 and, in the light of these large numbers, the Committee made the decision to limit their visits to one initial visit per family.[198] After this introductory visit, it was left to families to contact the Committee if and when they needed help. In many cases the most immediate help required was with the preparing and packing of next of kin parcels that the Committee undertook in a room at the Women's War Time Bureau on Thursday afternoons.[199] Although some relatives initially preferred to manage parcels by themselves, the Committee noted that 'in most cases they drift to us in the end' whether more for practical help or for moral support it remains impossible to tell.[200] Aside from help with parcels, the Committee provided a wide range of other practical help. In February 1941, Mrs Firth, the mother of Trooper Arnold Firth of the Cavalry and Armoured Corps who was prisoner in Stalag XXA, was taken ill.[201] The minutes of the Committee Meeting of the time record that the Committee undertook to 'send her Ovaltine or something nutritious'.[202] At the other end of the scale the Committee undertook to pay for boots for many local prisoners of war, as the expense of these was more than many wives could manage.[203] The boots were to be paid for by chit provided by the Committee and redeemable at the local shoe shops, Stead and Simpsons and Timpsons, in Huddersfield.[204]

The Committee also responded to special cases of need. For example, through SSAFA it learned that a Mr Lindsay, probably the father of Private Jack Lindsay of the Gordon Highlanders, prisoner in Stalag XXB, was in need of a new suit of clothes.[205] The Committee undertook to do whatever was possible, not, however, because of Mr Lindsay's need, but because 'we should do all we can in so far as it would affect the peace of mind of a prisoner'.[206] From this we must assume that the work of the Committee in overseeing prisoner of war families was at times incomplete. If Mr Lindsay had not written to his son making him aware of the situation the Committee would have either remained unaware of it or not done anything about it. Its prime concern appears to have been the peace of mind of a prisoner of war himself rather than the need of his father. In the event the suit was purchased jointly by the Committee and SSAFA with one of the Committee members making a personal donation of £1.[207] In April of the same year the Committee was again contacted by SSAFA with regard to Mrs Lewis, the wife of William Lewis, a Driver in the RASC captive in Singapore, who needed help with the purchase of spectacles. Although, in this case, the Committee agreed to pay the whole amount, they were at pains to point out that this was provided 'no precent [*sic*] should be so created'.[208]

It is difficult from these few examples to ascertain on what basis the Committee made their decisions with regard to such payments. Whether decisions were made solely on the basis of family need or on the degree of involvement of the serviceman concerned remains unclear. What is certain is that, where financial assistance was required for goods to be sent to prisoners themselves, there was no hesitation. During the course of the war the Committee donated £4,500 to the BRC for such goods.[209] However, in cases where the need was for financial assistance for items for the family there was rather more discussion and consideration of the individual merits of each case.

By the spring of 1945 the work of the Committee in relation to relatives was beginning to lessen, and the Garden Party of that year was cancelled.[210] Instead the Committee decided to make a donation of £5 to each returning prisoner, with the donation being given to relatives in the case of prisoners of war who had died in captivity. By July 1945, 336 local men had been welcomed back at thirteen receptions and, in October 1946, the Committee's final event, a Social Evening and Dance, was held.[211] A final 'winding up' meeting was held in November 1946 at which it was decided that the remaining funds should be distributed in gifts of £8 to relatives of those servicemen who had died as a direct result of their imprisonment.[212] It was as a direct result of this decision that some of the most moving letters from next of kin were received.

Mrs F. Hanson of Kirkheaton, the wife of Private Leslie Hanson who had been missing in the Far East since March 1942, wrote saying 'its been a comfort to know that someone thought about the one's that are left'.[213] E. Hall of Slaithwaite, possibly the wife of Leslie Hall believed to have been taken prisoner in Borneo, wrote in 1949:

> It is nearly two years since my husband died and I cannot get my business straightened out with the RAF . . . It makes me wonder why and for what our loves ones sacrificed there lives for, but someday we shall understand . . . It will give me great pleasure and comfort to recieve such a large amount.[214]

As we saw with the case of Mrs Truman in the previous chapter, once the serviceman himself had ceased to be of further use to his country, the plight of his family often became unimportant to official agencies.

Throughout this chapter we have seen a differentiation between two types of support agencies for prisoner of war families. On a local level, families tended to gravitate towards the support group, normally a local prisoner of war committee, which had been established in their home town and in direct response to the captivity of local men. Through these groups, families were assisted in a number of ways both financially, as we have seen in the case in Huddersfield where wives were helped to provide boots for their menfolk, and in terms of moral support through a network of visits, talks and shared information. Although there are some instances of relatives attending meetings in more diverse locales, the overall picture is that these occasions arose as a supplement to the immediate local provision or where other support groups provided more specialised information. The minutes of the Huddersfield Prisoner of War Committee, for example, record that, in July 1945, a number of relatives of men held captive in Japanese hands had been attending meetings in Halifax where there were a greater number of families in the same situation.[215] Although there was some discussion as to whether or not monthly meetings should be held in Huddersfield for these families, the emphasis is clearly on meeting the needs of the families concerned.

With national charities, however, the picture is rather more complex. The British Red Cross, SSAFA and POWRA each seems to have been in competition to be recognised in its own right as the primary support agency for prisoners of war's relatives. To some extent this perception is necessarily coloured by the sources themselves, none of which can be regarded as unbiased in this matter. The supposed public perception that the BRC was the agency to which the public turned is taken from Cambray and Briggs's sympathetic *Red Cross and St. John*. The perception that SSAFA was the prime agency providing support to all service families is taken from 'History of SSAFA', written for its own publication, *SSAFA News*. The authority of POWRA to speak for the vast majority of parents and wives of prisoners of war comes from its own correspondence. In this we see a parallel with the situation in both Canada and France. In Canada the Red Cross Society, the Canadian POWRA and the War Prisoners Aid of the World Alliance of YMCAs all believed that they were the agency best suited to answer the needs of prisoners of war and their families.[216] Similarly, in France, the Famille du Prisonnier and the Commissariat Général aux Prisonniers de Guerre Repatriés et aux Familles de Prisonniers de Guerre, both created specifically to provide moral and financial support for prisoners' wives, also competed to extend their respective power bases.[217]

In the cases of both Canada and Great Britain, governmental strategy for dealing with prisoner of war matters was not clearly defined. A number of government departments shared responsibility but there was no overall structure of responsibility. As we have already seen, this lack of coherence led to confusion amongst next of kin as to the best department to contact for advice and information. In the face of this lack of a clear lead from government, it is not surprising that other agencies should have attempted to fulfil this role. However, as no one government department held overall responsibility for deciding policy in these matters, all were free to deal with whichever charitable organisation suited their purpose at any particular moment. Hence the situation where, when information needed to be provided to servicemen regarding their families following the bombing of London, the War Office contacted SSAFA to supply this information but, with regard to contacting families regarding homecoming prisoners, the same government department contacted the Red Cross. This diversity may be regarded as giving government departments the flexibility to deal with whichever organisation was best suited for any particular task. For the families concerned, the lack of coherent policy and the competition for ascendancy between charitable organisations can only have increased and mirrored the confusion caused by lack of an overall policy between government departments and motivated the desire to establish their own action groups. The lack of coherent policy regarding the dissemination of information, however, cannot totally explain the rapid proliferation of local prisoner of war committees and support groups. In France, where from the autumn of 1940 most families of prisoners were aware of their fate and had established postal contact, similar self–help groups also formed. Regional groups, such as the Fédération des Associations de Femmes de Prisonniers, were supplemented by groups reflecting class or political divisions.[218] Whilst communist women in the Resistance established their own prisoners of war's wives' section, officers' wives in Paris, generally *bourgeoises*, formed the Femmes d'Absents.

Regardless of the degree of official information available and the level of governmental support, prisoners' wives of all nations exhibited a natural need to meet other wives in a similar situation with whom to discuss their problems and from whom to gain mutual and personal support.

Notes

1 A copy of this Act can be found in NA/PIN15/2663.
2 A copy of this Act can be found in NA/PIN15/2663.
3 Standing Conference of Voluntary Organisations in Time of War. December 1938. NA/PIN15/2663.
4 SSAFA Council Minutes. 11 February 41. SSAFA Archive.
5 Prisoners of War Central Enquiry Bureau. Draft Handbook. NA/WO32/1118. See also Work of the YMCA in Connection with POWs. NA/FO916/549.
6 Reports of Citizens' Advice Bureau. 07 January 43 and 13 July 45. Social Welfare Committee Minutes April 1943–June 1947. Norfolk Archives. N/TC31/1/7.
7 Reports of Citizens' Advice Bureau 07 January 43 and 13 July 45. Social Welfare Committee Minutes April 1943–June 1947. Norfolk Archives. N/TC31/1/7.
8 SSAFA continues its work to the present day. In 1998, the Association was still aiding 80,000 people. Report of the Council for the year ending 31 December 1998. SSAFA Archive.
9 SSAFA Annual Report. Year ended December 1942. SSAFA Archive.
10 SSAFA Annual Report Year ended December 1942. SSAFA Archive.
11 In this case the children were placed by SSAFA in permanent homes and the wife helped to find a job so that she could support herself. SSAFA Annual Report Year Ended December 1943. SSAFA Archive.
12 'History of SSAFA'. *SSAFA News*, Summer 1985. SSAFA Archive.
13 Parker, *Struggle for Survival*. p. 293.
14 'History of SSAFA'.
15 'History of SSAFA'.
16 'History of SSAFA'.
17 Letter SSAFA to Major–General the Viscount Bridgeman, War Office. 26 December 44. NA/WO32/11125 [105A].
18 Letter SSAFA to Major–General the Viscount Bridgeman, War Office. 26 December 44. NA/WO32/11125 [105A].
19 Draft Letter War Office to SSAFA, undated. NA/WO32/11125[106A]
20 SSAFA Council Minutes. 14 December 43. SSAFA Archive.
21 SSAFA Council Minutes. 14 December 43. SSAFA Archive.
22 SSAFA Council Minutes. 07 May 40. SSAFA Archive.

23 SSAFA Council Minutes. 11 June 40. SSAFA Archive.

24 SSAFA Council Minutes. 11 March 41. SSAFA Archive.

25 Second report of the BRC War Organisation 1940–41. p. 29. BRC Archive.

26 Cambray and Briggs. *Red Cross and St. John.* Introduction.

27 Belfield Report. p. 4. NA/FO916/14.

28 Belfield Report. p. 4. NA/FO916/14.

29 Whatever the official line, it appears to have proved impossible to prevent 'private' confiscation from parcels. During the Second World War reports existed of Italian guards confiscating 'clean' decks of playing cards from Red Cross parcels intended for British prisoners – although playing cards were originally on the list of banned items for parcels and should not, actually, have been accepted in parcels in the first place. War Diaries November 1941 – September 1944. NA/WO165/68.

30 Belfield Report. p. 4. NA/FO916/14.

31 Belfield Report. p. 6. NA/FO916/14.

32 Belfield Report. pp. 4, 6 and 7. NA/FO916/14.

33 Cambray and Briggs, *Red Cross and St. John.* p. 136.

34 Cambray and Briggs, *Red Cross and St. John.* p. 136.

35 This despite the fact that the peak period for sending food parcels actually occurred in 1942 when, at one stage, over 20,000 such parcels were being sent every week with a total of 5,552,151 in the year as a whole. Cambray and Briggs, *Red Cross and St. John.* p. 147.

36 For further details of this campaign see NA/PREM4/98/1.

37 Rolf, 'Blind Bureaucracy'. p. 51.

38 Rolf, 'Blind Bureaucracy'. p. 51.

39 In a letter to the War Office dated 17 November 44 Col. S.J. Cole, Temporary Administration Officer, Colonial Office, speaks of the 'vendetta' conducted by the POWRA against the BRC. See also Rolf, *Blind Bureaucracy.* pp. 51–53. The work of the POWRA is dealt with in greater detail later in this chapter.

40 Confidential note to Irene Ward from W.C.T. 2 July 1942. Irene Ward Papers, 19, New Bodleian Archive.

41 Confidential note to Irene Ward from W.C.T. 2 July 1942. Irene Ward Papers, 19, New Bodleian Archive.

42 BRC War Organisation First Annual Report 1939–40. p. 17. BRC Archive.

43 Rolf, 'Blind Bureaucracy'. pp. 51–52.

44 Cambray and Briggs, *Red Cross and St. John.* p. 179.

45 Cambray and Briggs, *Red Cross and St. John.* p. 179.

46 Cambray and Briggs, *Red Cross and St. John.* p. 198.

47 BRC War Organisation, Second Annual Report 1940–41. p. 23. BRC
    Archive.
48 Cambray and Briggs, *Red Cross and St. John*. p. 185.
49 Cambray and Briggs, *Red Cross and St. John*. p. 178.
50 Cambray and Briggs, *Red Cross and St. John*. p. 183.
51 In September 1942 the scarcity of clothing supplies in the UK as a
    whole led to a revision of this policy. From this date, 40 clothing
    coupons were issued for the first parcel and 20 for all subsequent
    parcels. Cambray and Briggs, *Red Cross and St. John*. p. 187.
52 Fishman, *We Will Wait*. p. 61.
53 Fishman, *We Will Wait*. p. 60.
54 Cambray and Briggs, *Red Cross and St. John*. p. 200.
55 Cambray and Briggs, *Red Cross and St. John*. p. 199.
56 Fishman, *We Will Wait*. p. 46.
57 Fishman, *We Will Wait*. pp. 60 and 144.
58 Cambray and Briggs, *Red Cross and St. John*. p. 200.
59 Cambray and Briggs, *Red Cross and St. John*. p. 200.
60 Cambray and Briggs, *Red Cross and St. John*. p. 185.
61 Figures from Cambray and Briggs, *Red Cross and St. John* p. 187.
    Parcels were despatched daily rather than in batches every three
    months, with an average despatch of 1,000 parcels per day in 1942.
62 The BRC parcel service continued throughout the war, until it was
    finally suspended by the Postmaster General on 16 February 45 for
    camps in Poland and Eastern Europe and until 22 March 45 for
    camps elsewhere in Germany. BRC War Organisation Sixth Annual
    Report 1944–45. BRC Archive.
63 Cambray and Briggs, *Red Cross and St. John*. p. 233.
64 Cambray and Briggs, *Red Cross and St. John*. p. 233.
65 Cambray and Briggs, *Red Cross and St. John*. p. 234.
66 Cambray and Briggs, *Red Cross and St. John*. p. 234.
67 Cambray and Briggs, *Red Cross and St. John*. p. 287, and Prisoners
    of War Central Enquiry Bureau: formation and functions. NA/
    WO32/11118.
68 Cambray and Briggs, *Red Cross and St. John*. p. 287
69 Cambray and Briggs, *Red Cross and St. John*. p. 287
70 Cambray and Briggs, *Red Cross and St. John*. p. 288, and Fourth
    Annual Report of BRC War Organisation, 1942–43. BRC Archive.
71 Cambray and Briggs, *Red Cross and St. John*. p. 234.
72 Cambray and Briggs, *Red Cross and St. John*. p. 236.
73 Cambray and Briggs, *Red Cross and St. John*. p. 236 and Phillimore
    Report. p. 50. NA/WO366/26.
74 Barnes, 'History of SSAFA'.
75 Barnes, 'History of SSAFA'.

76 Annual Report of the BRC War Organisation. 19940–41. p. 29. BRC Archive.
77 *The Prisoner of War* Issue 1, May 1942. BRC, and Cambray and Briggs, *Red Cross and St. John.* p. 229.
78 *The Prisoner of War* Issue 1, May 1942. BRC Archive.
79 Cambray and Briggs, *Red Cross and St. John.* p. 229.
80 *The Prisoner of War* Issue 1, May 1942. BRC Archive.
81 *The Prisoner of War* Issue 1, May 1942. BRC Archive.
82 *The Prisoner of War* Issue 4, August 1942. BRC Archive.
83 Cambray and Briggs, *Red Cross and St. John.* p. 229.
84 Cambray and Briggs, *Red Cross and St. John.* p. 229.
85 Cambray and Briggs, *Red Cross and St. John.* p. 230.
86 Cambray and Briggs, *Red Cross and St. John.* p. 230.
87 Resolution of the Rochdale and District Prisoner of War Committee to Harold Sutcilffe MP. 30 July 41. NA/FO916/34.
88 Resolution of the Rochdale and District Prisoner of War Committee to Harold Sutcilffe MP. 30 July 41. NA/FO916/34.
89 Cambray and Briggs, *Red Cross and St. John.* p. 288, and *Far East.* February 44. BRC Archive.
90 Cambray and Briggs, *Red Cross and St. John.* p. 288.
91 Letter from George Ford. *The Times.* 26 October 43. NA/CO980/207. This letter also drew a speedy response from the POWRA that its own News Sheet contained a section devoted to news from the Far East.
92 *Prisoner of War* continued to be published and issued to next of kin until September 1945, *Far East* until December of the same year. BRC War Organisation, Sixth Annual Report, 1944–45. BRC Archives.
93 Cambray and Briggs, *Red Cross and St. John.* p. 288.
94 Cambray and Briggs, *Red Cross and St. John.* p. 288.
95 *Far East.* First Edition, February 1944. BRC Archive.
96 *Prisoner of War.* May 1943 issue. BRC Archive
97 Editorial *Far East.* Final edition, December 1945. BRC Archive.
98 BRC Annual Reports 1942–43, 1943–44. BRC Archive.
99 British Red Cross War Organisation Annual Reports 1942–43, 1943–44 and 1944–45. BRC Archive. No information is contained in the archive to suggest how the films were received by the public nor the numbers who attended their showings.
100 Cambray and Briggs, *Red Cross and St. John.* p. 640.
101 There is no suggestion in Cambray and Briggs in either the introduction or the section specifically devoted to Joint County Committees (pp. 638–643) that these Joint County Committees followed a model established in the First World War.

102 British Red Cross War Organisation, First Annual Report 1939–40. BRC Archive.
103 Cambray and Briggs, *Red Cross and St. John*. p. 639.
104 BRC War Organisation. Fourth Annual Report 1942–43. BRC Archive.
105 BRC War Organisation. Fourth Annual Report 1942–43. BRC Archive.
106 BRC War Organisation. Fourth Annual Report 1942–43. BRC Archive.
107 BRC War Organisation. Fourth Annual Report 1942–43. BRC Archive.
108 BRC War Organisation. Fourth Annual Report 1942–43. BRC Archive.
109 Cambray and Briggs, *Red Cross and St. John*. p. 288.
110 Cambray and Briggs, *Red Cross and St. John*. p. 289.
111 Cambray and Briggs, *Red Cross and St. John*. p. 186.
112 Cambray and Briggs, *Red Cross and St. John*. p. 289.
113 Cambray and Briggs, *Red Cross and St. John*. p. 289.
114 Cambray and Briggs, *Red Cross and St. John*. p. 289.
115 Booklet of Daily Telegraph Prisoner of War Exhibition, Huddersfield Prisoner of War Committee Archive KC825/1/112 1943–46. Kirklees Archive, Huddersfield.
116 Booklet of Daily Telegraph Prisoner of War Exhibition, Huddersfield Prisoner of War Committee Archive KC825/1/112 1943–46. Kirklees Archive, Huddersfield.
117 Foreword to booklet accompanying Daily Telegraph Prisoner of War Exhibition, Clarence House. Kirklees Archive, KC825/1/12 1943–46.
118 Foreword to booklet accompanying Daily Telegraph Prisoner of War Exhibition, Clarence House. Kirklees Archive, KC825/1/12 1943–46.
119 Cambray and Briggs, *Red Cross and St. John*. pp. 356 and 236.
120 Cambray and Briggs, *Red Cross and St. John*. Footnote p. 243.
121 POWRA Newsheet 38. June 43. NA/FO916/550.
122 Phillimore Report. p. 53. NA/WO366/26.
123 Letter Sir Harold Satow, KCMG, OBE, Foreign Office, to Sir G. Warner. 16 March 43. NA/FO916/550. The Imperial Lists for the period of the Second World War do not attribute any official position to Sir Harold Satow, who had officially retired at this period. Foreign Office lists note that he was 're–employed in the Foregin Office from February 1940' without specifiying the capacity in which he was re–employed.
124 Minutes of Huddersfield Prisoner of War Committee. 18 February 42, 18 March 42 and 15 July 42. Kirklees Archive KC825/1/1.

125 Note, Mann, Colonial Office. 30 September 43. NA/CO980/207.
126 Note, Mann, Colonial Office. 30 September 43. NA/CO980/207.
127 Letter Prisoner of War Dept to Major–General E.C. Gepp, CB, DSO, Director of Prisoners of War, War Office. 28 June 43. NA/FO916/550.
128 Note, Mann, Colonial Office. 05 October 43. NA/CO980/207.
129 Belfield Report. p. 6. NA/FO916/12/32749.
130 Letter Sir O. Sargeant, Under–secretary of State, Foreign Office, to the Earl of Galloway referring to his letters of 26 September 40 and 19 September 40. 15 October 40. NA/FO916/562.
131 Letter Walsall and District Co–operative Society to W.M. Adamson MP. 05 January 42. NA/FO916/562.
132 Letter Walsall and District Co–operative Society to W.M. Adamson MP. 05 January 42. NA/FO916/562.
133 Draft letter Sir Harold Satow, Foreign Office, to Sir G. Warner. 16 March 43. NA/FO916/550.
134 Draft letter Sir Harold Satow, Foreign Office, to Sir G. Warner. 16 March 43. NA/FO916/550.
135 Draft letter Sir Harold Satow, Foreign Office, to Sir G. Warner. 16 March 43. NA/FO916/550.
136 Letters from Sir Harold Satow, Foreign Office, to Sir G. Warner. 09 March 43 and 16 March 43. NA/FO916/550.
137 Robert Vansittart began his career in the Foreign Office in 1911. During the First World War he served with the Prisoner of War Department, gaining some success in improving conditions in which both British prisoners of war and civilian internees were held. In 1918–1919 he was involved in the Paris Peace Conference negotia-tions on the issues of the Turkish Treaty and the Palestine Mandate. In 1920 he returned to the FO as Assistant Secretary before becom-ing Private Secretary to the Prime Minister, Stanley Baldwin, in 1928, a position he retained when Ramsay MacDonald took office. In 1930 he became Permanent Under–secretary for State at the Foreign Office, a position he held until 1938 when he was removed, by Anthony Eden, to a specially created post of Diplomatic Adviser. In 1941 he retired and entered the House of Lords. Rose, N., *Vansittart. Study of a Diplomat* (London: Heinemann, 1978); and Williams, E.T. and Palmer, H.M. (eds), *The Dictionary of National Biography 1951–1960.* Oxford: Oxford University Press, 1971. p. 1005.
138 Letter Rt Hon. Sir Anthony Eden, Secretary of State for Foreign Affairs, to Robert, Lord Vansittart. 21 May 43. NA/FO916/562/19.
139 Letter Rt Hon. Sir Anthony Eden, Secretary of State for Foreign Affairs, to Robert, Lord Vansittart. 21 May 43. NA/FO916/562/19.

140 Letter Rt Hon. Sir Anthony Eden, Secretary of State for Foreign Affairs, to Robert, Lord Vansittart. 21 May 43. NA/FO916/562/19.

141 Letter Robert, Lord Vansittart, to Sir Anthony Eden. 24 May 43. NA/FO916/562/21.

142 Letter Sir David Scott, KCMG, Assistant Under–secretary of State, Foreign Office, to Robert, Lord Vansittart, POWRA. 14 April 43. NA/FO916/562.

143 Letter Sir David Scott, KCMG, Assistant Under–secretary of State, Foreign Office, to Robert, Lord Vansittart, POWRA. 14 April 43. NA/FO916/562.

144 The information contained in this letter is not strictly accurate. Whilst Vansittart may have regarded himself as having been in charge of the day–to–day running of the department, the actual head of the Prisoner of War Department was Lord Newton. Letter Robert, Lord Vansittart, to Foreign Office. 01 April 43. NA/FO916/562.

145 Belfield Report. p. 2. NA/FO916/14.

146 See, for example, unsigned letter from POWRA to Rt Hon. R. Law, Minister of State, Foreign Office. 16 December 43.

147 Cambray and Briggs, *Red Cross and St. John*. Footnote p. 243.

148 Letters Sir Harold Satow, Foreign Office, to Lt–Col. P.E.A. Elwes, POW Dept Foreign Office. Undated; and Gepp, Director of Prisoners of War, War Office, to W. St. C.H. Roberts, Counsellor, Foreign Office. 16 June 43. NA/FO916/550.

149 Gepp, Director of Prisoners of War, War Office, to W. St. C.H. Roberts, Counsellor, Foreign Office. 16 June 43. NA/FO916/550.

150 Cambray and Briggs, *Red Cross and St. John*. Footnote. p. 243.

151 Cambray and Briggs, *Red Cross and St. John*. Footnote. p. 243.

152 Cambray and Briggs, *Red Cross and St. John*. Footnote. p. 243.

153 Letter Prisoner of War Dept, Foreign Office, to Gepp, Director of Prisoners of War, War Office. 28 June 43. NA/FO916/550.

154 Phillimore Report. p. 53. NA/WO366/26.

155 See correspondence contained in NA/CO980/207.

156 Note, Cole, Temporary Administative Officer, Colonial Office. 05 October 43. NA/CO980/207.

157 Letter Mrs Stewart, organising Secretary, POWRA, to Cole, Temporary Administrative Officer, Colonial Office. 23 November 43. NA/CO980/207.

158 Note Mann, Colonial Office. 12 August 43, and Cole, Temporary Administrative Officer, Colonial Office, 05 October 43. NA/CO980/207.

159 Letter Mrs Stewart to Cole, Temporary Administrative Officer, Colonial Office. 01 May 45. Mrs Stewart also wrote of her son, saying he 'was one of the first prisoners and it looks as if he'll be one of the last' and asking 'How will they [prisoners of war] fare under Doenitz? A nasty piece of work!'

160   Letter from W. Laing, Organising Secretary, POWRA, to Cole, Temporary Administrative Officer, Colonial Office. 20 December 45; and vice versa. 07 January 46. NA/CO980/207.

161   Note Mann, Colonial Office. 08 November 44. NA/CO980/207.

162   Vance, J., 'Candian Relief Agencies and Prisoners of War, 1939–45' in *Journal of Canadian Studies*. Vol. 31, No. 2, Summer 1996. p. 135.

163   Letter Mrs Stewart, POWRA, to Cole, Temporary Administrative Officer, Colonial Office. 04 April 44. NA/CO980/207.

164   George McGill Papers quoted in Vance, 'Canadian Relief Agencies and POWs 1939–45'. p. 135.

165   Letter Co–operative Party, Westminster, to Rt Hon. Richard Kidson Law, Minister of State, Foreign Office. 22 October 43. NA/FO916/562/23.

166   Letter Rt Hon. Richard Kidson Law, Minister of State, Foreign Office, to the Co–operative Party, Westminster. 08 November 43. NA/FO916/562[23].

167   Rolf, D, 'Blind Bureaucracy'. p. 47.

168   Fishman, *We Will Wait*. p. 63.

169   Fishman, *We Will Wait*. pp. 100 and 101.

170   Fishman, *We Will Wait*. p. 99.

171   Report of the Citizens' Advice Bureau. 13 July 445. Norwich Record Office.

172   See *Henley Standard*. 18 February 44, 03 January 44, 23 August 40, 16 August 40, 11 October 40. Centre for Oxfordshire Studies.

173   Letter. *Henley Standard*. 16 August 40. Centre for Oxfordshire Studies.

174   Letter. *Henley Standard*. 30 August 44. Centre for Oxfordshire Studies.

175   Reports of WI meetings. *Bicester Advertiser*. 09 July 43. Centre for Oxfordshire Studies.

176   *Henley Standard*. 20 December 40. Centre for Oxfordshire Studies.

177   Report of Henley Prisoner of War Committee. *Henley Standard*. 20 September 40. Centre for Oxfordshire Studies.

178   Report of Henley Prisoner of War Committee. *Henley Standard*. 20 September 40. Centrre for Oxfordshire Studies.

179   Front page, *Yorkshire Evening News*. 12 June 41. Local Studies Archive, Leeds.

180   Front page, *Yorkshire Evening News*. 12 June 41. Local Studies Archive, Leeds.

181   'It Happened in Yorkshire', *Yorkshire Evening News*. 01 July 42. Local Studies Archive, Leeds.

182   'It Happened in Yorkshire', *Yorkshire Evening News*. 13 July 42. Local Studies Archive, Leeds.

183 'It Happened in Yorkshire', *Yorkshire Evening News*. 13 July 42. Local Studies Archive, Leeds.

184 'It Happened in Yorkshire', *Yorkshire Evening News*. 13 July 42. Local Studies Archive, Leeds.

185 Deeds of Trust relating to the Barnsley and District Prisoners of War Fund. 01 June 88. Borough Secretary's Department, Barnsley Town Hall.

186 The houses in question were at 338, 340, 370 and 372 Doncaster Road, Barnsley. Deeds of Trust relating to the Barnsley and District Prisoners of War Fund. 01 June 88. Borough Secretary's Department, Barnsley Town Hall.

187 Deeds of Trust relating to the Barnsley and District Prisoners of War Fund. 01 June 88. Borough Secretary's Department, Barnsley Town Hall.

188 Deeds of Trust relating to the Barnsley and District Prisoners of War Fund. 01 June 88. Borough Secretary's Department, Barnsley Town Hall.

189 From this time onwards an item, 'News of Some Local Soldiers', became a regular feature in the *Huddersfield Weekly Examiner*, bringing people up to date with information regarding local men who were reported missing, prisoner of war or dead.

190 Minutes of Huddersfield Prisoner of War Committee. 16 October 40. Kirklees Archive KC825/1/1.

191 Minutes of the Huddersfield Prisoner of War Committee. 21 August 40. Kirklees Archive KC825/1/1.

192 Minutes of the Huddersfield Prisoner of War Committee. 16 October 40. Kirklees Archive KC825/1/1.

193 Minutes of the Huddersfield Prisoner of War Committee. 30 November 40. Kirklees Archive KC825/1/1.

194 Minutes of Huddersfield Prisoner of War Committee. 14 November 44 and 12 December 44. The actual size of a 'large' family is not made clear. Kirklees Archive KC825/1/1.

195 Minutes of the Huddersfield Prisoner of War Committee. 21 May 41. Kirklees Archive KC825/1/1.

196 Minutes of Huddersfield Prisoner of War Committee. 20 April 43, and Fourth Annual Report of the Huddersfield Prisoner of War Committee. 18 July 44. Kirklees Archive KC825/1/1.

197 Minutes of Huddersfield Prisoner of War Committee. 18 June 43. Kirklees Archive KC825/1/1.

198 Minutes of the Huddersfield Prisoner of War Committee. 16 September 42. Kirklees Archive KC825/1/1.

199 Minutes of the Huddersfield Prisoner of War Committee. 18 June 43. Kirlees Archive KC825/1/1.

200 Minutes of the Huddersfield Prisoner of War Committee. 18 June 43. Kirlees Archive KC825/1/1.

201 Minutes of the Huddersfield Prisoner of War Committee. 19 February 41. Kirklees Archive KC825/1/1.

202 Minutes of the Huddersfield Prisoner of War Committee. 19 February 41. Kirklees Archive KC825/1/1.

203 Minutes of the Huddersfield Prisoner of War Committee. 20 August 41. Kirklees Archive KC825/1/1.

204 Minutes of the Huddersfield Prisoner of War Committee. 20 August 41. Kirklees Archive KC825/1/1.

205 Minutes of Huddersfield Prisoner of War Committee. 15 February 44. Kirklees Archive KC825/1/1. Details of Pte Lindsay's captivity appear in KC825/1/7.

206 Minutes of Huddersfield Prisoner of War Committee. 15 February 44. Kirklees Archive KC825/1/1.

207 Minutes of the Huddersfield Prisoner of War Committee. 15 February 44. Kirklees Archive KC825/1/1.

208 Minutes of Huddersfield Prisoner of War Committee. 25 April 44. Kirklees Archive KC825/1/1. Details of William Lewis's captivity appear in KC825/1/10.

209 Minutes of the Huddersfield Prisoner of War Committee. 19 June 45. Kirklees Archive KC825/1/1.

210 Minutes of the Huddersfield Prisoner of War Committee. 10 April 45. Kirklees Archive KC825/1/1.

211 Minutes of the Huddersfield Prisoner of War Committee. 17 July 45 and 11 October 46. Kirklees Archive KC825/1/1.

212 Minutes of Huddersfield Prisoner of War Committee. 11 October 46 and 06 November 46. KC825/1/1.

213 Undated letter Mrs F. Hanson to Huddersfield Prisoner of War Committee. Kirklees Archive KC825/1/9.

214 Letter E. Hall to Huddersfield Prisoner of War Committee. 15 January 49. Kirklees Archive KC825/1/9.

215 Minutes of Huddersfield Prisoner of War Committee. 17 July 45. Kirklees Archive, KC825/1/1.

216 Vance, 'Canadian Relief Agencies and Prisoners of War, 1939–45'. p. 133.

217 Fishman, *We Will Wait*. p. 77.

218 This particular association later became the basis of the largest of all French prisoners of war's wives' groups with forty thousand members by 1943. Fishman, *We Will Wait*. p. 101.

'The rate for the job' – debates on postwar service allowances

As we have seen in earlier chapters, from early 1942 onwards regular reports were compiled relating to overall morale in the army and showing that throughout 1942, 1943 and 1944 the worries of soldiers focused mainly such issues as allowances for families, how families were coping financially, family illness and the fidelity of wives.[1] By early 1945, as the war was reaching its end, the concerns highlighted in these reports had turned more towards future reintegration into civilian life, employment and housing. The Morale Report of March to May 1945 reported that the reduction in the number of Allied and Dominion troops in the United Kingdom had led to reduced concerns amongst servicemen abroad regarding infidelity.[2] Similarly, a report of late 1945 recorded that the issue of pay and allowances, which had been constantly present in these reports since their inception, was now 'the least cause of discontent to the troops'.[3]

For most servicemen, this change in priorities reflected an assumption that, on return to the United Kingdom, they would be demobilised from the services and resume their former employment or seek new civilian employment. For those concerned with manpower levels within the services, however, the situation was rather different. British postwar political aims included not only the occupation of Germany and the safeguarding of the Empire but also involvement in other international task forces to prevent threats to the peace of Europe. All these ambitions involved the maintenance of a military presence in a wide variety of locations. In addition the war had seen the eclipse of British military power by the United States and, to retain some credibility as a major international power, it was necessary that this imbalance should not be worsened.[4] This ambition was patently not attainable if large numbers of men immediately left the armed services for civilian employment. To this end it was necessary for action to be taken, largely by the War Office and Treasury, so that remaining in, or joining, the armed services could be seen as an attractive career option. For the navy and the air force the problems of maintaining the requisite levels of recruitment were regarded as less severe.[5] Sir John Grigg at the War Office, writing to Sir John Anderson, Chancellor of the Exchequer, in February 1945, felt it unlikely that either of these services would 'find it difficult to fill their postwar complements'.[6]

The necessity to maintain a high military profile had not only political but also economic implications. In August 1945 John Maynard Keynes warned that the country faced 'a financial Dunkirk'.[7] In addition to financing the new welfare state, the Labour government elected in the summer of 1945 also wished to maintain Britain's international role as a major political power. Although it may have been prepared to negotiate a withdrawal from some areas such as India and Palestine, it was by no means prepared to relinquish all its colonies.[8] Overseas development, particularly in Africa, was viewed as a means of aiding the recovery of the British economy; but ensuring the security of these colonies required a military presence. In addition to these international concerns, the government was also faced with domestic pressures from a general population who expected that wartime sacrifices would now be rewarded by improved employment and housing conditions at the very least[9] – an expectation shared by those now preparing to leave the services.

In fact, the problem of presenting a career in the services as an attractive option was not new to the postwar era. In 1937 Leslie Hore-Belisha, Secretary of State for War, considered that the army was suffering in the eyes of potential recruits as 'its officers were too old'.[10] Retirement pay for army officers at the time was based on two elements – length of service and rank – and maximum retirement pay could not be attained unless a certain length of service had been achieved.[11] A major, for example, could attain maximum retirement pay only if he had achieved a total of 27 years of service, including ten years at the rank of major. Consequently, many officers were reluctant to retire before absolutely necessary as potential retired pay continued to increase as long as they were in service. Effectively, this created a predominance of older officers, blocking promotion routes and making the army unattractive for those wishing to pursue a career in the services.[12] Hore-Belisha's aim was to ensure that there were no serving officers in the army over the age of 55.[13] To achieve this, from August 1938 pensions were calculated by a combination of age and total length of service up to the rank of Colonel, after which a fixed rate applied for each rank.[14]

In 1945, however, the problems associated with retaining and recruiting career soldiers incorporated a much wider range of issues than just pension levels. As we have already seen, the well-being of families was a major concern for soldiers on active duty. However, improvements granted in the levels allowances mainly resulted from public interest in service families at any given time. In Chapters 1 and 2, we saw how the profile of service families had historically been raised by concerns over recruitment and conscription. In 1939 Hore-Belisha went as far as to suggest that the success of conscription would be 'made or marred' by the way in which the state treated the relatives of servicemen.[15] However, in peacetime, provision for service families had received little public attention, a fact recognised in 1944 by the Army Council which acknowledged that 'past consideration of allowances questions had been characterised by cycles of opinion'.[16] To retain and recruit personnel following the cessation of hostilities, this issue needed to be addressed, so that peacetime servicemen could be assured that, if their families were left behind while they served abroad, they would be adequately cared for. With the large numbers of servicemen who would regularly serve abroad in Germany and in parts of the Empire in the immediate postwar period, the matter now became one of some urgency. In this the Army Council felt that it was to some extent fighting a losing battle as 'the position would never be really satisfactory until there were some prospects of soldiers having their families with them'.[17]

In 1944 Fred Bellinger (Labour MP, Bassettlaw) had referred in the House of Commons to the 'chaotic maner [sic] . . . in which the Army settles its pay rates'.[18] This was an issue recognised by the War Office, which, even before the end of hostilities, had begun to discuss the need for a simplified code for pay and allowances for the postwar army.[19] As we have already seen, during the course of the war, many financial problems had resulted from a misunderstanding of regulations governing the admission and payment of allowances. As a consequence, by April 1945, there was an expectation within the services that a full-scale governmental review of pay and allowances was called for and, in the light of this, the War Office formed a committee specifically charged with the task of devising a new pay code, that was 'simple to understand and operate'.[20]

This Committee on the Postwar Emoluments of Army Officers established a number of general principles to be applied to any postwar pay code.[21] Firstly, the code should be simple and easy to operate. Secondly, there should be close parity between the emoluments payable to fighting men and those employed in technical work. As a result, both technical and military qualifications should count towards pay supplements.[22] In previous pay codes there had been a tendency for technical skills to be more highly prized in peacetime and military skills more in times of conflict. As a result of these recommendations, the Committee envisaged that any new pay code would apply equally to all service whether it was at home, on long-term overseas postings such as in Germany or the Dominions, or in times of war.[23] By establishing a 'universal' pay and allowances code, some of the problems encountered by dependants during the Second World War, such as delays in obtaining allowances and problems with their administration, would be removed.[24] In addition, any new pay code was envisaged as carrying with it the expectation of a guaranteed career progression to the age of 47, to encourage more men into the Army as a positive career move.[25]

At the same time, the Chancellor of the Exchequer, Sir John Anderson, established an Inter-departmental Committee on Postwar Pay, Allowances and Pensions in the Armed Services (the Bridges Committee), under the Chairmanship of Sir Edward Bridges, Secretary of State at the Treasury.[26] Starting from a similar standpoint to that of the War Office Committee, that existing arrangements for service pay and allowances were 'extremely complex', the Committee's first task was to have been to consider the gradual phasing out of special wartime considerations such as JCP and WSG.[27] However, with the sudden end of the war in the Far East which, as Sir Eric Speed, Joint Permanent Under-secretary of State for War, suggested, had 'taken us by surprise in many respects', the problems before the Committee became more urgent.[28] Sir Eric felt that unless new terms were proposed to the existing troops 'pretty

quickly', there 'wouldn't be any troops to put them before' as soldiers would have already been demobilised and returned to civilian
occupations.[29]

In addition to a review of pay and conditions of service, the
Bridges Committee also considered allowances made to wives and
dependants of servicemen.[30] Between 1938 and 1945 the total cost
of allowances had risen by 58 per cent in the navy and 63 per cent
in the air force with an increase in total expenditure on Family
Allowances of 213.5 per cent from £937,000 in 1938 to just under
£2 million in 1945.[31] Although these increases may appear substantial, a number of other factors need to be borne in mind. Firstly,
the size of the services had also increased dramatically during the
period of the war. The navy, for example, had seen a rise in personnel of over 300 per cent, while air force personnel had risen by
almost 400 per cent.[32] Effectively, then, families in both these services were probably worse off than they had been at the commencement of the war. The disadvantage to service families becomes
especially clear when the differential between the increases in their
allowances and the increases in civilian wages is taken into consideration. In the engineering and shipbuilding industries, average
weekly earnings for men over the age of 21 had increased by 76
per cent.[33] Although, as they were reserved occupations, few men
were likely to have been conscripted from these trades, making
comparisons not completely valid, men would, however, have been
conscripted from the food, drink and tobacco trades. Here increases
had been in the region of 70 per cent and men were more able to
make some comparison between the wages they earned as servicemen and those they would have earned in their normal, civilian
occupations.[34]

The Bridges Committee was asked to consider a number of specific issues in relation to allowances for the postwar services.[35]
Firstly, it was asked to examine the advantages and disadvantages
of paying both officers and men a salary or wage based on their
conditions of service without consideration of their marital status.
As an alternative, it was also requested to consider the implications
of continuing to pay servicemen higher emoluments as a direct
result of their marital status. Finally, it was asked to 'comment' on
the desirability of making marriage allowance subject to income
tax.[36] Although these considerations had implications for the
services with regard to recruitment into the armed forces, the

conflicting economic concerns of the Treasury can be seen through-out the discussions. Whilst on the one hand it was keen to create a pay and allowances structure which would present the armed forces as a viable career, on the other hand the economic implica-tions of increased pay and allowances continued to weigh heavily. Consequently, even when faced with direct comparisons with civil-ian wages, it persisted in regarding the increased levels of allow-ances as generous and as having come about 'as a result of special war conditions'.[37] In its view, the effects of these special conditions were not a satisfactory basis on which to establish postwar allowances.

These investigations also had political implications. The Chancellor had already outlined that one aim of the Committee was to simplify the pay and allowance structure and, where pos-sible, to apply the same conditions to all three services.[38] In addition he had called for a pay code that was more easily understandable not only by the men concerned but also by the general public. From 1942 onwards much discussion had arisen in reviews of service pay and allowances around the comparisons between levels of service and civilian pay. Both the government and the services regarded a great deal of this controversy as having been caused by the fact that, for the layman, any real comparison of the two systems was wellnigh impossible.[39] The vast range of allowances available to servicemen ranging from housing and fuel allowances through to allowances for children meant that the general public would not be able to translate service pay into a comparable civilian rate.

The first interim report of the Committee made it clear that, even within the services themselves, agreement on a common pay and allowance structure would not be an easy matter.[40] The main problem arose from a fundamental difference between the War Office on one hand and the Air Ministry and Admiralty on the other as to the basis for the new pay structure. The Air Ministry wished to retain its existing system whereby other ranks were divided into five major pay groups according to degree of technical knowledge and skill. The Admiralty had in operation at the time a complicated system whereby pay was supplemented by additions in respect of certain qualifications but was already investigating the possibility of moving to a system very close to that of the air force. The War Office, however, operated a system of different pay levels for four different trade groups together with a separate set of pay rates for non-tradesmen, i.e. fighting soldiers, up to the rank of sergeant. Above this rank, pay was only differentiated into that for tradesmen or non-tradesmen. Although the War Office was also considering changes to its existing code, what was proposed was a single pay code for tradesmen and non-tradesmen alike which would allow all soldiers to attain the highest level of pay, subject to qualifications and experience, regardless of whether their expertise lay in a trade or in military skill.

In fact the War Office proposals were already close to those the government had already outlined creating parity between fighting and technical skills as one means of helping to make the services a viable career option. However, the Admiralty and Royal Air Force could not be persuaded to agree. Their argument was that military skills could not be prized as highly as technical expertise under peacetime conditions, particularly as the latter normally entailed a long apprenticeship. This opinion was further supported by the assertion that prizing such technical skills was more in keeping with pay structure in civilian employment where skills gained through a long apprenticeship normally accrued higher rates of pay. The matter proved insoluble in Committee and was referred for ministerial decision.[41] However, when the White Paper was presented to Parliament in December 1945, it was noted that it still had not been possible to arrive at parity across the services in these matters although a 'close uniformity' had been attained.[42] Despite this professed 'uniformity', obvious differences were still clearly apparent, not least that the army and air force continued to refer to their allowances to married servicemen as 'Family Allowance' while the navy persisted with the term 'Marriage Allowance'.[43]

The second issue considered by the Committee was that of Children's Allowances.[44] One of the major anomalies of service allowances during the war period was that, unlike civilian families, service personnel actually benefited from having large families. Children's Allowances were normally paid to servicemen for each and every child in the family, a fact often quoted by civilian workers to help refute the claims that their wages were much greater than those of servicemen during the 1942 campaign for increases in service allowances.[45] Although the public regarded the system as unfairly rewarding servicemen for having large families, these payments had, in fact, been introduced as part of a series of measures to compensate older men with existing families for the drop in

remuneration they would inevitably experience as a result of conscription.[46] The government had always regarded these payments
as 'not suitable' to form part of a pay code after the end of the war
as they were at odds with the established principle of paying the
'rate for the job'.[47] Instead, it was envisaged that service Family
Allowances in respect of children would be brought into line with
Family Benefit available to civilian families. Under the 1943 Family
Allowances Act, child benefit of 5s per week would be paid for the
second and all subsequent children of all families, regardless of
whether civilian or service families. This allowance would be paid
direct to mothers and, for service families, was not dependent on
any prior contribution by the serviceman. All service families would
receive a Family Allowance at a standard rate of 35s per week,
excluding qualifying allotment, regardless of family size, replacing
earlier allowances, which differed in relation to number of children.[48] Based on the rates of allowances which had originally been
proposed for the postwar period, service families with one child
effectively lost 7s per week; those with two children lost 13s 7d;
those with three 19s 1d and those with four £1 5s 9d.[49]

An undated note from Sir Edward Bridges suggests that the
introduction of Family Allowances in this form would 'leave
responsibility for the maintenance of his family, [. . .], to the serviceman'.[50] Although this would have the effect of bringing service pay
and allowances more into line with civilian wages, it can also be
seen as a retrograde step in relation to the administration of service
allowances. As detailed in Chapter 1, before the First World War
the amount given by servicemen to their families had been left solely
to their own discretion and the campaign to force the state to accept
some responsibility for its soldiers' dependants had been long and
difficult. From the 1920s onwards the state reluctantly accepted
responsibility for the maintenance of these families through allowances for other ranks paid directly to the families concerned. As a
result, men who joined up to escape family responsibilities no
longer left families destitute. Now, although women would receive
Family Allowance direct, any additional financial provision for
their families was once again devolved to the serviceman.

Although for service families as a whole this was a retrograde
step, for the families of some categories of future prisoners of war
the decision of the state to pay national Family Allowance to service
families would have a potential benefit. As this allowance was paid

directly to wives, the wives of officers who were taken captive, and who, during the Second World War, had been unable to access their husbands' bank account, would in the future have an allowance paid directly to them. Although this allowance alone would not be sufficient to maintain a family in the absence of any other income, it did provide for a minimal constant income. In fact, the Bridges Committee also made further recommendations to address this particular problem by recommending that, during short peacetime separations and in times of war, payment of allowances should continue to be made directly to the wives of other ranks.[51] A similar recommendation that, in time of war only, allowances should be paid direct to the wives of officers resulted in considerable discussion across the services and, despite the fact that both the Treasury and War Office were in agreement that payments should be made in this way, the matter remained unresolved.[52]

In December 1950 this discussion was reopened: at this time all parties concerned agreed that, although cases of hardship might occur where the officer was posted abroad at short notice, allowances should remain payable to the officer rather than his family unless he elected otherwise.[53] To change this policy was regarded as running the risk of appearing to doubt the officer's integrity, and cases where the officer deliberately failed to make provision were regarded as being 'very rare'.[54] As, however, the services continued not to place any emphasis on preparing either men or officers for a time when they might be taken captive it seems unlikely that officers would place any priority on making arrangements for such an eventuality. Consequently, their families might still find themselves with no way of accessing funds. However, the Army Council continued to insist that

> It was of paramount importance that officers should be treated as officers despite any administrative difficulties which might arise. It was also wrong to change the practice of previous wars merely because a small minority of officers had evaded their domestic responsibilities.[55]

Thus, the service authorities reduced the plight of families facing possible destitution to a mere 'administrative difficulty'.[56]

In addition to these questions on the administration of Family Allowances in time of war, the Committee also brought to light two further issues, which had proved problematic for the administration of allowances in 1939. These issues were to be investigated by a Technical Sub-committee on Financial Concessions Received by Service Personnel – the Wilson-Smith Sub-committee.[57] Firstly, the Committee requested guidance on the issue of qualifying age for Marriage Allowance.[58] At the start of the Second World War, as a result of the conscription of young married men, it was eventually agreed that all married servicemen would be eligible for Marriage Allowance regardless of age. Before this date the policy for career soldiers had largely been governed by the policy that 'junior officers and short service other ranks were required as far as possible to be unmarried'.[59] Initially the Army Council now agreed that eligibility for Marriage Allowance should begin at the age of 23 for other ranks and 'about 25 or 26' for officers based on the rationale that, by this age, most servicemen would have completed their first overseas tour of duty.[60]

However, as the Working Party pointed out, in any postwar conscript army there were bound to be a number of younger married men and, from a political standpoint, it would be inadvisable to deny allowances to their families. This point is aptly illustrated by the case of a young man from Maling in Kent who married at the age of 19 and was subsequently called up for national service.[61] Before his call-up, the man had been earning in the region of £4 per week but, on entering the services, he was ineligible for Family Allowance because of his age. As a result, his pregnant wife was left 'absolutely penniless'.[62] This particular case was brought to the attention of SSAFA, which subsequently passed the following resolution at its 1946 Branch Conference: 'We strongly recommend to the Service Authorities that payment of marriage allowance shall be made to the wife of any serving soldier, sailor or airman irrespective of age.'[63]

The Bridges Committee was also aware that, if the government was determined to pursue a policy of increasing birth rate, it would be impossible to regard marriage 'solely from the aspect of military efficiency and administrative convenience'.[64] To achieve the desired outcomes of government in relation to birth policy, the dictates of military efficiency and the economic concerns of the Treasury, a compromise would have to be reached. In the event the War Office 'reluctantly agreed' that any new allowance system would have to be drawn up on the assumption that all marriages of both officers and men would be officially recognised for allowances.[65]

Although the subject of a qualifying age for Marriage Allowance then disappears from the sources, it does not seem to have been settled for once and for all. In 1968 the army was not recruiting married men or granting Marriage Allowance to other ranks under the age of 21 or officers under the age of 25, suggesting that 'officers who marry at say 20 are unlikely ever to learn their jobs properly'.[66] However, it was, apparently, under some pressure to change its thinking on this matter. Major-General H.E.N. Bredin, Director of Volunteers, Territorials and Cadets at the Ministry of Defence, felt that, as neither the air force nor the navy applied such restrictions, the army was 'being dragged at the chariot wheels of the other two services'.[67] In what appears to be a change from the 1945 position on recruitment, he also suggests that if the army was doing this 'to scrape up a few more recruits' then 'it was doubly wrong'.[68] By 1968 the pressure on the government to maintain an Imperial presence in diverse areas of the world had, presumably, decreased and it could afford to consider the prospect of a smaller army to meet decreased demands. A new line of argument was also introduced at this stage suggesting that it was not actually legal to forbid anyone to marry and that soldiers of any age could not, in fact, be prevented from marrying if they so wished.[69] Presumably, however, the argument was not whether or not soldiers could be forbidden to marry but whether or not they should be granted Marriage Allowances if they later married in defiance of the conditions of service that they had agreed to abide by when enlisting.

The second problematic issue faced by the Bridges Committee was the recurring problem of allowances for 'unmarried' wives.[70] As we have already seen, throughout the late 1930s and early 1940s problems occurred where servicemen claimed Family Allowance in respect of women whom they were living with but not married to. Although the services were reluctant to make allowances to these women, the whole rationale for the granting of allowances was predicated on the assumption that they would be used to maintain the serviceman's home against his return. If, therefore, a serviceman had set up home with a woman to whom he was not married, this home would, nevertheless, be the one to which he would return and which should be maintained. Although a compromise position had been reached in cases where legal and 'unmarried' wives made competing claims, no satisfactory general ruling had been agreed. Now the War Office made a recommendation designed to settle the matter once and for all by suggesting that:

> All officers and soldiers who are married, whether estranged from their families or not, should be entitled to a family allowance in respect of their wives, subject to liability to make a prescribed contribution to the family in the event of separation; that officers and soldiers should be entitled to an allowance in respect of their divorced wives only to the extent that they can prove they are legally liable to support such wives, and subject to the further conditions that the wife's allowance should be payable; and that they should be entitled to family allowance in respect of their and their wife's legitimate children, and any other children living in their home unless the children are maintained without expense to the officer or man (e.g. in an institution).[71]

The Executive Committee of the Army Council endorsed this view, stating that Family Allowance should be payable to all officers and men with families 'whatever their situation *vis-a-vis* their families' and, as a result, Special Dependants' Allowances for 'unmarried' wives were abolished.[72]

Finally, the Bridges Committee turned its attention to whether or not service allowances should be made subject to income tax.[73] This discussion hinged on two main issues: whether for civilian workers all additions were subject to income tax and whether or not allowances could be counted as additions to pay. Within the services themselves, and especially in the air force, exemption from tax on Family Allowance was regarded as part compensation for long periods of separation from families. As a consequence the UAB, which was fully involved in these discussions, felt that to begin taxing such allowances would cause greater resentment than any other part of the new tax code.[74] The War Office, again mindful of possible effects on recruitment, was also against the introduction of this tax.[75] However, although this argument continued to inform many discussions on postwar pay and allowances, its actual validity must be open to question. A confidential letter from the RAF Technical Training Headquarters in Huntingdon to the Air Ministry asserted that 'A very large proportion of the airmen now serving are completely disinterested in the new pay proposals, as they only have one aim in view – to complete their RAF service as soon as possible and return to occupations in civilian life'.[76] In the event, Family Allowance across all three services became taxable from 1 April 1947.[77]

Three other forms of payment to servicemen and their families during the war also came under general consideration at this time. Dependants' Allowances, which had been introduced as a result of conscription in 1939, were now regarded by the Treasury as being 'inappropriate as part of a peacetime code of pay and allowances'.[78] As such they were discontinued for the dependants of all recruits after 1 January 1946.[79] No discussion has come to light regarding the possibility of allowances for men called up for national service although a number of families must have faced the same issues that resulted in the granting of these allowances in 1939. Similarly, despite the professed War Office intent of devising a code of pay and allowances equally applicable in times of both war and peace, there is no mention of how dependants were to be provided for in the event of a future war. However, in both cases, the advent of National Assistance may have alleviated the need to formulate specific policy. War Service Grant, which had been made to families of conscripted men to offset hardship resulting from loss of income following compulsory service, was also deemed inapplicable to new recruits. Grants already in existence were reviewed following the introduction of the new Pay Code in July 1946 and then again in July 1947.[80] Japanese Campaign Pay, for example, introduced in November 1944, was continued up to the first anniversary of VJ Day in August 1946 and then ended.[81]

Overall, the new rates of pay and allowances suggested in the White Paper were estimated to show a 61 per cent increase in costs from the 1938 level (see Table 4).[82] These figures are, however,

Table 4: Changes in total amounts payable in service allowances 1938–46, based on 1938 strength

	Army	Navy	Air force	Overall
1938 Rate	11,473,000	11,279,500	6,511,000	29,263,500
Postwar	19,308,000	17,842,000	9,789,000	47,025,000
Per cent increase	69	58	50	61

Source: Figures taken from Inter-departmental Committee on Postwar Pay and Allowances. NA/WO32/11565.

based on the strength of the services in 1938, and the White Paper does point out that the figures do not 'enable accurate conclusions to be drawn' because of unknown factors such as the comparative ages and ranks of servicemen before and after the war.[83]

It is difficult to imagine just what the Committee hoped to gain by presenting these figures. In terms of estimating future expenditure they were, by the Committee's own admission, of limited use. Not only was the future constituency of the services in terms of age, marital status and rank unknown, but also no adjustments had been made for the greatly increased size of the services as a whole – a factor that was likely to be perpetuated in the postwar era. If the figures were designed to demonstrate a generous increase in service allowances during the period of the war, they are misleading as they make no mention of the fact that these increases barely kept pace with increases in the cost of living during the same period.[84] Finally, although the White Paper on Postwar Pay and Allowances made it clear that these new rates of pay would be 'subject to review from time to time', it was also made clear that such reviews would take place only in the event of a 'marked alteration in circumstances'.[85] No suggestion was made that pay and allowances should be linked to the Cost of Living Index. In addition no changes were proposed to the way in which service pay and allowances were negotiated. All discussion of changes still had to be negotiated through the floor of the House of Commons – a time-consuming practice at best and directly at odds with the rationale of bringing conditions surrounding service pay more in line with that of civilian workers.

In fact, by mid-1946 the Ministry of Defence was already expressing doubts as to whether or not married men, especially those with families to maintain, would be able to cover their expenses within the existing rates of Family Allowance.[86] The War Office expressed similar concerns although, in its case, concern was more directed towards possible effects on recruiting levels than towards the welfare of the families involved.[87] As a result a sub-committee of the Bridges Committee, the Wilson-Smith Sub-committee, proposed a range of increases to allowances ranging from 3s for a Leading Seaman, Corporal or other rank below age 25 to 15s for a Warrant Officer.[88] The Treasury also focused on the possible repercussions for recruitment rather than the welfare of the families.[89] Its argument was that recruitment was more likely to be affected by the fact that men had already been separated from their families for long periods of time. As a consequence, men now sought employment that would enable them to stay at home, regardless of comparative rates of remuneration. In their view, therefore, increasing rates of pay would not solve the recruitment problem and the thorny question of service pay would have been reopened to no good effect. With the cessation of hostilities, service families had once again lost their high public and political profile. Increases in service pay and allowances would now be regarded purely in the light of comparative civilian employment rather than as a reward for service to king and country.

In addition to the immediate financial considerations of pay and allowances, all three services also began to review their overall welfare provision for service families. As with new pay regulations, one of the underpinning concerns was to attempt to standardise, and possibly amalgamate, provision across all three services.[90] A report of May 1946 from the Committee on the Organisation of Common Services, established specifically to investigate this matter, agreed that provision generally fell into two areas.[91] Firstly, each service, and particularly the commanding officer in each case, was regarded as being directly responsible for the welfare of men and women under his command. However, with the introduction of National Service and continuing high numbers of personnel in the services, it was noted by the War Office that the traditional role of the Regimental Officers in this respect was becoming impossible.[92] The sheer weight of numbers involved meant that it was no longer feasible for every Regimental Officer to have detailed knowledge of every man under his command in terms of personality, career and family matters.[93] Many Regimental Officers, themselves recruited during the war, did not have the knowledge and had not had the time to gain the experience of welfare matters acquired by long-term career officers before the war.[94] All three services clearly felt that the traditional role of commanding officer as 'guide, philosopher and friend' had been eroded.[95] However, as large numbers of army personnel, at least, would remain overseas for some time, it was necessary to establish and maintain channels for dealing with personal and family problems.

The nature of the required provision had also changed during the course of the war. Before 1939 service welfare had largely concerned itself with the needs of the soldier as most had either been unmarried or had had their families with them. During the war, however, a large number of men who were already married were drafted into the services. This, together with the separation of families as a consequence of the war, had resulted in both the army and air force welfare services beginning to deal with the welfare of the families concerned. The Committee on the Organisation of Common Services, in a meeting in June 1946, reported on the 'considerable development' of this family welfare in response to the special needs of 'citizen forces', who had left families behind them.[96] It is, however, difficult to ascertain exactly where and how this 'considerable development' had taken place, and charitable organisations, such as SSAFA, continued to play a crucial part in the well-being of service families. In the navy the picture was slightly different.[97] In theory at least, the existence of families in overseas naval bases before the war meant that Welfare Officers already existed to deal with family problems. In reality, most welfare outside of ships was, as in the cases of the army and air force, conducted through SSAFA or other voluntary organisations whose work was regarded as both 'invaluable' and 'of an unfailingly high standard'.[98]

Partly as a result of this existing provision, all three services agreed that family welfare should continue to be the province of voluntary organisations and that a common policy should be established for dealing with these organisations.[99] However, with the ending of hostilities the voluntary organisations were also beginning to limit their activities. From 1946 onwards SSAFA began gradually to close its overseas bureaux that had served the Navy so well, although one representative was retained in each major overseas command.[100] For SSAFA the major problem, both in Britain and overseas, was one of diminishing funds.[101] The ending of the war meant that the welfare of service families once again ceased to be a matter of national concern and donations began to fall. Although the Association was invited to administer the balance of the Queen's Canadian Fund, which has been replenished by the Queen up to the present day, donations fell sharply after the war.[102] In 1948 donations totalled £127,547; by 1949 they had fallen to £94,573, contributing to a cumulative overspend of £184,212 and to the Association beginning to reconsider its role in postwar service welfare.[103]

The Branch Conference in October 1945 had already heard a report from the Chairman on the widely held belief that the work carried out during the war by SSAFA 'should now be a government concern undertaken by a government department'.[104] Indeed, for many servicemen, this seemed a logical extension of the way in which the government had directed every part of their lives, and those of their families, during the war years. SSAFA, however, did not agree. The Committee saw its independent status as a guarantee of its ability to petition all government departments – a freedom it did not believe would be open to a governmentally funded and administered agency.[105] It also believed that its independence made it the best-equipped organisation to support and campaign for 'special cases'.[106] The experience of the Second World War had shown that it was almost impossible to legislate for all possible family circumstances in relation to allowances, and an independent body willing to support those who had fallen outside the normal pattern had proved essential. SSAFA's last argument for its welfare work to remain independent of government is, however, rather more contentious. The Committee argued for continued independence on the grounds of the expense that would be incurred if this work were to be taken over by a government department.[107] Although SSAFA had not been directly instrumental in encouraging the state to accept its responsibility for the welfare of service families, to argue that the financial burden for this welfare should be now be taken back by charitable organisations as a money-saving measure seems a dangerous political argument.

While questions of future pay, allowances and welfare in the services occupied much of the thinking of the War Office, Air Ministry and Admiralty, for returning servicemen and especially for returning prisoner of war and their families there were often more immediate concerns. As we have already seen, by March 1945, 150,000 British servicemen were being held prisoner in both Europe and the Far East. The numbers of men held captive and the length of time they had been held are shown in Table 5. The War Office considered that all men who had been held captive for longer than four years, the majority of those who had been held for over three years and 20 per cent of those who had been held for less than this period would require some degree of mental rehabilitation on their release. A total of some 71,000 men would, therefore, need support of some kind to facilitate their reintegration into civilian life. In fact the War Office had been considering this question since October 1944 but, as had been the case with information and allowances for prisoner of war families, no coherent policy was formulated.[108]

Table 5: Number of prisoners of war and length of captivity

Duration of captivity	Held in Europe	Held in Far East	Total
Less than 1 year	9,000	2,000	11,000
Over 1 year	94,000	45,000	139,000
Over 2 years	92,000	45,000	137,000
Over 3 years	58,000	45,000	103,000

Source: NA/WO32/11129.

Some within the War Office suggested that families should be sent a letter, possibly written by a repatriated prisoner of war, giving advice based on personal experience. Others felt that this might be seen as 'interfering in private lives' and wished to avoid any suggestion that former prisoners of war were 'peculiar' or would 'require humouring by their relatives'.[109] In the event, although a pamphlet was distributed to all British Commonwealth personnel awaiting repatriation from prisoner of war camps in Germany, no specific advice was given to relatives beyond suggesting that personal or domestic problems could be referred to an Army Welfare Officer, SSAFA, CAB or BRC.[110] In many cases specific arrangements were left to local groups who, as was the case for the Huddersfield Prisoner of War Committee, often appeared to consider their duties discharged or felt unqualified to assist further once the serviceman had been welcomed home. Perhaps more appropriate, but similarly uncoordinated, was the assistance provided by regiments such as the Cambridge and Isle of Ely Territorial Association, who regarded the provision of 'a friend from whom to seek advice' as a natural extension of the care which regiments offered to their servicemen and their families.[111]

The problems faced by returning prisoners of war and indeed servicemen in general, have been widely investigated in many studies from the 1940s to the present day.[112] For many, fears held during their absence, and recorded through the Army Morale Reports, of the infidelity of wives, in contemporary parlance 'drifting', proved only too real.[113] Vivienne Chatfield, in her unpublished biography, notes that 'there were many unpleasant shocks for returning prisoners from the Far East. Many wives had remarried when their husbands were missing and others were living with other men.'[114] By late 1945 the national divorce rate had risen 250 per cent on the 1939 figure and, in contrast with the prewar picture where most divorce petitions had been brought by wives, most petitions in that year were brought by husbands on the grounds of adultery.[115] Generally, women's magazines of the war period had advised women who had been unfaithful to wait until their husbands came home and 'were not taken up with the business of fighting for life' before breaking the news.[116] Consequently, many men were deprived of the support of their partners at the same time as having to adjust to civilian life. For wives who had become pregnant, the advice was to 'tell him the truth and ask his forgiveness' and figures seem to suggest that a significant number of returning service men may have been faced with this 'truth'.[117] In 1945 illegitimate births made up 9.1 per cent of all total births, and a survey conducted in Birmingham in 1944–45 showed that 18 per cent of all illegitimate children in this area had been born to servicemen's wives.[118]

Even for those not faced with evidence of their wives' infidelity, readjusting to home and family life often proved problematic. Many men who had been taken prisoner were changed by their experiences, some irrevocably, although few can have changed to the extent of Celia Mitchell's prisoner of war husband in *The Captive Heart* who returned, quite literally, a different man.[119] Similarly, many prisoners of war and their wives had changed in ways that called for long periods of adjustment. Many women had experienced taking complete responsibility for their families and working outside the home, perhaps for the first time. For both parties, the reality of their reunion often failed to live up to their expectations. Turner and Rennell cite the case of a returning prisoner of war who had been in a prison hospital for nearly four years.[120] All through his time in hospital he had imagined his wife and family in their home, as he had left them. In reality the wife had had to leave her home and put the children into a nursery so that she could take a part-time factory job to make ends meet. She, in turn, had dreamt of her husband returning and taking all the cares from her shoulders. Inevitably their reunion was a disappointment for both parties and they subsequently divorced.[121]

This example also serves to highlight the problems faced by servicemen coming home to Britain and to a civilian population that had also suffered deprivation and hardship. Reese, in

Homecoming Heroes, suggests that the general public in Britain was less likely to be 'generous' to returning prisoners of war than in the USA and Canada because, although 'no doubt many prisoners of war had suffered terribly, so had Mrs Jones'.[122] To prepare returning prisoners of war for this eventuality, the DPW in September 1944 had suggested they should be provided with information on conditions at home before they were actually repatriated.[123] This information was to include: the part played by industry 'so that he learns to appreciate the civilian workman's point of view'; the work of the Home Guard 'so that he appreciates the civilian's point of view'; the part played by women 'so that he appreciates the women's point of view'; accommodation problems 'so that he does not imagine that his difficulties are unique'; and wartime restrictions such as coupons and rationing 'so as to give him a balanced picture of England in wartime'.[124] No information has been located to suggest that this recommendation was acted on and, as a result, both returning servicemen and their families often felt that they were not accorded the recognition of their suffering they believed they deserved, thereby making readjustment that much harder. In contrast to the British attitude, Canadian former prisoners of war and civilians alike were issued with a pamphlet of almost 40 pages, *Back to Civil Life*, giving general information on repatriation issues.[125] This pamphlet proved so popular that by August 1945 it was already in its second edition.[126]

Servicemen had also changed in ways not directly engendered by their experience of combat or imprisonment. Army education, begun with the objective of motivating troops and alleviating boredom, had also taken on the task of educating servicemen to be better informed on current affairs and more responsible citizens.[127] As a result, demobilised servicemen had gained not only in maturity and experience during the course of the war but also in political awareness. For many, returning to their prewar employment only led to frustration and restlessness;[128] a situation worsened by the failure of the Government Training Scheme which, from the outset, was problematic in that it required mature experienced servicemen to undergo an 'apprenticeship' which many felt to be humiliating.[129] Even for those who did qualify in a trade, employment was often hard to come by, especially within the building trade. An official report of 1948 on ex-service employment reported that the

Government Training Scheme had failed 'because they have trained men in such trades as plastering and bricklaying and now there was no work for them'.[130]

Many of the sources dealing with repatriation issues, however, rely largely on evidence from the returning servicemen themselves or the memories of their children. There is little direct testimony from the wives of returning prisoners of war regarding their own readjustment. Many speak of 'just doing what any loving mother would do' and 'keeping the home together for when they came home' but, by and large, their own support networks of prisoner of war committees and relatives' associations ended with the return of their husbands and sons.[131] Although the Barnsley Prisoner of War Fund continues to operate to the present day, what evidence is available suggests that many more local committees followed the example of the Huddersfield Committee and wound up their affairs following the repatriation of local prisoners of war.

For some families, however, there was neither the joy occasioned by the return of family members nor the comfort provided by the gifts and thoughts of local support groups. Following the general repatriation of prisoners of war, a number of men who, although they were 'not missing in the proper sense of the word', failed to return home.[132] From the army, eight officers and 362 other ranks apparently chose not to return, whilst seven men from both the navy and the air force remained unaccounted for.[133] Of the sailors who did not return, at least three had married foreign nationals and were awaiting permission to bring their wives home to Britain.[134] It would seem reasonable to assume that such cases also existed within the other branches of the services, although no direct evidence for this has been located. However, there can be no doubt that some men, although they had survived captivity, chose not to return to their families in Britain. For example, Leading-Stoker T.H. Barker, who was captured after the loss of S/M *Saracen* in August 1943, was known to have been released from captivity in Italy but failed to return to his family in Britain or to make contact with them in any way.[135] Richard Lamb records that, when the war ended, more than two thousand prisoners of war were missing, a proportion of whom were 'living happily with Italian families and did not want to return to their homeland'.[136] Similarly, Ministry of Pensions files contain a number of case studies of men who had disappeared at the end of the war, some of whom were known to have 'made arrangements to meet other women' in France and India.[137]

In all such cases the Interdepartmental Prisoner of War Co-ordinating Committee (Finance) decided that allowances should continue only for thirteen weeks after commanders from the various locations reported that there were no prisoners of war remaining in their area 'so far as they could trace'.[138] When questioned by the Air Ministry as to why these allowances were not continued for the more normal 26-week period, the Chairman of the Committee replied that this was accepted as an 'appropriate' length of time for families to 'reasonably adjust their standard of living'.[139] For the families of all those who had been held captive in Europe, this decision was implemented by October 1945 – the date by which the War Office considered that all former prisoners of war had had sufficient time to contact some authority representing the British government.[140] In all, a total of 381 families were accorded a scant thirteen weeks to come to terms with the fact that their loved ones had chosen not to return to them and to adjust their lives accordingly. For the Treasury this decision resulted in a saving in the region of £9,000 – a minuscule amount in an overall expenditure on service allowances which was in excess of £42 million.[141]

What this decision suggests is that, despite the professed intention of the War Office, in particular, to attempt to promote the army as an attractive postwar career option, other factors militated against this. Following the 1945 election, Hugh Dalton, as Chancellor of the Exchequer, inherited major economic problems.[142] Britain's exports stood at only 46 per cent of their 1938 level, largely as a result of the diversion of resources into war production, and the country's liabilities had risen to £3,500 million.[143] Not surprisingly, the Treasury was keen to economise wherever and whenever possible resulting in a conflict between the aims of maintaining Britain as a major military presence overseas and concentrating all possible resources on rebuilding the national economy.

For service families this tension often resulted in allowances that continued to be issued at levels below that necessary to maintain an adequate standard of living. Five years after the end of the Second World War, Ellen Porter, the wife of a rifleman in the Royal Enniskillen Fusiliers, was still struggling to keep her family on a meagre service allowance.[144] Her husband, who had been held captive in Germany for five years during the Second World War, was recalled for service in Korea in August 1950 with just 21 days of his time as a reservist left. Mrs Porter received an allowance of just £2 12s 6d for herself and two small children, which she supplemented by working. When her third child was born handicapped in May 1951, she was no longer able to work and had to support the whole family on just £3 10s per week.[145]

What Mrs Porter's case suggests is that the problems associated with service allowances apparent throughout the whole of the Second World War were not addressed by the subsequent postwar strategy. Despite the professed intent of the War Office, Admiralty and Air Ministry to simplify allowances and to make the services an attractive postwar career, overall economic factors linked to postwar reconstruction militated against this. Coupled with a lowering in the public profile of service families once hostilities had ended, these factors led to a continuation of allowances at a level barely above that sufficient to ensure survival which persisted up to the outbreak of war in Korea. Although Ferguson and Fitzgerald, in their official history of the Second World War volume on the social services, claim that the war 'brought about a remarkable development of the Welfare organisations of all three Services' they cite no specific examples of this development.[146] In the light of the continued problems of service families demonstrated in this chapter, it is difficult to see how such a claim can be justified.

Notes

1   Reports of the War Office Morale Committee. NA/WO32/15772.
2   Report of the War Office Morale Committee. March–May 1945. NA/WO32/15772.
3   Report of the War Office Morale Committee. September–Nov. 1945. NA/WO32/15772.
4   In 1938 the British armed forces had actually been slightly larger than those of the USA at 381,000 and 323,000 respectively. By 1945 the balance had been reversed with USA figures standing at 12,123,00 against a British figure of 4,682,000. Warner G., 'The Impact of the Second World War upon British Foreign Policy' in Brivati, B., and Jones, H. (eds), *What Difference Did the War Make?* London and New York: Leicester University Press, 1995.

5 Letter Sir John Grigg, Permanent Under-secretary of State, War Office, to Sir John Anderson, Chancellor of the Exchequer. 19 February 45. NA/WO32/11981[4A].

6 Letter Sir John Grigg, Permanent Under-secretary of State, War Office, to Sir John Anderson, Chancellor of the Exchequer. 19 February 45. NA/WO32/11981[4A].

7 Taylor, A.J.P., *English History 1914–1945.* Oxford and New York: Oxford University Press. 1975 edition. p. 599.

8 Taylor, *English History 1914–1945.* p. 599.

9 Pugh, *State and Society.* p. 235.

10 Memo, Leslie Hore-Belisha, Secretary of State for War. 30 August 37. NA/T162/524/35479.

11 Memo, Leslie Hore-Belisha, Secretary of State for War. 30 August 37. NA/T162/524/35479.

12 In the navy, officers could already achieve maximum pension much more quickly.

13 Memo, Leslie Hore-Belisha, Secretary of State for War. 30 August 37. NA/T162/524/35479. In his proposals, Hore-Belisha seems to have ignored those at the rank of Field Marshal who, a pencilled marginal note from the Treasury suggests, 'presumably serve until they drop'.

14 Memo, Leslie Hore-Belisha, Secretary of State for War. 30 August 37. NA/T162/524/35479.

15 Minutes of Conference of Ministers. 16 July 39. NA/T162/573/E38866/01.

16 Minutes of the 149th Meeting of the Executive Committee of the Army Council. 18 February 44. NA/WO32/9822[12A].

17 War Office Morale Report. November 1945–April 1946. NA/WO32/15772[92A].

18 Debate in the House of Commons. 02 March 44. NA/WO32/10448.

19 See, for example Minute Sheet 1. 08 February 45. NA/WO32/11981, and Directors Conference on Postwar Emoluments of Army Officers. 17 January 45. NA/WO32/11186.

20 Report of the Committee on the Postwar Emoluments of Army Officers. 13 June 45. NA/WO32/11186.

21 Report of the Committee on Postwar Emoluments of Army Offices. 13 June 45. NA/WO32/11186.

22 Consideration of General Principles. Director's Conference on Post-war Emoluments of Army Officers. 22 February 45. NA/WO32/11186.

23 Report of the Committee on Postwar Emoluments of Army Offices. 13 June 45. NA/WO32/11186.

24 Brief for Meeting on Service Pay. 26 April 45. NA/T213/7/DP611/37/06.

25 Committee on the Postwar Emoluments of Army Officers. April 1945. NA/WO32/11186.

26 Inter-departmental Committee on Postwar Allowances and Pensions of the Armed Forces (Bridges Committee). April 1945. NA/T213/7/DP611/37/06.

27 Letter Sir John Anderson, Chancellor of the Exchequer, to War Office. 02 February 45. Referred to in Brief for the First Meeting of the Inter-departmental Committee on Postwar Allowances etc. and in White Paper 'Postwar Code of Pay & Allowances' NA/T213/DP611/37/06.

28 Letter Sir Eric Speed, War Office, to Sir Edward Bridges, Treasury. 17 August 45. NA/T213/DP611/37/06.

29 Letter Sir Eric Speed, War Office, to Sir Edward Bridges, Treasury. 17 August 45. NA/T213/DP611/37/06.

30 Brief for meeting on Service Pay. 26 April 45. NA/T213/7/DP611/37/06.

31 Figures based on 1932 distribution of personnel across ranks and on a 1936 figure assuming that 23 per cent of all servicemen would be married. NA/T2113/4/DP43/09.

32 Central Statistical Office, *Fighting with Figures*. Table 3.4 Strength of the Armed Forces and Women's Auxiliary Services. p. 39.

33 Most of the increase in the Cost of Living Index had, in fact, taken place between 1939 and 1941; following that time the Index remained relatively stable for the rest of the period of the war. Figures taken from Tables 12.3 Average weekly earnings in manufacturing and certain other industries and 12.6 Wage rates and cost of living. Central Statistical Office, *Fighting with Figures*. pp. 236 and 237.

34 Table 12.5 Average Weekly Earnings in Certain Industries. Central Statistical Office, *Fighting with Figures*. p. 237.

35 General Points for Consideration. Bridges Committee. April 45. NA/T213/7/DP611/37/06.

36 Before the war only naval officers' Marriage Allowances had been subject to tax. NA/T213/4/DP43/09.

37 White Paper 'Postwar Code of Pay, Allowances and Service Pensions and Gratuities for Members of the Forces below Officer Rank'. December 1945. NA/WO32/11565/7A. A further copy of this White Paper can also be found in WO32/11981/29A.

38 Brief for meeting of the Bridges Committee. 26 April 45. NA/T213/7/DP611/37/06.

39 White Paper 'Postwar Code of Pay, Allowances and Service Pensions and Gratuities for Members of the Armed Forces below Officer Rank'. December 45. NA/WO32/11565[7A]. A copy of this White Paper is also present in NA/WO32/11981[29A].

40 First Interim Report of the Bridges Committee. 20 June 45. NA/ T213/7/DP611/37/06.

41 First Interim Report of the Bridges Committee. 20 June 45. NA/ T213/7/DP611/37/06.

42 White Paper 'Postwar Code of Pay, Allowances and Service Pensions and Gratuities for Members of the Forces below Officer Rank'. December 1945. NA/WO32/11565[7A].

43 White Paper 'Postwar Code of Pay, Allowances and Service Pensions and Gratuities for Members of the Forces below Officer Rank'. December 1945. NA/WO32/11565[7A].

44 General Points for Consideration. Bridges Committee. April 45. NA/ T213/7/DP611/37/06.

45 Sir Edward Bridges, Secretary of State for War. 01 January 42. NA/ T162/646/E44411/1.

46 Draft broadcast by the First Lord of the Admiralty. 20 December 44. NA/T162/801/E45396/01/2.

47 Draft broadcast by the First Lord of the Admiralty. 20 December 44. NA/T162/801/E45396/01/2.

48 White Paper 'Postwar Code of Pay, Allowances and Service Pensions and Gratuities for Members of the Forces below Officer Rank'. December 45. T213/7/DP611/37/06.

49 Calculated on proposed figures for postwar allowances. NA/ T162/692/45396/1.

50 Note from Sir Edward Bridges. Undated but probably around June 1945. NA/WO32/11565.

51 Principles Governing Service Emoluments in Respect of Dependants. Item 3, Payment of Marriage Allowance in Time of War. Undated, but probably early December 1945. NA/WO32/11598.

52 Principles Governing Service Emoluments in Respect of Dependants. Item 3, Payment of Marriage Allowance in Time of War. Undated, but probably early December 1945. NA/WO32/11598.

53 Executive Committee of the Army Council. Payment of Marriage Allowance in Times of War. 28 December 50. NA/WO32/11598[38A].

54 Executive Committee of the Army Council. Payment of Marriage Allowance in Times of War. 28 December 50. NA/WO32/11598[38A].

55 Extract from the Minutes of the 363rd Meeting of the Executive Committee of the Army Council. Item 3, Payment of Marriage Allowance in Time of War. 05 January 51. NA/WO32/11598.

56 Extract from the Minutes of the 363rd Meeting of the Executive Committee of the Army Council. Item 3, Payment of Marriage Allowance in Time of War. 05 January 51. NA/WO32/11598.

57 Interim Report of the Technical Sub-committee on Financial Concessions received by Service Personnel (Wilson-Smith Sub-committee). January 1945. NA/WO32/10972.

58 Interim Report of the Technical Sub-committee on Financial Concessions received by Service Personnel (Wilson-Smith Sub-committee). January 1945. NA/WO32/10972.

59 Interim Report of the Wilson-Smith Sub-committee. January 1945. NA/WO32/10972.

60 Report of the Executive Committee of the Army Council. Undated, but probably December 1945. NA/WO32/11598/7. See also Draft regulations for Postwar Allowances (1946–49). NA/WO32/119984.

61 SSAFA Branch Conference 09 and 10 October 46. p. 11. SSAFA Archive.

62 SSAFA Branch Conference 09 and 10 October 46. p. 11. SSAFA Archive.

63 SSAFA Branch Conference 09 and 10 October 46. p. 11. SSAFA Archive.

64 SSAFA Branch Conference 09 and 10 October 46. p. 11. SSAFA Archive.

65 Brief for Meeting on Service Pay and Allowances. 26 April 45. NA/T213/7/DP611/37/06.

66 Letter Major-General H.E.N. Bredin, Director of Volunteers, Territorials and Cadets, Ministry of Defence, to Major-General D.A. Beckett. 30 December 68. NA/WO32/14364.

67 Letter Major-General H.E.N. Bredin, Director of Volunteers, Territorials and Cadets, Ministry of Defence, to Major-General D.A. Beckett. 30 December 68. NA/WO32/14364.

68 Letter Major-General H.E.N. Bredin, Director of Volunteers, Territorials and Cadets, Ministry of Defence, to Major-General D.A. Beckett. 30 December 68. NA/WO32/14364.

69 Note re Under Age Marriage. 09 October 68. NA/WO32/14364.

70 Draft Regulations, Postwar Allowances. 01 January 46. NA/WO32/119984.

71 Report of the War Office Working Party on Married Allowances. 07 August 45. NA/WO32/11598/16A.

72 Executive Committee of the Army Council, Committee on the Simplification of Allowances. 15 November 45. NA/WO32/11598.

73 General Points for Consideration. Bridges Committee. April 45. NA/T213/7/DP611/37/06.

74 Unsigned letter, UAB to Treasury. 18 February 46. NA/T213/4/DP43/09.

75 Unsigned letter, UAB to Treasury. 18 February 46. NA/T213/4/DP43/09.

76 Letter marked 'confidential'. RAF Technical Training Command HQ, Huntingdon (signature indecipherable), to Group Captain G.H. White, Air Ministry. 18 February 46. NA/T213/4/DP43/09.

77 General Correspondence re White Paper on Service Pay and Allowances, 1945. NA/T213/4/DP43/09.

78 White Paper 'Postwar Code of Pay, Allowances and Service Pensions and Gratuities for Members of the Forces below Officer Rank'. p. 10. NA/T213/7/DP611/37/06.

79 White Paper 'Postwar Code of Pay, Allowances and Service Pensions and Gratuities for Members of the Forces below Officer Rank'. p. 10. NA/T213/7/DP611/37/06.

80 White Paper 'Postwar Code of Pay, Allowances and Service Pensions and Gratuities for Members of the Forces below Officer Rank'. p. 11. NA/T213/7/DP611/37/06.

81 White Paper. 'Postwar Code of Pay, Allowances and Service Pensions and Gratuities for Members of the Forces below Officer Rank'. p. 11. NA/T213/7/DP611/37/06.

82 White Paper 'Postwar Code of Pay, Allowances and Service Pensions and Gratuities for Members of the Forces below Officer Rank'. p. 17. NA/WO32/11565.

83 White Paper 'Postwar Code of Pay, Allowances and Service Pensions and Gratuities for Members of the Forces below Officer Rank'. p. 17. NA/WO32/11565.

84 Table 12.6 Wage rates and cost of living. Central Statistical Office, *Fighting with Figures*. p. 237.

85 White Paper 'Postwar Pay & Allowances'. NA/T213/7/DP611/37/06.

86 Minutes of the 12th Meeting of the Inter-departmental Committee on Postwar Pay, Allowances and Pensions of the Armed Forces, Wilson-Smith Sub-committee. 12 August 46. NA/T213/58.

87 Minutes of the 12th Meeting of the Inter-departmental Committee on Postwar Pay, Allowances and Pensions of the Armed Forces, Wilson-Smith Sub-committee. 12 August 46. NA/T213/58.

88 Minutes of the 12th Meeting of the Inter-departmental Committee on Postwar Pay, Allowances and Pensions of the Armed Forces, Wilson-Smith Sub-committee. 12 August 46. NA/T213/58.

89 Minutes of the 12th Meeting of the Inter-departmental Committee on Postwar Pay, Allowances and Pensions of the Armed Forces, Wilson-Smith Sub-committee. 12 August 46. NA/T213/58.

90 Report on the Organisation of Welfare Services. 23 May 46. NA/WO32/12222.

91 Report on the Organisation of Welfare Services. 23 May 46. NA/WO32/12222.

92 Report on the Organisation of the Welfare Services. 23 May 46. NA/WO32/12222/6A.

93 Report on the Organisation of the Welfare Services. Part IV, Section 13. 23 May 46. NA/WO32/12222.

94	Minutes of the 21st Meeting of the Committee on the Organisation of the Common Services. 21 June 46. NA/WO32/12222.

95	Report on the Organisation of the Welfare Services. 23 May 46. NA/WO32/12222/6A.

96	Extract from the minutes of the 21st Meeting of the Committee on the Organisation of Common Services. 21 June 46. NA/WO32/12222/7A.

97	Report on the Organisation of the Welfare Services. Appendix B, Navy. 23 May 46. NA/WO32/12222.

98	Extract from the minutes of the 21st Meeting of the Committee on the Organisation of Common Services. 21 June 46. NA/WO32/12222/7A.

99	Minutes of the 21st Meeting of the Committee on the Organisation of the Common Services. 21 June 46. NA/WO32/12222.

100	'History of SSAFA'.

101	'History of SSAFA'.

102	'History of SSAFA'.

103	'History of SSAFA'.

104	SSAFA Branch Conference and Annual Meeting. 4 and 5/10/45. SSAFA Archive.

105	SSAFA Branch Conference and Annual Meeting. 4 and 5/10/45. SSAFA Archive.

106	SSAFA Branch Conference and Annual Meeting. 4 and 5/10/45. SSAFA Archive.

107	SSAFA Branch Conference and Annual Meeting. 4 and 5/10/45. SSAFA Archive.

108	Army Council Secretariat brief for the Secretary of State for War. 01 September 44. NA/WO32/11129.

109	Report on giving information and advice to the next-of-kin of prisoners of war in Germany. November 1944. NA/WO32/11125.

110	Report on giving information and advice to the next-of-kin of prisoners of war in Germany. November 1944. NA/WO32/11125.

111	Meeting of Honorary Colonel and Officers of the Cambridge Regiment for Arrangements for Repatriated Prisoners of War. Item 3, 27 October 44. Cambridge Archives.

112	See, for example: Hartley, *Hearts Undefeated*; Howard, *Sex Problems of the Returning Soldier*; Reese, *Homecoming Heroes*; Shephard, 'A Clouded Homecoming' in *History Today*. Vol. 46, August 1976; Turner and Rendell, *When Daddy Came Home*. In addition Susan Hartmann's article 'Prescriptions for Penelope: Literature on women's Obligations to Returning World War II Veterans', *Women's Studies*. Vol. 5, 1978. pp. 223–239. This lists numerous American sources covering this theme.

113 Gardiner, J., 'Over Here'. The GIs in Wartime Britain. London: Collins & Brown, 1992. p. 213.

114 Chatfield, V., 'Theirs Not to Reason Why' (unpublished biography). 461. IWM Department of Documents.

115 Braybon and Summerfield, Out of the Cage. p. 214.

116 Advice from 'Leonora' in Woman's Own. 27 August 43, quoted in Waller, J., and Vaughan-Rees, M. Women in Wartime: The Role of Women's Magazines, 1939–45. London: MacDonald 1987, p. 76.

117 Waller, and Vaughan-Rees, Women in Wartime. p. 76.

118 Figures taken from Table 1.6 Births in the United Kingdom, Central Statistical Office, Fighting with Figures. p. 6, and Braybon and Summerfield, Out of the Cage. p. 216.

119 The Captive Heart (1946), Director: Basil Dearden. In this film a Czech escapee from Dachau (Michael Redgrave) takes on the identity of Capt. Geoffrey Mitchell of the 5th Oxford Light Infantry who has been killed.

120 Turner and Rendell, When Daddy Came Home. p. 148.

121 Turner and Rendell, When Daddy Came Home. p. 148.

122 Reese, Homecoming Heroes. p. 210.

123 Meeting of the Directorate of Prisoners of War. 21 September 44. NA/WO32/11125.

124 Meeting of the Directorate of Prisoners of War. 21 September 44. NA/WO32/11125.

125 A copy of this pamphlet can be found in NA/WO32/11125 [112A].

126 A copy of this pamphlet can be found in NA/WO32/11125 [112A].

127 Turner and Rennell, When Daddy Came Home. pp. 166–168.

128 Turner and Rennell, When Daddy Came Home. pp. 166–168.

129 Turner and Rennell, When Daddy Came Home. p. 175.

130 Standing Consultative Committee for Ex-Service Employment. 05 April 48. Quoted in Turner and Rennell, When Daddy Came Home. p. 177.

131 Mrs Parkes and Alice Truman. IWM Sound Archives 12864/1 and 12365/2 respectively.

132 Minutes of the 19th Meeting of the Inter-departmental Prisoner of War Co-ordinating Committee (Finance) p3, item 4. 20 February 45. NA/WO163/639.

133 War Office memo. Submitted for consideration at the 25th meeting of the Inter-departmental Prisoner of War Co-ordinating Committee (Finance). 27 October 45. NA/WO163/639.

134 Of all three services, only the navy appears to have been able to name its prisoners of war who had not returned. NA/WO163/639.

135 War Office memo. Submitted for consideration at the 25th meeting of the Inter-departmental Prisoner of War Co-ordinating Committee (Finance). 27 October 45. NA/WO163/639.

136 Lamb, R., *War in Italy, 1943–1945. A Brutal Story*. London: Penguin Books, 1995. p. 167.

137 Widows (1939) War. Claim to pensions where death has been presumed. NA/PIN15/3467.

138 Minutes of the 19th Meeting of the Inter-departmental Prisoner of War Co-ordinating Committee (Finance) p3, item4. 20 February 45. NA/WO163/639.

139 Roseway, Director of Finance, Inter-departmental Prisoner of War Co-ordinating Committee (Finance), in reply to question from Rew, Air Ministry. Minutes of the 19th Meeting of the Inter-departmental Prisoner of War Co-ordinating Committee (Finance) p3, item 4. 20 February 45. NA/WO163/639.

140 War Office memo. Submitted for consideration at the 25th meeting of the Inter-departmental Prisoner of War Co-ordinating Committee (Finance). 27 October 45. NA/WO163/639.

141 Figures based on the 1945 rate of Family Allowance for Petty Officers and Sergeants aged over 25 of 40's per week.

142 Pugh, *State and Society*. p. 225.

143 Pugh, *State and Society*. p. 229.

144 Letter Ellen Porter to Iris Strange. 26 February 74. Box 44, Iris Strange Collection, University of Stafford.

145 Letter Ellen Porter to Iris Strange. 26 February 74. Box 44, Iris Strange Collection, University of Stafford.

146 Ferguson and Fitzgerald, *Studies in Social Services*. p. 8.

Conclusions

What conclusions then can be drawn about the development of British welfare policy from this study of service families in general and prisoner of war families in particular during the Second World War?

Firstly, it is clear that government agencies largely ignored the experiences of the First World War in relation to both service allowances and prisoner of war matters. During this war many service families had suffered financial hardship because of delays in payment of both Family and Dependants' Allowances. Despite the fact that SSAFA drew this to the attention of the War Office and Treasury in 1924, no action was taken to devise a better system to operate in the event of future wars. In fact, both the Treasury and the War Office were unwilling to admit that such a problem really existed. The War Office, with what proved to be unwarranted complacency, felt that its own machinery for the administration of allowances was already perfectly adequate. The Treasury, with its mind on national economic problems, took the view that, as Marriage Allowance was now issued as the norm, the mechanisms for payment were already in place and would merely be extended in the event of future conflicts. In this it completely overlooked the problems that might be caused by a decision to issue Dependants' Allowances, payable in time of war only, to other dependants such as parents who were not eligible for Family Allowances.

An equally serious oversight was the fact that both the War Office and Treasury appeared to ignore the possible effects of mass conscription. Leaving aside particular problems posed by the enforced service of a broad section of young men, some of whom were married but below the age at which Family Allowance was normally paid to servicemen, the sheer weight of numbers of those immediately eligible to apply for allowances was bound to stretch any system to breaking point. Between the outbreak of war in September and November 1939, three hundred thousand Family Allowances alone were granted as men conscripted into the services claimed benefits for their wives and children.[1] Figures for Dependants' Allowances during the same period are not available but by March 1941, well after the first major influx of applications from conscripts, new applications for these allowances were still running at 4,500 per week.[2] These allowances posed particular problems as, in each and every case, the exact level of prior dependency had to be established – a sensitive and time-consuming exercise.

Similarly, no action was taken in the aftermath of the First World War to ensure better provision in the event of a future conflict for the families of those taken captive. Despite the fact that the Belfield Report had highlighted a number of areas of dissatisfaction, and proposed a number of concrete measures to prevent these problems surfacing again in future conflicts, no measures were instigated to implement these recommendations. Many of the problems identified, such as an uncertainty as to which authority held ultimate responsibility for prisoner of war matters and where to apply for information, resurfaced immediately following the first capture of large numbers of men from the BEF in May 1940. This problem was inevitably exacerbated by the fall of Singapore and Hong Kong and the subsequent lack of notification by the Japanese of the status of British servicemen.

Gillian Thomas, in the conclusions to her study of separation allowances and pensions during the First World War, opts for a feminist reading of government action in relation to service allowances following that conflict. However, by suggesting that allowances were used largely as a means of controlling social behaviour and participation in employment, Thomas overlooks a wider historical perspective on the perceived national importance of service allowances. The cyclical pattern by which soldiers, and all matters affecting them, attain a high political profile in times of war and then disappear from the political agenda in times of peace was already well established. The pattern of soldiers being reviled in times of peace and revered in times of war was already enshrined in popular literature by 1890:

For it's Tommy this, an' Tommy that, an' 'Chuck him out, the brute!'
But it's 'Saviour of 'is country' when the guns begin to shoot.[3]

This perception clearly informed discussions relating to service pay
in times of war as is evidenced by the level of popular campaigning
for increased allowances in the press. In addition the role of families
in influencing the willingness of men to enlist and their effectiveness
in action was also widely acknowledged. In 1939 Leslie Hore-
Belisha, Secretary of State for War, wrote, 'to send a soldier to fight
knowing that those whom he leaves behind are in want may well
endanger his morale and reduce his value as a soldier'.[4] Thus the
government, and the nation as a whole, had a duty to maintain a
soldier's family while he fought to protect the national 'family'.
From 1942 onwards the reports of the War Office Morale
Committee emphasised the role that families, and the knowledge
of their well-being, played in maintaining the morale and effectiveness of soldiers.[5] Towards the end of the Second World War a
further dimension was added to these concerns of government. The
imminence of a general election following the ending of the war
provided servicemen with an immediate means of registering protest
if they felt that the government had not fulfilled its responsibility
to their families.

As Thomas suggests, once hostilities ended, the upkeep of their
families reverted to being the responsibility of the individual serviceman.[6] Whilst it is most likely that these changes resulted from
an overall lessening of interest in service issues as a whole, it is also
possible that the government again sought to reinstate traditional
family values at the end of the Second World War as Thomas suggests they had at the end of the First. However, rather than viewing
this as a deliberate measure by the government to reinforce traditional family values and the economic dependence of women, it
seems more likely to be indicative of an overall lessening of interest
in service issues as a whole. As the need to provide for service
families in order to bolster the morale and effectiveness of soldiers
decreased, so the whole subject of service pay and allowances
slipped from the national agenda, and administrative procedures
reverted to their prewar practice.

Generally, the re-emergence of issues highlighted from the experience of the First World War once again failed to result in the
framing of long-term policy to address these issues. Although some

short-term solutions were advanced, these were, by and large, effective only 'for the duration'. Qualifying age for Marriage Allowance
proves a case in point here. The introduction of conscription in
April 1939 had led to protracted discussions on the topic of the
eligibility of conscripted soldiers, under the normal qualifying age
for Marriage Allowance, to claim these allowances. As a result this
qualifying age was suspended during the period of the war. However,
no lasting decisions were made regarding the eligibility of men who
married before undertaking involuntary service in the armed forces.
Consequently, despite the fact that the National Services Acts of
1948 demanded that all men over the age of 18 should serve in the
armed forces for eighteen months, no provision was made for
allowances to be paid to the wives of men who married before being
conscripted into National Service. During discussions in 1939 prior
to the introduction of conscription, the service hierarchy had argued
that men choosing to serve in the armed forces, as a career, did so
knowing that they would not be eligible for allowances before a
certain age.[7] Presumably the government now felt that, as men
knew they would be called up for national service, they should not
undertake the financial responsibilities of marriage before this was
completed. The subject was still proving to be a contentious matter
within the services in the late 1960s when the War Office was
arguing for the retention of qualifying ages of 21 for army other
ranks and 25 for officers whilst the navy and air force favoured a
reduction in these ages.[8]

Perhaps more importantly, given postwar attempts to promote
the services as an attractive career, no changes were made as a result
of the Second World War to the way in which increases to service
pay and allowances were negotiated. No formal channels were
developed through which servicemen could campaign for pay
increases nor were any prescribed links forged whereby service pay
would automatically increase in response to inflation or rises in the
cost of living. Throughout the course of the war and in the postwar
period, all changes to service pay and allowances continued to be
negotiated through the floor of the House of Commons, a cumbersome and time-consuming exercise. The high public profile achieved
by servicemen and their families during the war did not immediately
translate into a governmental concern to ensure that service families
received adequate financial provision. Indeed, in some respects the
professed concern of the nation and government in this respect

made the situation even more difficult. Servicemen, despite the fact that they had first-hand knowledge from their families of financial hardship, were not in a position to campaign themselves for increased allowances when the vaunted national care of their families proved inadequate. To do so would have suggested disloyalty to their country and might, during a time of war, have appeared akin to blackmail.

To effect any increases to service pay and allowances necessitated a concerted campaign to engage the attention of MPs so that the matter would be raised and debated in the House of Commons. This was no easy matter when the attention of the nation was focused on the business of waging war and particularly when many of the general public must have believed that the government was already dealing adequately with the matter. Campaigns for increases in service pay and allowances were, therefore, left to the vagaries of public opinion. Pressure for such increases normally followed a pattern of MPs' attention being drawn to the plight of a local group of service wives and so generating publicity through the local press. This, in turn, led to interest from national groups such as SSAFA and POWRA which together with local MPs acted to increase national interest and publicity in the subject. From this increased national interest, sufficient momentum was generated for the matter to be raised in the House of Commons. Generally, with the exception of continual campaigning by POWRA over specific prisoner of war issues, these campaigns remained uncoordinated. Although national figures such as Sylvia Pankhurst and Eleanor Rathbone were prominent in a number of campaigns, at no time did a popular champion of service families come forward. Possibly as a result of this lack of a national pressure group, increases in service pay and allowances failed to attain a formal review system during the course of the war. With the cessation of hostilities, public interest in levels of service pay waned and no pressure was brought to bear on the government to adopt a negotiating structure for pay increases more closely aligned to that operating in industry.

To some extent this lack of a co-ordinated pay review system seems surprising, as one concern of the services towards the end of the war and in the immediate postwar period was to attempt to make the armed services appear an attractive career. In both 1942 and 1944 campaigns for increases in service pay had utilised unfavourable comparisons between service and civilian pay as an argument for increasing service pay, and a more transparent pay scheme for servicemen was viewed by the services as one means of highlighting career prospects.[9] However, in the immediate postwar period, the two ways in which the government acted to make the systems more comparable were both detrimental to service families.

Children's Allowances had traditionally been granted for all children within a serviceman's family in addition to other allowances such as Marriage or Family Allowance. In contrast, civilian workers had not received any extra allowances for their children. During the course of the war, campaigners had argued that civilian wages were much higher than those payable to servicemen. The Treasury, however, had claimed that, to calculate the full extent of service pay, all allowances including those made for children, needed to be included in the calculations. The actual 'pay' component of service pay was argued as being the equivalent of the disposable income left to civilians after all financial commitments had been met – effectively 'spending money'. With the introduction of the 1945 Family Allowances Act, Children's Allowances to service families were abolished, being replaced by the national allowance of 5s per week for the second and every subsequent child in a family. Some commentators such as Braybon and Summerfield have argued, with justification, that from a feminist standpoint this change proved to be a beneficial move.[10] Whereas service Children's Allowance, for other ranks, was paid directly only to the women involved in times of war, Family Allowance was as a matter of course paid to mothers. However, although the gross financial implications of this are impossible to calculate, there can be no doubt that this measure effected a substantial saving to the Treasury in service spending.[11] A combination of diminishing public interest in service matters after the cessation of hostilities and the preoccupation of government, including MPs, with both social and economic reconstruction, meant that no agency existed to safeguard the interests of service families in this matter. Without exciting any public debate on the issue, by changing families from service Children's Allowance to national Family Allowance, the Treasury was able to effect a saving in the region of £700 per annum in allowances paid to each service family with two children.[12]

In a further move designed to increase parity between service pay and its civilian equivalent, the Treasury, through the medium of the

Bridges Committee, began discussions on the introduction of income tax to service allowances. Previously service allowances had remained exempt from tax whilst additions for civilian workers were taxed. Despite resistance from the War Office in particular, the Treasury view prevailed and income tax on service Family Allowances was introduced from April 1947. Again, actual figures for the income the Treasury generated by this move are impossible to calculate. However, some estimates can be made. In June 1945 the total strength of the armed forces stood at 4,653,000.[13] If even two-thirds of these servicemen were married and claiming Family Allowance, then close to £2.5 million in service allowances instantly became subject to income tax. In both of these instances, issues raised as arguments for increasing service pay and allowances during the course of the war were used to effectively decrease the value of service pay after its end. The diminishing public interest in service matters after the conclusion of the war meant that such changes, presented to the general public as a means of establishing parity between service and civilian pay, were unlikely to generate debate.

For prisoner of war families, a similar lack of change can be identified in the particular administrative problems associated with their allowances. In these instances, however, this inertia resulted from military policy rather than from the cyclical nature of public interest in service matters. For the families of officers taken prisoner, especially those captured in the Far East, particular problems had arisen during the course of the war around their ability to access funds. The wives of ordinary soldiers who were captured continued to be able to draw their allowances by means of the books of drafts issued directly to them. Officers' allowances, however, were issued to the men themselves together with their pay, and often paid direct into their bank accounts. All three services stressed that they encouraged their officers to make arrangements for their families to be able to access these funds before they were posted overseas and faced the possibility of being taken prisoner. At the same time, however, all three also exhibited a reluctance to interfere directly in the family life of their officers. Instead they chose to believe that they had played their part by suggesting that financial provision should be made and that officers would naturally look after the best interests of their families. The actual level of encouragement to make this provision must, however, be open to doubt. In military terms, any discussion of the possibility of capture was seen as defeatist and, as a result, men were provided with only minimal training on how to prepare for capture and how to conduct themselves if capture occurred. If men were not encouraged to consider this eventuality, then it was unlikely that they would recognise the importance of making such provision for their families.

Although this matter was the subject of some discussion in the wake of the Second World War, little concern was shown by the services for families. Instead, attention once again focused on respecting the integrity of the officers involved. Similarly, postwar official histories concerned with prisoner of war matters, such as Cambray and Briggs's *Red Cross and St. John* and Satow and Sée's *The Work of the Prisoners of War Department during the Second World War*, failed to address the problem. Only the Phillimore Report mentions the topic and then solely in connection with the RAF – the only one of the services to have existing provision to order all or part of an officer's pay and allowances to be paid directly to his wife to prevent hardship. In his summary of the provisions made by the other two services, Colonel Phillimore does not raise the issue. Instead he merely reiterates the suggestion that officers should make such provision for their families and proposes that, in cases where this had not happened, the officer could subsequently rectify the situation by sending a letter to his bank manager.[14] Although this possibility did exist for officers held prisoner in Europe, such a solution was patently not possible for those held prisoner in the Far East. In fact the whole question of service training for the eventuality of capture changed not as a result of the Second World War but with the later experience of the Korean War. Reports on prisoner of war conduct after capture between 1951 and 1953 were clear in their conclusions that increased training was necessary to help servicemen to prepare for the possibility of ill-treatment, including interrogation.[15] Although these changes were driven by military necessity rather than concern for family welfare, it seems likely that an increased awareness of the realities of capture would have encouraged soldiers to ensure that they had made adequate provision for their families.

Similarly the administration of allowances for the families of servicemen who were reported 'missing in action' but whose ultimate fate was not known was not altered as a result of the war.

Throughout the Second World War, families of those reported missing were allocated 'missing' allowances for a specified time after the serviceman went missing. If no word was received of prisoner of war status within that period, the serviceman was presumed to be dead and allowances reduced to pension rates. However, after the fall of Singapore in 1942 and other actions in the Far East, it became clear that the Japanese authorities would not forward notification of capture within the set time and as a consequence allowances were extended until notification could be received. In many cases this notification was never forthcoming and allowances were extended in three-month periods for the duration of the war. At no time during the Second World War did the government seem to consider the possibility of implementing a new category, already adopted by the Indian government, of 'Missing, believed POW'. Nor is there any suggestion that the possibility of a 'holding' category was discussed in the postwar years. Again, changes to this policy resulted only from the experience of the Korean War.[16] However, changes remained superficial and in reaction to an international initiative rather than through the government responding to the needs of service families. During the course of the Korean War, the British Repatriated Prisoner of War Interrogation Unit with the Headquarters of UN Command established the use of this category of missing personal, largely in response to the testimony of repatriated prisoners of war on the status of their companions still in captivity.[17] Even then, the services were keen to make it clear to relatives that this was a 'limited' category. The men involved were still officially posted missing and their allowances calculated accordingly.

Finally, the government in the Second World War, as during the First, failed to ensure an adequately clear channel of communication through which prisoner of war families could make enquiries and seek advice. Sources suggest that, throughout the war, the War Office in particular was at best uncomfortable dealing directly with a civilian population and at times openly inconsiderate in its dealings with these families. An Enquiry Centre for the relatives of those missing or held captive in the Far East was established only in response to persistent campaigns by relatives supported by both MPs and POWRA. Even then, for many families, the Enquiry Centre proved to be only the first stage in their quest for information. Few enquiries were dealt with direct and the majority of families were merely directed to one of eleven further possible sources of information.

Following the war the Phillimore Report noted the resistance of both the Foreign and War Offices to the proposal to establish a separate Minister for Prisoner of War matters.[18] However, in its analysis of the pros and cons of the argument the Report argues purely from the standpoint of what would be best for the government departments concerned rather than for prisoners of war themselves or their families. For example, the Report acknowledges that delays in information had occurred but views the importance of these as being that they resulted in 'a storm of public indignation' which had serious results for the 'standing of the government' rather than the worry that they caused for the families concerned.[19] The stated objective of the report 'to preserve the experience gained during the Second World War [...] in selected fields of military staff work and administration' is then utilised solely to suggest changes which would benefit the service departments in general, and the War Office in particular, rather than to highlight ways in which the services could improve their administrative systems to benefit prisoners of war and their families.[20]

Again, changes to the provision of information to families resulted only as a by-product of changes to military strategy in the wake of the Korean War. Once the decision had been taken to increase the amount of training on conduct and possible treatment after capture, a decision was also taken to increase the amount of information provided to relatives.[21] During the Second World War the British government had withheld information regarding the possible mistreatment of prisoners by the Japanese from the general public. In the late 1950s, however, the American government made the decision that publicising Communist treatment of prisoners of war was an effective propaganda tool.[22] In addition, it hoped that acknowledging this possible mistreatment linked with the fact that servicemen were now being trained to cope with this eventuality would minimise the fears of families. In this the British government followed suit. However, although this may have gone some way towards allaying fears, problems associated with lack of notification of status remained. Later studies on American prisoner of war families show that many wives during the Vietnam War were dissatisfied with the level of information provided.[23] As a result they, like their British counterparts before them, often participated in both local and national initiatives to clarify their husbands' status. What these studies also show, however, is the importance of such clarification for the adjustment and coping strategies of the families involved. Whilst the families of all servicemen may experience hardship in adjusting to long-term separation, for the families of those whose status remains unknown the burden is doubled. Families are faced with the necessity to plan both for the eventual return of their husbands and fathers and for the possible confirmation of their death. For the families of British prisoners of war during the Second World War, the administrative systems adopted by the Services made no concessions towards helping families cope with these stresses.

In general, comparatives for this study have proved almost impossible to locate. Although Sarah Fishman's study *We Will Wait* also deals with prisoner of war wives during the Second World War, it is written from a different perspective. Whilst this book concentrates on governmental treatment of and reaction to service families and prisoner of war families, in particular using evidence taken largely from official, written sources, Fishman's study is written from the standpoint of the testimony of the wives themselves and relies largely on oral testimony. The two investigations, therefore, provide different perspectives on similar problems. The whole political context of the experience of French prisoner of war families is also markedly different from that of families in England. The expectations of British families of a government negotiating the treatment of those held captive in enemy hands was markedly different from French expectations of the Vichy government. In addition, French families did not experience to the same degree the problems of British families in connection with lack of information regarding their menfolk. For French families the longest delay in notification of capture was in the region of twelve weeks, while some British families were without news for upwards of three years. Allowances too, although often similarly inadequate, posed different problems for French and British families. The families of British officers experienced problems accessing allowances whilst their husbands were captive in the Far East, whereas French wives, by and large, were generally in contact with their husbands and so were able to overcome problems of this nature.

In one respect, however, there do seem to have been great similarities. Although not the focus of this book, the effect that the experience of being the wife of a prisoner of war had on the lives of the women involved needs some consideration. In *We Will Wait*, Sarah Fishman reports that, following the repatriation of their husband, most wives resumed their interrupted domestic duties and relinquished the public roles they had assumed in local and national associations. Incidental information gleaned during the course of this book suggests a similar pattern for British prisoner of war wives. As local committees and national organisations such as POWRA were wound up, so the women involved resumed their domestic spheres. A number of wives interviewed by the Imperial War Museum described their wartime activities in terms of preserving home and family. Alice Truman, mentioned earlier in connection with the requisition of her house, had fought a long campaign with her local authority to be allowed to return home, even to the extent of involving the Home Secretary in her campaign. However, after her husband returned home she described her actions as 'just doing what any loving mother would do for her children'.[24] Whilst this may well be true, any lasting effects of her action, such as increased self-confidence in dealing with authority or ability in dealing with financial matters, appear to be discounted. Although such considerations may well have affected subsequent resumption of married life, the women concerned generally discount their own experiences, choosing instead to allow their husbands and their experiences to claim priority. In this they were generally following the advice provided to them by both government and services but it is difficult to imagine that their experiences did not colour their subsequent lives. Whilst some wives may have been happy to relinquish the responsibility involved in being 'head' of the family, many must surely have resented their displacement and their loss of influence within the family sphere.

Despite the fact that T.H. Marshall considers that the experience of total war is 'bound to have an effect on both the principles of social policy and the methods of social administration', the direct impact of the Second World War on British government and service departments' policies towards service families in general, and prisoner of war families in particular, was minimal.[25] During the course of the war, action by service families had succeeded in drawing attention to the low levels of service allowances and the differential between service allowances and civilian pay. Although in 1942 and 1944 this action had resulted in increases to service pay and allowances, in the postwar years this comparison worked to their detriment. In its attempt to present service pay and allowances in a way in which both servicemen and the general public could make comparisons between the different pay structures, the government implemented changes that actually decreased the level of payments to service families. Income tax was introduced on Marriage Allowance, and the Children's Allowance was discontinued in favour of national Family Allowances. As had been the previously established pattern, once the actual conflict had ended the welfare service families again faded into the background. The cumbersome machinery by which pay and allowances were negotiated remained unchanged and the lack of coherent policy for the payment of allowances to the families of those believed to have been taken captive remained unaltered. Any momentum which campaigns for improved conditions might have gained whilst the need to maximise the effectiveness of soldiers remained a political issue was once again lost. However, for service families generally there had been at least some attempt to devise a coherent and comprehensible policy, albeit that the result of this was to the detriment of the families concerned. For prisoner of war families the situation proved even more complex. At the outset of this study there was an expectation that systems for administering allowances and disseminating information to prisoner of war families might well have been altered by the experience of the Second World War, particularly in the light of the experience of the families of those held captive in the Far East. It had seemed possible that the problems faced by these families might have informed postwar discussions and contributed to the development of more efficient mechanisms for dealing with families undergoing these particular problems. What has actually emerged, however, is that the treatment of these families was not an issue that the services were actually able to deal with directly. There was, in fact, a 'missing link', which made it impossible for them to devise such a policy until it had been resolved. During the Second World War no coherent policy existed within the services for preparing men for the eventuality of capture and consequently, despite the professed encouragement of service departments, many men failed to make adequate preparations for their families to be provided for in this eventuality. For whatever reason, a specific policy was not devised to deal with these issues, and this lack resulted in an inability to devise lasting solutions to particular problems, such as those of extending allowances for families whose menfolk were missing but likely to prove to have been taken captive. All action to address the problems was devised on a reactive basis and only as short-term solutions. Until the services faced the fact that a policy towards educating men in preparing for the possibility of capture and more comprehensive education on behaviour after capture were needed, then suffering of the families concerned was bound to continue. Although the behaviour of the Japanese should have suggested the need to address the problems of capture by enemies who were not party to the Geneva Convention for implementation in the event of a future conflict, no action was taken. As a result servicemen, and their families, were similarly unprepared for the experience of capture in Korea. When changes to policy did come, these were largely as a result of pressure being brought to bear on the British government through the actions of other agencies such as the United Nations. Although further investigation is obviously needed into the policy of the British government towards preparing their servicemen for the possibilities of capture in the 1950s, this is beyond the scope of this book. However, what these initial findings do suggest is that the government continued to formulate policy towards prisoners of war and their families reactively. Furthermore, neither the decision to implement the informal category of 'missing believed prisoner of war' nor the action in publicising possible communist treatment of prisoners of war was developed in response to the concerns or needs of the men and families concerned. Instead both resulted from action by outside agencies and in response to military need.

Notes

1 Report of the Inter-departmental Committee on Dependants' Allowances. 06 November 40. NA/WO32/9444.
2 Minute Sheet. 20 March 41. NA/AST11/145.
3 Kipling, R., 'Tommy' in Karlin, D. (ed.) *The Oxford Authors: Rudyard Kipling*. Oxford: Oxford University Press, 1999. p. 434.
4 Letter, Hore-Belisha to Lady Astor, 31 December 39. NA/WO32/4679.
5 Reports of the War Office Morale Committee. January 1942–February 1948. NA/WO32/15772.
6 Thomas, *State Maintenance for Women during the First World War*. Conclusions.

7 Fighting Services Separation Allowances. Men called up under the Military Training Act, 1939. NA/T162/573/E388866/01.

8 Letter Major-General H.E.N. Bredin, Director of Volunteers, Territorials and Cadets, Ministry of Defence, to Major-General D.A. Beckett. 30 December 68. NA/WO32/14364.

9 See for example: Improvements in Service Pay and Allowances 1942, NA/WO32/10448, NA/T162/692/45396/1 and NA/T162/692/E45396/2; Revision of Service Pay and Allowances 1944, NA/WO32/10975 and NA/T162/801/E45396/01.

10 Braybon and Summerfield, *Out of the Cage*. p. 277.

11 Care needs to be taken over the terminology used in relation to these various allowances. Within the services the terms Family Allowance (for the army and air force) and Marriage Allowance (for the navy) both refer to allowances paid to wives. The service equivalent of the national Family Allowance is, therefore, Children's Allowance, and not Family Allowance.

12 Figure calculated using rate of National Family Allowance and figures given for Children's Allowances in the services April 1945. NA/T213/4/DP43/09.

13 Table 3.4 Strength of the Armed Forces and Women's Auxiliary Services. Central Statistical Office, *Fighting with Figures*. p. 39.

14 Phillimore Report. p. 284. NA/WO366/26.

15 Treatment of Returned POWs from Korea. NA/AIR8/2473.

16 Korean Casualties – Proposed new category 'Missing Believed POW'. NA/ADM1/24704.

17 Korean Casualties – Proposed new category 'Missing Believed POW'. NA/ADM1/24704.

18 Phillimore Report. p. 20. NA/WO366/26.

19 Phillimore Report. p. 20. NA/WO366/26.

20 Phillimore Report. Introduction. NA/WO366/26.

21 Service Ministers Meeting. 18 January 56. NA/AIR8/2473.

22 Service Ministers Meeting. 18 January 56. NA/AIR8/2473.

23 See for example: McCubbin, H.I., Hunter, E.J., and Dahl, B.B., 'Residuals of War: Families of Prisoners of War and Servicemen Missing in Action' in *Journal of Social Issues*. Vol. 31, No. 4, 1975. pp. 95–109; MacIntosh, H., 'Separation Problems in Military Wives' in *American Journal of Psychiatry*. Vol. 125, No. 2, August 1968. pp. 156–161; McCubbin, H., Dahl, B.B., Lester, G.R., Benson, D., and Robertson, M.L., 'Coping Repertoires of Families Adapting to Prolonged War-induced Separations' in *Journal of Marriage and the Family*. August 1976. pp. 461–471.

24 Truman Alice Kathleen, IWM Sound Archive 12365/2.

25 Marshall, *Social Policy*. p. 82.

Bibliography

Primary sources

The Army Benevolent Fund, 41 Queen's Gate, London SW7 5HR

Army Historical Branch, Ministry of Defence, 3–5 Great Scotland Yard, London SW1A 2HW

Army Staff College, Camberley

Barnsley Prisoner of War Fund, Borough Secretary's Department, Town Hall, Barnsley, South Yorkshire S70 2TA
Deeds of the Barnsley Prisoner of War Fund

Black Watch Regimental Headquarters, Balhousie Castle, Hay Street, Perth PH1 5HR

Bodleian Library, Oxford
Irene Ward – Private Papers

British Red Cross Archive, 9 Grosvenor Crescent, London SW1X 7EJ
Annual Report of the BRC War Organisation 1939–1945
'The Prisoner of War', Issues May 1942–July 1945
'Far East', Issues February 1944–December 1945
Miscellaneous files N5, P41

British War Widows Association Archive (The Iris Strange Collection), University of Stafford
POW Journal – William Percy Scott RA 802209
Letters Robert Strange to Iris Strange 1940–1941
Letters Iris Strange to Robert Strange 1941–1942
Box 5   Far Eastern POW (FEPOW) Newsletters
Box 7   FEPOW Magazines
Box 43   Miscellaneous Items
Box 44   Unusual Items and Correspondence

Cambridgeshire County Council Archive, Shire Hall, Castle Hill, Cambridge CB3 0AP

Meeting of Hon. Colonel and Officers of Cambs Regiment for arrangements for reception of POWS 27/10/44

Reports of Welfare Committee

Annual Meeting   05 November 43

Annual Meeting   27 October 47

Annual Meeting   26 October 45

Quarterly Meeting   26 January 45

Quarterly Meeting   06 July 45

Meeting of General Purposes Committee 06 November 45

Centre for Oxfordshire Studies, Central Library, Oxford

COS, WLWO 71

Bicester Advertiser, 16 July 43, 09 July 43

Henley Standard, 16 August 40, 23 August 40, 20 September 40, 11 October 40, 03 January 44, 18 February 44

Centre for Prisoner of War Studies, Naval Health Research Centre, San Diego, CA 92152, USA

The Churchill Archive, Churchill College, Cambridge

Private Papers of Alfred Duff-Cooper, Lord Norwich, Secretary of State for War 1935–1937

Private Papers of Leslie Hore-Belisha

HOBE 1/5   Diaries 19/12/38–09/08/39

HOBE 5/1–5/7   Correspondence 1937

HOBE 5/9–5/26   Correspondence 09/37–04/38

HOBE 5/46–5/63   Correspondence 01/39–03/39

HOBE 5/70–5/80   Correspondence 09/39–10/39

HOBE 5/81–5/93   Broadcasts

HOBE 6/1–6/6   Correspondence 1944–55

Private Papers Captain David Margesson, Secretary of State for War, 1941

Private Papers of Sir Edward Grigg, Permanent Under-secretary of State for War, 1940

PJG 9/7   Army Morale

Far Eastern Prisoners of War (and Internees) Association, 30 Copsewood Way, Bearsted, Maidstone, Kent ME15 8PL

Imperial War Museum, London

Sound Archive

8448/4   Tokeley

8454/1   Goode

12864/1   Parkes

12866/1   Heath

12861/2   Ford Edie

7276/3   Buswell

11520/2	Hill
15893/1	Morris
14618/1	O'Brien
15980/1	Summers
12365/2	Truman

Department of Documents

P461	Mrs V. Chatfield
97/25/1	Mrs V.K. Franklin
94/32/1	R.A. Graydon, G.A. Griffiths, W.M. and Mrs E. Innes-Ker
88/5/1	L.J. Rookwood
95/30/1	Captain G.W. Smith
1333	Miscellaneous
1434	Miscellaneous
1585	Miscellaneous

Liverpool/Merseyside Record Office, Central Library, William Brown Street, Liverpool L3 8EW

Local Studies Unit (Archives) Manchester City Council Department of Libraries and Theatres, Central Library, St Peter's Square, Manchester M2 5PD

National Archives, Kew, London
Admiralty
ADM1

11909	Extended Periods of Payment of Allowances to Dependants of Naval personnel Missing in Far East
24704	Korean Casualties – Proposed new category 'missing, believed, POW'

Air Ministry
AIR2

6177	Prisoner of War in German hands. Pay and Allowances, reciprocal arrangements
6200	Suggestions for exchange of information of POWs through Apostolic Delegations
6223	Italian Prisoners of War – Issue of Emoluments
6408	Hong Kong – Malaya etc. Pay and Allowances of Missing and Captured Personnel
6587	Prisoners of War – correspondence concerning awards
8621	1943–46 Postwar Repatriation POW Committee
10199	Missing research in SE Asia
10860	1948 Revision of Geneva Conventions
11025	1951–54 Use of Japanese assets in UK for benefit ex-POW and dependants

11026   Disposal of Japanese Assets
11027   Disposal of Japanese Assets
12305   Works Directorate. Officials posted as missing – Policy as to emoluments and payments to dependants
AIR8
2473   Treatment of Returned POWs from Korea
Unemployment Assistance Board
AST11
122   Policy and procedure in payment of allowances 1914–39
123   Policy and procedure 1939–40
124   Policy and procedure 1940–41
125   Policy and procedure 1941–42
126   Policy and procedure 1942–43
127   Policy and procedure 1943–49
128   Investigation procedures Oct. 1944–Dec. 1948
129   Territorial Army Proficiency Grant – treatment in assessing need
130   Service in HM Forces – 'normal occupation' qualification
131   Military Training Act 1939 – allowances to dependants of men called up – investigation of claims by Board: Procedure
132   Military Training Act 1939 – allowances to dependants of men called up – investigation of claims by Board: Procedure
133   Military Training Act 1939 – allowances to dependants of men called up – investigation of claims by Board: Procedure
134   Allowances for dependants of personnel serving with HM Forces' Procedure under Military Service (Special Allowances) Advisory Committee. War Service Grants Advisory Committee.
135   Dependants Allowances Advisory Committee Dec. 39–April 40
136   Dependants Allowances Advisory Committee April 40–March 42
137   Service Dependants etc. Allowances and/or National Service Grants. Treatment in assessing need 1939–40
138   Service Dependants etc., Allowances and/or National Service Grants. Treatment in assessing need. 1940–46
139   Military Service (Armed Forces) Act 1939: Allowances to Dependants of Members of HM Forces: Investigation of Claims: Procedure
140   Service in HM Forces: Scope position following discharge after the termination of the War
141   Service Dependants Allowances Scheme: consideration of improvements in rates and conditions. 1940 June–July
142   Members of HM Forces. Welfare Facilities. Particulars of Board's Functions

143 Allowances to dependants of members of HM Forces: Inter-Departmental Committee set up to investigate delay in settlement of claims

144 Service Dependants' Allowances. Notification to Service Department of a payment by the Board; Notification by a Service Department of issue of a Service Allowance

145 Service Dependants' Allowances Scheme: Effect of Determination of Needs Bill 1941

146 Army Allowances. Co-ordinating (Inter-departmental) Committee on Dependants Allowances etc.

147 Agricultural Occupations

148 Interim Allowances to dependants of Home Guard reported killed or missing as a result of operations against the enemy. Payment by Board on behalf of War Office

149 S.D.A. and W.S.G. Verification of Earnings

150 Allowances for dependants of men of the Hong Kong and Malaya Volunteer Forces. Investigation of applications on behalf of the Colonial Office

151 Service Dependants' Allowances and War Service Grants Revision of procedure consequent on investigation by Treasury Official

152 Personnel of HM Forces and National Service: Postwar civil liabilities and resettlement: General Policy

153 Personnel of HM Forces and Auxiliary Services: Civil Liabilities Scheme

154 Personnel of HM forces and other forms of National Service: Scheme for Resettlement Grants

155 Rates of Service Pay and Allowances: Comparison with Board's Allowances

156 Service in HM Forces: Scope position of Commissioned Officers following discharge

157 National Insurance Act 1946: Effect on Service Dependants' Allowances

Colonial Office

CO 980

204 Publicity and Press Releases on POW and Internment Camps

205 Setting up an enquiry centre for information regarding POWs in the Far East

207 British POWs Relatives Association

Foreign Office

FO383 POWs and Aliens Department. General correspondence 1915–1919

FO916

2 Functions of POW Information Bureau

22   Reports of visits to POW camps in German occupied territory
42   POW welfare, Norway
45   POW Food and Clothing
46   POW Food and Clothing
47   Repatriation of Allied POW from Germany/Italy
52   POW welfare, Indian, New Zealand, Australian
53   POW welfare, Indian, New Zealand, Australian
54   POW welfare, Indian, New Zealand, Australian
151   1941 Imperial War Graves Commission
152   Imperial War Graves Commission
181   Parcels received by British POW in Italy
226   POW welfare in Japanese hands
227   POW Information Bureau – lists of internees
230   1942 POW Information Bureau functions
256   1942 Lists of POW in Germany
257   1942 Lists of POW in Germany
352   POW in unoccupied France – financial questions
489   1942 POW and internees in Japanese hands – nos
549   YMCA work for POWs 1943
550   Relatives Association, British POWs 1943
562   Setting up of POW Dept. 1943
671   1943 Italian POWs – remittances to relatives
676   POWs in Italy, credit balances
696   POWs French Colonies, financial matters
782   1943 POW and internees in Japanese hands
785   POWs Far East, financial matters
843   1944 POWs in camps in Germany – nos
876   1944 burial arrangements for deceased POWs
993   1944 POWs in Greece – lists/nos
1056   1944 POWs in Japan – lists/nos
1358   1945 POWs in Japan – lists/nos
2573   Financial matters concerning POWs
2578   POWs in German territory, individual financial cases
2579   Credit balances due to POWs on repatriation
Home Office
 HO45
 21875   POW employment, repatriation, fraternisation 1940–47
Ministry of Pensions
 PIN3
  63   Family Allowances Bill 1945
 PIN4
  153   1939–46 War Occupations Collection of National Insurance
            Contributions

154   1939–58 Mobilisation of Reservists – National Insurance Contributions

PIN15

2634   Missing Personnel – arrangements regarding inter-departmental procedure

2635   Missing Personnel – arrangements regarding inter-departmental procedure

3339   Missing Personnel – arrangements regarding inter-departmental procedure

2299   National Service Act 1941. Effect on Civil Defence Services. Sick-pay, injury allowances etc.

2300   National Service Act 1941 Effect on Civil Defence Services. Sick pay, injury allowances etc.

2663   Financial relations between the Government and Voluntary Organisations during a war

2705   Naval and Royal Marine Officers. Re-employment in a rank lower than that held on the retired list. Rates of Pension for widows

3467   Entitlement – Widows (139 war) Claim to pension where death has been presumed

PIN91   Ministry of Pensions: Second World War Pensions Award Files of Far Eastern POWs

Prime Minister's Office

PREM3   Operational correspondence and papers. 1938–1946

PREM4   Confidential correspondence and papers. 1936–1946

Treasury

T162

470   Dependants' allowances in the event of a future war. 1924–38

524   Air Force/Navy allowances to dependants (reserves)

524   Conditions of service pensions for Army, Navy and Air Force. Hore-Belisha's proposals

563   Dependants' allowances in a future war – machinery for administration

573   Fighting Services Separation Allowances. Men called up under Military Training Act 1939

646   Revision of pay and allowances 1941–42

647   Service pay and allowances. Joint Standing Committee

692   Issue of White Paper 1942. Service pay and allowances

692   Issue of White Paper 1942. Service pay and allowances

733   1920–44 Annual lists of grants of pay and allowances

792   Members of fighting services missing or POW, methods of payment of allowances

801   Payment of allowances to service personnel with families located in enemy occupied territory
       White Paper April 1941. Service pay and allowances
875   Armed Forces Dependants' Postwar Allowances, White Paper 1946
972   Fighting Services pay and allowances – Air Force
973   Language Qualifications
978   Fighting Services. Mother/Child Welfare Centres
989   Fighting Services Family Welfare
999   Fighting Services Pay and Allowances – escapees
T163   General Registered Files (G series). 1888–1948
T172
41   Family Allowances – memo on letter in Times
T211
39   1930–48 Fighting Services, Pay and allowances
T225
26   Cost and maintenance of POW and internees in other countries
T265
34   Indices to minutes of meetings 1936–50 Defence Policy and Materials Division
35   Indices to minutes of meetings 1936–50 Defence Policy and Materials Division
36   Indices to minutes of meetings 1936–50 Defence Policy and Materials Division
37   Indices to minutes of meetings 1936–50 Defence Policy and Materials Division
38   Indices to minutes of meetings 1936–50 Defence Policy and Materials Division
39   Indices to minutes of meetings 1936–50 Defence Policy and Materials Division
40   Indices to minutes of meetings 1936–50 Defence Policy and Materials Division
41   Indices to minutes of meetings 1936–50 Defence Policy and Materials Division
T213
3   Revisions of pay and allowances
4   White Paper on Pay and Allowances, General correspondence
5   1945–6 Inter-departmental committee on Postwar pay and allowances and pensions
6   Minutes of inter-departmental committee meetings on Postwar allowances etc.
7   General papers of Inter-departmental Committee on Postwar allowances/pay – correspondence

56	Wilson-Smith sub-committee to inter-departmental committee – minutes
57	Minutes of sub-committee meetings
58	Post 1946

War Office

WO32

3153	1932/3 amendments to FS regulations
3169	1934–6 Marriage allowance for those over 26
4249	1937/8 Families of non-European soldiers in Hong Kong
4854	Separation allowances to families of military prisoners 1920
4679	Separated and 'unmarried' wives 1939–41
4680	Age of marriage allowance 1938–39
9444	1940–41 Report of inter-departmental committee on dependants' allowances
9445	1940 repercussions in army from improvements in marriage allowance in war-time RAF
9817	Payments after death, family resident abroad 1940–41
9818	Separated wives 1940–47
9819	POWs, repayment of interest on balances of pay due 1941–42
9821	1941–45 Czech/Slovak land forces: Family Allowances
9822	1941–45 Simplification of Army pay codes
9823	1941–47 War Service Grants. Increase pay/allowances other ranks
9824	Overpayment of family allowances, bigamy 1941–47
9906	British POWs publicity and press announcements
9909	Pay for Missing and POW 1939–41
9910	Penal stoppages imposed by enemy governments. 1941–45
9924	1941–43 Junior married officers: allowances
10189	Overseas Service Families Committee 1942–47
10298	Pensions (Navy, Army RAF and Mercantile Marine) Bill 1939
10448	1942–44 Improvements pay and allowances
10449	Family Allowance for wife (without children) in rate aided institution
10477	1942 US Forces in UK: pay
10715	Pay and allowances to POW families 1942–45
10715	Pay for Missing and POW 1942–45
10740	Working pay to POWs
10757	Rehabilitation 1943–46
10798	Disposal of effects of personnel reported missing or prisoner of war
10972	1944–45, (a) Simplification of allowance regulations, (b) Consolidation of Army Pay and Allowances
10975	1944–7 Revision of services pay/allowances
11116	Pay of Air Force personnel who are prisoners in Germany

11118   Formation and functions of POW Central Enquiry Bureau
11125   1944–5 Rehabilitation of returned prisoners
11129   1944 rehabilitation of British ex-POWs
11186   1944–5 Pay of Officers in Postwar army
11986   Stoppage of Family Allowance and allotments after 7 days AWOL
11490   1945–50 Inter-departmental Committee of the Wilson-Smith Committee on Postwar pay, allowances and pensions. 1945–50
11564   1945–52 Simplification of allowances
11565   Inter-departmental Committee on Postwar pay, allowances and pensions. 1945–46
11598   1945–51 Simplification of Married Allowances
11599   Marriage between British personnel and women of other nationalities
11743   1945–50 Services Committee for Welfare of Forces
11981   1945–6 Interdepartmental Committee on Postwar pay/allowances
11982   1946–7 amendments to allowances regulations
11984   1946–7 Postwar allowances. Draft regulations
11985   1946–7 Postwar allowances. Lump sum compensation awards to workmen
12170   1939–45 Proposed Marriage Act for men in the services
12222   1946 Amalgamation of Common Services: Welfare services
14361   1940–2 Officers married to women in the Women's Services. Entitlement to Married Allowance
14362   1942–4 Officers married to women in Women's Services. Colonial Cases – Bermuda and Malta
14364   1946–69 Allowances for under-age married officers and other ranks
14518   1941–2 Procedure in cases of POW for adoption of children (summary jurisdiction) Rules 1936
15543   SHAEF Board of Enquiry – report of treatment of USA/GB POW
15760   Review of Army Welfare Service in Home Commands
15772   1942–48 War Office Morale Committee reports
WO113
21   Officers' pay 1928–45
23   NCO pay
29   Officers, NCO, men – family allowances 1938–58
WO163
152   Imperial POW Committee 1941–43
582   Imperial POW Committee Minutes, summary of action, progress reports August 1941–1947

583 Imperial POW Committee. Sub-Committee 'A' Minutes and Special Meetings June 1941–April 1942

584 Imperial POW Committee Sub-Committee 'A' Meetings 7–14

585 Imperial POW Committee Sub-Committee 'A' Meetings 15–20

586 Imperial POW Committee Sub-Committee 'A' Meetings 21–30

587 Imperial POW Committee Sub-Committee 'A' Meetings 31–40

588 Imperial POW Committee Sub-Committee 'A' Meetings 41–52

589 Imperial POW Committee Sub-Committee 'B' Meetings 11–29

590 Imperial POW Committee Sub-Committee 'B' Meetings 30–40

591 Directorate of Prisoners of War. Repatriation Committee No 1, Policy. Minutes of meetings and selected papers

592 Directorate of POW. Repatriation Committee No 2, Administration. Minutes of meetings and selected papers

593 Combined Repatriations Committee – Europe

608 Conditions of Military Service July 1938

638 Imperial POW Committee – subcommittee B

639 Interdepartmental POW Co-ordinating Committee (Finance) Meetings 1–26

WO165

59 War Diaries

60 War Diaries

61 War Diaries

62 War Diaries

63 War Diaries

64 War Diaries

65 War Diaries

66 War Diaries

67 War Diaries

68 War Diaries

69 War Diaries

70 War Diaries

71 War Diaries

WO219

1402 SHAEF Papers Tables of Organisation POW Executive

1448 Care and repatriation of Allied POW 1944/45

1452A Allied POW misc. correspondence 1944/45

WO259

12 Compensation for ex-POW in Japanese hands

17 Daily Worker – Govt. denial of accredited war correspondent

30 Relations with press

36 Army Manpower requirements January 1941

37 PM minutes and replies – Army Intake Feb.–March 1941

44 Army morale: Paper by Adjutant General May 1944

53   Mr Clemens Datt of Daily Worker not accredited as War
      Correspondent. 1944 January–October
56   Daily Worker request for a War Correspondent in Italy. 1947
      July–August
62   Morale in Army – press criticism
WO307
2   POW Information Bureau: Correspondence and Papers, Second
      World War
3   POW Information Bureau: Correspondence and Papers, Second
      World War
WO366
25   Phillimore report – draft
26   Phillimore Report – bound draft
80   British POW in Italy
116   British POW repatriated 1943–4

National Army Museum, Royal Hospital Road, Chelsea, London SW3
4HT

Norfolk Record Office, Gildengate House, Anglia Square, Upper Green
Lane, Norwich NR3 1AX
  N/LM/1/34–36, Committee appointed at request of Ministry of
    Information for keeping up morale and disseminating information.
    19940–45
  N/TC 31, Norwich City Council Social Welfare Committee 1929–70
  N/TC 28/29–30, Norwich City Council Emergency Committee 1939–
    45
  C/C482–501, Norfolk County Council Public Health and Assistance
    Committee 1930–48

The Not Forgotten Association, Buckingham Palace Road, London

The Officers Association, Pall Mall, London

The Officers Pension Society, Vauxhall, London

Royal British Legion, 48 Pall Mall, London SW1Y 5JY

Royal Norfolk Regimental Museum, Shirehall, Market Avenue, Norwich
NR1 3JQ

Royal Patriotic Fund, Queen Anne's Gate, London

Scottish United Services Museum, Crown Square, The Castle, Edinburgh
EH1 2NG

SSAFA, Queen Elizabeth the Queen Mother House, 19 Queen Elizabeth
Street, London SE1 2LP
  Annual Reports: 1923, 1938, 1939, 1940, 1941
  Report of Branch Conference: 1942, 1946

Emergency Conference of Secretaries of Branches: 1943, 1944, 1945
Council Minutes: 1939–1946
SAFFA News: Winter 1984, Spring 1985, Summer 1985, Autumn 1985

Sheffield Archives, 52 Shoreham Street, Sheffield S1 4SP

CA 43/1   Sheffield Information Committee 1941–44
CA 538/60 City Archives – allowances to dependants of Council employees reported dead or missing 1940–42
CA 39
41   Emergency Committee and Public Assistance and Social Welfare Committee
157   Emergency Committee and Public Assistance and Social Welfare Committee
186   Emergency Committee and Public Assistance and Social Welfare Committee
196   Emergency Committee and Public Assistance and Social Welfare Committee

Surrey History Centre, 130 Goldsworth Road, Woking Surrey GU21 1ND

Waltham Forest Archives, Vestry House Museum, London Borough of Waltham Forest, Vestry Road, Walthamstow, London E17 9NH

West Yorkshire Archive Service – Kirklees, Central Library, Princess Alexandra Walk, Huddersfield, W. Yorkshire HD1 2SU
Huddersfield POW Committee
KC825/1/12 1943–46 – Booklet Daily Telegraph POW Exhibition May 1944
KC825/1/13 1945–47
KC825/1/10, Letter Mrs D. McGeoch
KC825/1/9, Letter Mrs F. Hanson, Letter Mrs Ethel North, Letter E. Hall
KC825/1/1, Minute Books

Wiltshire and Swindon Record Office, Bythesea Road, Trowbridge, Wiltshire BA14 8BS

Official publications

History of the Second World War Series
UK Medical Series:
Crew, P.A.B., *The Army Medical Services (Administration) Vols 1 and 2*. London: HMSO, 1953.
MacNalty, A.S., *The Civilian Health and Medical Services. Vols 1 and 2*. London: HMSO, 1953.

Military Series:
Butler, Sir James, *U.K. Military*. London: HMSO, 1956.
Hancock, W.K., and Gowing, M.M., *British War Economy*. London: HMSO, 1949, and Kraus Reprint (revised edition), 1975.
Donnison, F.S.V., *Civilian Affairs and Military Government. Central Organisation and Planning*. London: HMSO, 1966.
Woodward, Sir Llewellyn, *British Foreign Policy in the Second World War*. London: HMSO, 1976.
Gibbs, N.H., *Grand Strategy. Vol. 1. Rearmament Policy*. London: HMSO, 1976.
Butler, J.R.M., *Grand Strategy. Vol. 2. Sept. 1939–1941*. London: HMSO, 1957.
Gwyer, M.A., *Grand Strategy. Vol. 3, Pt I. June 1941–Aug. 1942*. London: HMSO, 1964.
Butler, J.R.M., *Grand Strategy. Vol. 3, Pt II. June 1941–Aug. 1942*. London: HMSO, 1964.
Howerd, M., *Grand Strategy. Vol. 4. Aug 1942–Sept. 1943*. London: HMSO, 1972.
Ehrman, J., *Grand Strategy. Vol. 5. Aug 1943–Sept. 1944*. London: HMSO, 1956.
——*Grand Strategy. Vol. 6. Oct 1944–Aug. 19445*. London: HMSO, 1956.
UK Civil Series:
Sayers, R.S., *Financial Policy 1939–45*. London: HMSO, 1956
Titmuss, R.M., *Problems of Social Policy*. London: HMSO, 1976.
Ferguson, S., and Fitzgerald, H., *Studies in Social Services*. London: HMSO, 1978.
Donnison, F.S.V., *Report of the International Committee of the Red Cross on its activities during the Second World War (September 1, 1939–June 30, 1947)* Vol. 1, General Activities. Geneva: 1948.
Satow, Sir H., and Sée, M.J., *The Work of the Prisoners of War Department during the Second World War*. London: Foreign Office, 1950.

Unpublished theses

Lomas, J. *War Widows in British Society, 1914–90*. Unpublished PhD thesis, University of Stafford, 1997.
Thomas, G., *State Maintenance for Women during the First World War: The Case of Separation Allowances and Pensions*. Unpublished PhD Thesis, University of Sussex, 1989.

Selected secondary sources

Books

Addison, P., *The Road to 1945. British Politics and the Second World War*. London: Jonathan Cape, 1975.

—— *Now the War Is Over. A Social History of Britain 1945–1951*. London: BBC and Jonathan Cape, 1985.

Allat, P., 'Men and War' in Garmarnikow, E., et al. (eds) *The Public and the Private*. London: Heinemann, 1983.

Anderson, B., *We Just Got On With It. British Women in World War II*. Chippenham: Picton Publishing, 1994.

Andrzejewski, S., *Military Organisation and Society*. London: Routledge, 1954.

Armitage, M.J., *The Royal Air Force*. London: Arms and Armour, 1995.

Ashford, D.E., *The Emergence of the Welfare State*. Oxford: Blackwell, 1986.

Balfour, M., *Propaganda in War 1939–1945. Organisations, Policies and Publics in Britain and Germany*. London: Routledge and Kegan Paul Ltd, 1979.

Bamfield, V., *On The Strength. The Story of the British Army Wife*. London: Charles Knight, 1974.

Barker, A.J., *Behind Barbed Wire*. London: William Clowes & Sons Ltd, 1974.

Barnett, C., *The Audit of War. The Illusions and Reality of Britain as a Great Nation*. London: Macmillan, 1986.

—— *Britain and Her Army: A Military, Political and Social History of the British Army, 1509–1970*. London: Cassell, 2000.

Bedarida, F., *A Social History of England, 1851–1990* (2nd ed.). London and New York: Routledge, 1991.

Bessel, R., *Germany after the First World War*. Oxford: Clarendon Press, 1993.

Birch, R., *The Shaping of the Welfare State*. London: Longman, 1974.

Braybon, G., and Summerfield, P., *Out of the Cage*. London: Pandora, 1987.

Brickhill, P., *The Great Escape*. New York: Norton, 1950.

Brivati, B., and Jones, H. (eds), *What Difference Did the War Make?* London and New York: Leicester University Press, 1995.

Brooke, S. (ed.), *Reform and Reconstruction. Britain after the War, 1945–51*. Manchester and New York: Manchester University Press, 1995.

Bruce, M., *The Coming of the Welfare State* (4th ed.), London: Batsford Ltd, 1961.

—— *The Rise of the Welfare State. English Social Policy 1601–1971*. London, Fakenham and Reading: Cox & Wyman Ltd, 1973.

Bruley, S., *Women in Britain since 1900*. Basingstoke: Macmillan, 1999.

Burton, E., *What of the Women? A Study of Women in Wartime*. London: Frederick Muller, 1941.

Calder, A., *The People's War: Britain 1939–1945*. London: Granada, 1971.

Calder, A., and Sheridan, D., *Speak for Yourself. A Mass-Observation Anthology, 1937–49*. London: Jonathan Cape, 1984.

Cambray, P.G., and Briggs, G.G.B., *Red Cross and St. John. The Official Record of the Humanitarian Services of the War Organisation of the British Red Cross Society and Order of St. John of Jerusalem, 1939–1947*. London: Sumfield and Day Ltd, 1949.

Central Statistical Office. *Fighting with Figures. A Statistical Digest of the Second World War*. London: HMSO, 1995.

Chandler, D. (general ed.), *The Oxford History of the British Army*. Oxford: Oxford University Press, 1996.

Clark, D. (ed.), *Marriage, Domestic Life and Social Change. Writings for Jacqueline Burgoyne (1944–88)*. London and New York: Routledge, 1991.

Coleman, P., *Rosie the Riveter. Women Working on the Home Front in World War II*. New York: Crown Publishers, 1995.

Cook, C., and Sked, A., *Postwar Britain. A Political History*. London: Penguin Books, 1979.

Cordingly, D., *Heroines and Harlots. Women at Sea in the Great Age of Sail*. London, Basingstoke and Oxford: Macmillan, 2001.

Cox, M., *British Women at War*. London: John Murray and Pitot Press, 1941.

Crew, D.F. (ed.), *Nazism and German Society 1933–1945*. London and New York: Routledge, 1994.

Daniel, U., *The War from Within: German Working-Class Women in the First World War* (trans. Margaret Reis). Oxford and New York: Berg Publishers, 1997.

Daws, G., *Prisoners of the Japanese. POWs of World War II in the Pacific*. New York: William Morrow & Co. Inc., 1994.

Dear, I.C.B. (ed.), *The Oxford Companion to the Second World War*. Oxford: Oxford University Press, 1995.

Dennis, P., *Decision by Default. Peacetime Conscription and British Defence 1919–39*. London, Routledge and Kegan Paul, 1972.

Devine, E.T., and Brandt, L., 'Disabled Soldiers & Sailors Pensions and Training' In Kinley, D. (ed.), *Preliminary Economic Studies of the War. Carnegie Endowment for International Peace*. New York: Oxford University Press, 1919.

Douie, V., *The Lesser Half: A Survey of the Laws, Regulations and Practices Introduced during the Present War, Which Embody*

Discrimination against Women. London: Women's Publicity Planning Association, 1943.

—— *Daughters of Britain. An Account of the Work of British Women during the Second World War.* London: Women's Library Service, 1949.

Duchen, C., and Bandhauer-Schoffmann, I. (eds), *When the War Was Over. Women, War and Peace in Europe, 1940–1956.* London and New York: Leicester University Press, 2000.

Elshtain, J.B., *Public Man, Private Woman. Women in Social and Political Thought.* Princeton, NJ: Princeton University Press, 1981.

—— *Women and War.* Brighton: Harvester, 1987.

Finch, J., and Summerfield, P., 'Social Reconstruction and the Emergence of Companionate Marriage, 1945–59' in Clark, D. (ed.), *Marriage, Domestic Life and Social Change. Writings for Jacqueline Burgoyne (1944–88).* London: Routledge, 1991.

Finlayson, G., *Citizen, State and Social Welfare in Britain 1830–1990.* Oxford: Claredon Press, 1994.

Fishman, S., 'Waiting for the Captive Sons of France: Prisoner of War Wives, 1940–1945'. Higonet, R. et al. (eds), *Gender and the Two World Wars.* New Haven: Yale University Press, 1987.

—— *We Will Wait. Wives of French Prisoners of War, 1940–1945.* New Haven and London: Yale University Press, 1991.

Foy, D.A., *For You the War Is Over. American Prisoners of War in Nazi Germany.* New York: Stein & Day, 1984.

Fraser, D., *The Evolution of the British Welfare State.* London: Macmillan, 1973.

Frei, N., *National Socialist Rule in Germany. The Fuhrer State 1933–1945.* Oxford: Blackwell, 1993.

Friedman, K.V., *The Legitimation of Social Rights and the Western Welfare State.* Chapel Hill: University of North Carolina Press, 1981.

Fussell, P., *Wartime: Understanding and Behaviour in the Second World War.* Oxford: Oxford University Press, 1989.

Gardiner, J., *'Over Here'. The GIs in Wartime Britain.* London: Collins and Brown, 1992.

Garmarnikov, E., et al. (eds), *The Public and the Private.* London: Heinemann, 1983.

Gilbert, A., *POW. Allied Prisoners in Europe 1939–1945.* London: John Murray, 2006.

Gledhill, C., and Swanson, G. (eds), *Nationalising Femininity. Culture, Sexuality and British Cinema in the Second World War.* Manchester: Manchester University Press, 1996.

Goldsmith, M., *Women at War.* London: Lindsay Drummond, 1946.

Gorst, A., Johnman, L., and Scott, L.W., *Postwar Britain 1945–64. Themes and Perspectives.* London and New York: Pinter Publications, 1989.

Gourvish, T., and O'Day, A., *Britain Since 1945.* Basingstoke: Macmillan, 1991.

Grant, M., *Propaganda and the Role of the State in Inter-war Britain.* Oxford: Clarendon Press, 1994.

Haldane, R.B., *Army Reform and Other Addresses.* London: T. Fisher Unwin, 1907.

Hall, P. Parker, R. Land R., and Webb, A. (eds), *Change, Choice and Conflict in Social Policy.* London: Heinemann, 1975.

Hall, P., *What a Way to Win a War.* Tunbridge Wells: Midas Books, 1978.

Harris, J., 'Social Policy Making in Britain During the Second World War' in Mommsen, W. (ed.), *The Emergence of the Welfare State in Britain and Germany.* London: Croom Helm, 1981.

Hartley, J. (ed.), *Hearts Undefeated. Women's Writing of the Second World War.* London: Virago Press, 1996.

Hicks, A.L., *Unfinished Business. Prisoner of War Slave Labour.* Oxford: Privately printed, 1999.

Higonet, M.R., Jenson, J., Michel, S., and Weitz, M.C. (eds), *Behind The Lines. Gender and the Two World Wars.* New Haven and London: Yale University Press, 1987.

Hill, R., and Boulding, E., *Families under Stress. Adjustment to the Crises of War, Separation and Reunion.* New York: Harper Bros, 1949.

Hodgson, V., *Few Eggs and No Oranges.* London: Persephone, 1946.

Honey, M., *Creating Rosie the Riveter: Class, Gender and Propaganda in World War II.* Amhurst: University of Massachusetts Press, 1984.

Howard, K., *Sex Problems of the Returning Soldier.* Manchester: Sydney Pemberton, 1945.

Hunter, E.J., and Nice S., *Military Families: Adaptation to Change.* New York: Praeger, 1978.

Hunter, E.J., 'Treating the Military Captive's Family' in Kaslow, F. and Ridenour, R.I. (eds), *The Military Family: Dynamics and Treatment.* New York: Guildford, 1984.

Izzard, M., *A Heroine in her Time.* Harmondsworth: Macmillan, 1969.

Janowitz, M., and Little, R.W., *Sociology and the Military Establishment* (3rd edition). Beverly Hills and London: Sage Publications, 1959.

Jeffrey, K., *War and Reform. British Politics during the Second World War.* Manchester and New York: Manchester University Press, 1994.

Jolly, M., *'Dear Laughing Motorbike': Letters from Women Welders of the Second World War.* London: Scarlet Press, 1997.

Jones, R.B., *Economic and Social History of England, 1770–1977.* Hong Kong: Sheck Wah Tong Printing Press Ltd, 1979.

Koonz, C., *Mothers in the Fatherland. Women, the family and Nazi Politics*. London: Methuen, 1988.

Kochavi, A.J., *Confronting Captivity. Britain and the United States and their POWs in Nazi Germany*. Chapel Hill and London: University of North Carolina Press, 2005.

Lamb, R., *War in Italy 1943–1945. A Brutal Story*. London: Penguin Books, 1995.

Lane, T., *The Merchant Seamen's War*. Manchester and New York: Manchester University Press, 1990.

Lang, C., *Keep Smiling Through. Women in the Second World War*. Cambridge: Cambridge University Press, 1989.

Lee, L.E. (ed.), *World War II. Europe, Africa and the Americas with General Sources: A Handbook of Literature and Research*. Westport, CT: Greenwood, 1997.

Lewis, J., *Politics of Motherhood. Child and Maternal Welfare in England 1900–39*. London: Croom Helm, 1980.

—— *Women in England 1870–1950*. Brighton: Wheatsheaf Books, 1984.

Liddell Hart, B.H., *History of the Second World War*. London: Cassell, 1970.

Litoff, J.B., and Smith, D.C., *Since You Went Away. World War II Letters from American Women on the Home Front*. Oxford: Oxford University Press, 1991.

Little, R.W., 'The Military Family' in Little, R.W. (ed.), *Handbook of Military Institutions*. Beverly Hills: Sage Publications, 1971.

Lowe, R., *The Welfare State in Britain since 1945*. Basingstoke: Macmillan Ltd, 1993.

Lukacs, J., *The Last European War. September 1939–December 1941*. London: Routledge & Kegan Paul Ltd, 1976.

MacDonald, S., 'Drawing in the Lines' in MacDonald, S. et al. (eds), *Images of Women in Peace and War: Cross-Cultural and Historical Perspectives*. London: Macmillan, 1987.

Mack, A., *Dancing on the Waves. A Wartime Wren at Sea*. Andover: Benchmark Press, 2000.

MacKay, R., *The Test of War: Inside Britain 1939–45*. London: UCL Press, 1999.

MacKenzie, S.P., 'Prisoners of War and Civilian Internees: The European and Mediterranean Theatres' in Lee, E.L. (ed), *World War II. Europe, Africa and the Americas, with General Sources: A Handbook of Literature and Research*. Westport, CT: Greenwood, 1997.

—— *British War Films, 1939–1945*. London and New York: Hambledon & London, 2001.

—— *The Colditz Myth*. Oxford: Oxford University Press, 2004.

McLachan, D. *Room 39*. London: Weidenfeld and Nicolson, 1968.

McLaine, I., *Ministry of Morale. Home Front Morale and the Ministry of Information in World War II*. London: George Allen and Unwin Ltd, 1979.

Macnicol, J., *The Movement for Family Allowances 1918–45*. London: Heinemann, 1980.

Marshall, T.H., *Citizenship and Social Class*. London: Hutchinson & Co., 1975.

——*Class, Citizenship and Social Development*. London: Heinemann, 1977.

Marwick, A., *Britain in the Century of Total War. War, Peace and Social Change 1900–1967*. London: The Bodley Head, 1968.

——*Women at War*. London: Croom Helm for the Imperial War Museum, 1977.

——*War and Social Change in the Twentieth Century: A Comparative Study of Britain, France, Germany, Russia and the United States*. London: Macmillan 1974.

Marwick, A., *British Society since 1945*. Harmondsworth: Penguin, 1982.

Marwick, A. (ed.), *Total War and Social Change*. London: Macmillan, 1988.

Mason, T., *Social Policy in the Third Reich*, ed. J. Caplan, trans. J. Broadwin. Oxford: Berg, 1993.

Mayer, S.L., and Koenig, W.J., *The Two World Wars. A Guide to Manuscript Collections in the United Kingdom*. London and New York: Bowker, 1976.

Milward, A., *War, Economy and Society, 1939–45*. London: Allen Lane, 1977.

Minns, R., *Bombers and Mash: The Domestic Front 1939–45*. London: Virago, 1980.

Mitchell, B.R., and Dean, P. (collaborator), *Abstract of British Historical Statistics*. Cambridge: Cambridge University Press, 1962.

Mommsen, W. (ed.), *The Emergence of the Welfare State in Britain and Germany 1850–1950*. London: Croom Helm on behalf of the German Historical Institute, 1981.

Moore, B., and Fedorowich, K. (eds), *Prisoners of War and Their Captors in World War II*. Oxford: Berg, 1996.

Moore, B., and Hately-Broad, B. (eds), *Prisoners of War, Prisoners of Peace*. Oxford: Berg, 2005.

Morgan, D., and Evans, M., *The Battle for Britain. Citizenship and Ideology in the Second World War*. London and New York: Routledge, 1993.

Morgan, K.O., *The People's Peace. British History 1945–1990*. Oxford: Oxford University Press, 1990.

Morton, D., *Fight or Pay. Soldiers' Families in the Great War*. Vancouver and Toronto: University of British Columbia Press, 2004.

Myrdal, A., and Klein, V., *Women's Two Roles: Home and Work*. London: Routledge and Kegan Paul, 1968.

Nicholson, M., *'What Did You Do in the War, Mummy?'* London: Chatto and Windus, 1995.

Noakes, J. (ed.), *Nazism 1919–1945: Volume 4 The German Home Front in World War II*. Exeter: University of Exeter Press, 1998.

Obelkevich, J., and Catterall, P. (eds), *Understanding British Postwar Society*. London: Routledge, 1994.

Oram, A., ' "Bombs Don't Discriminate!" Women's Political Activism in the Second World War' in Gledhill, C. and Swanson, G. (eds), *Nationalising Femininity. Culture, Sexuality and British Cinema in the Second World War*. Manchester: Manchester University Press, 1996.

Orwell, G., *The Lion and the Unicorn*. London: Penguin, 1941.

Pargeter, E., *She Goes to War*. London: William Heinemann, 1942. (London: Headline Publishing, 1989).

Parker, R.A.C., *Struggle for Survival. The History of the Second World War*. Oxford: Oxford University Press, 1989.

Pateman, C., 'The Patriarchal Welfare State' in Pierson, C. and Castles, F.G., *The Welfare State Reader*. Oxford and Malden, MA: Blackell, 2000.

Pelling, H., *Britain and the Second World War*. Fontana History of War and Society Series. London: Collins, 1970.

Pierson, C., and Castles, F.G., *The Welfare State Reader*. Oxford and Malden, MA: Blackwell, 2000.

Preston, A., *History of the Royal Navy*. London: Hamlyn, 1983.

Price, A., *What Did You Do in the War, Mam? Women Steelworkers at Consett during the Second World War*. Newcastle-upon-Tyne: Open University Northern Region, 1984.

Priestley, J.B., *Postscripts*. London: William Heinemann, 1940.

—— *British Women Go to War*. London: Collins, 1943.

Pronay, N., and Spring, D.W., *Propaganda, Politics and Film 1918–45*. London and Basingstoke: Macmillan Ltd, 1982.

Pugh, M., *State and Society. British Political and Social History 1870–1992*. London and New York: Arnold, 1994.

Reese, P., *Homecoming Heroes. An Account of the Re-assimilation of British Military Personnel into Civilian Life*. London: Leo Cooper, 1992.

Reynolds, D., *Rich Relations. The American Occupation of Britain 1942–1945*. New York: Random House, Inc., 1995.

Riley, D., *War in the Nursery. Theories of the Child and Mother*. London: Virago, 1983.

Roberts, E., *Women and Families. An Oral History 1940–1970*. Oxford and London: Blackwell, 1995.

Roland, C.G., *Long Night's Journey into Day. Prisoners of War in Hong Kong and Japan, 1941–1945*. Waterloo, Ontario: Wilfrid Laurier University Press, 2001.

Rolf, D., *Prisoners of the Reich: Germany's Captives, 1939–45*. London: Leo Cooper, 1988.

——' "Blind Bureaucracy": The British Government and Prisoners of War in German Captivity, 1939–45' in Moore, B., and Fedorowich, K. (eds), *Prisoners of War and Their Captors in World War II*. Oxford: Berg, 1996.

Roof, M., *A Hundred Years of Family Welfare. A Study of The Family Welfare Association (Formerly Charity Organisation Society) 1869–1969*. London: Michael Joseph, 1972.

Rose, N., *Vansittart, Study of a Diplomat*. London: Heinemann, 1978.

Samuel, R. (ed.), *Patriotism: The Making and Unmaking of British National Identity. Vols I, II and III*. London: Routledge, 1989.

Schweitzer, P., Hilton, L., and Moss, J. (eds), *'What Did You Do in the War, Mum?'* London: Age Exchange Theatre Co., 1985.

Scott, P., *British Women in War*. London: Hutchinson, 1940.

Settle, M.L., *All the Brave Promises. The Memories of Aircraftwomen Second Class*. London: Heinemann, 1966.

Sharpe, M., *History of the Royal Air Force*. Bath: Paragon, 1999.

Sheridan, D. (ed.), *Wartime Women*. London: Heinemann Ltd / Mandarin Paperbacks, 1990.

Short, K.R.M. (ed.), *Film and Radio Propaganda in World War II*. Beckenham: Croom Helm Ltd, 1983.

Skelley, A.R., *The Victorian Army at Home. The Recruitment and Terms and Conditions of the British Regular 1859–1899*. London: Croom Helm Ltd, 1977.

Skocpol, T., *Protecting Soldiers and Mothers*. Cambridge, MA., and London: The Belknap Press of Harvard University Press, 1992.

Slader, J., *The Fourth Service. Merchantmen and War 1939–1945*. London: Robert Hale, 1994.

Sleeman, J.F., *The Welfare State. Its Aims, Benefits and Costs*. London: George Allen and Unwin Ltd, 1973.

Smith, H.L., *War and Social Change. British Society in the Second World War*. Manchester: Manchester University Press, 1986.

——*Britain in the Second World War. A Social History*. Manchester and New York: Manchester University Press, 1996.

Somerville, C., *Our War. How the British Commonwealth Fought the Second World War*. London: Weidenfeld and Nicolson, 1998.

Sommer, D., *Haldane of Cloan. His Life and Times, 1856–1928*. London: George Allen and Unwin, 1960.

Sullivan, M., *The Development of the British Welfare State*. Hemel Hempstead: Prentice Hall/Harvester Wheatsheaf, 1996.

Summerfield, P., *Women Workers in the Second World War. Production and Patriarchy in Conflict*. London: Croom Helm, 1984; 2nd edition Routledge, 1989.

——*Reconstructing Women's Wartime Lives: Discourse and Subjectivity in Oral Histories of the Second World War*. Manchester: Manchester University Press, 1998.

——'British Women in Transition from War to Peace' in Duchen, C., and Bandhauer-Schoffmann, I. (eds), *When the War Was Over. Women, War and Peace in Europe, 1940–1956*. London and New York: Leicester University Press, 2000.

Summerfield, P., and Finch, J., 'Social Reconstruction and the Emergence of Companionate Marriage 1945–59' in Clark, D. (ed.), *Marriage, Domestic Life and Social Change. Writings for Jacqueline Burgoyne (1944–88)*. London and New York: Routledge, 1991.

Swinnerton, I.S., *An Introduction to the British Army: Its History, Traditions and Records*. Birmingham: Federation of Family History Societies, 1996.

Tanner, J., *Women and War*. London: Century, 1987.

Taylor, E., *Women Who Went to War. 1938–1946*. London: Grafton Books, 1989.

Taylor-Gooby, P., *Public Opinion, Ideology and State Welfare*. London: Routledge and Kegan Paul plc, 1985.

Thane, P., *Foundations of the Welfare State*. London: Longman, 1982.

——'Towards Equal Opportunities?' in Gourvish, T., and O'Day, A., *Britian Since 1945*. Basingstoke: Macmillan, 1991.

Titmuss, R.M., *Problems of Social Policy*. Westport, CT: Greenwood Press, 1950.

——'War and Social Policy' in *Essays on the Welfare State*. London: Allen and Unwin, 1958.

——*Social Policy. An Introduction*. London: George Allen and Unwin Ltd, 1974.

Towle, P., Kosuge, M., and Kibata, Y., *Japanese Prisoners of War*. London and New York: Hambledon and London, 2000.

Townsend, C., and Townsend, E., *War Wives*. Glasgow: William Collins and Sons, 1989.

Trustram, M., *Women of the Regiment. Marriage and the Victorian Army*. Cambridge: Cambridge University Press, 1984.

Turner, B., and Rennell, T., *When Daddy Came Home. How Family Life Changed Forever in 1945*. London: Hutchinson, 1995.

Ungerson, C., and Kember, M. (eds), *Women and Social Policy. A Reader*, 2nd ed. Basingstoke: Macmillan Ltd, 1997.

Vickers, J., *Women and War*. London: Zed, 1993.

Waller, J., and Vaughan-Rees, M., *Women in Wartime. The Role of Women's Magazines, 1939–1945*. London: MacDonald, 1987.

Warner, O.M.W., *The British Navy. A Concise History*. London: Thames and Hudson, 1975.

—— *Women in Uniform 1939–1945*. London: Papermac, 1989.

Wightman, C., *More than Munitions. Women, Work and the Engineering Industries 1900–1950*. London: Longman, 1999.

Wild, D., *Prisoner of Hope*. Lewes: The Book Guild, 1992.

Williams, A.S., *Women and War*. Hove: Wayland, 1989.

Williams, E.E., *The Wooden Horse*. New York: Harper, 1950.

Williams, E.T., and Palmer, H.M. (eds), *The Dictionary of National Biography 1951–1960*. Oxford: Oxford University Press, 1971.

Wilmot, C., *The Struggle for Europe*. Westport, CT: Greenwood Press, 1952.

Wilson, E., *Women and the Welfare State*. London: Tavistock, 1977.

—— *Only Halfway to Paradise: Women in Postwar Britain 1945–68*. London and New York: Tavistock Publications, 1980.

Wilson, T., *The Myriad Faces of War*. Cambridge: Polity Press, 1986.

Woolfitt, S., *Idle Women*. London: Benn, 1947.

Wootton, G., *The Politics of Influence. British Ex-servicemen. Cabinet Decisions and Cultural Change (1917–57)*. London: Routledge and Kegan Paul Ltd, 1963.

Articles

Anderson, O., 'Early Experiences of Manpower Problems in an Industrial Society at War. Great Britain 1854–1856' in *Political Science Quarterly*. Vol. 82, 1967.

Barrett Litoff, J., and Smith, D.C., 'U.S. Women on the Home Front in World War II' in *The Historian*. Vol. 57, No. 2, December 1995.

Beaumont, J., 'Rank, Privilege and Prisoners of War' in *War and Society* (Australia), Vol. 3, No. 1, 1983. pp. 67–94.

Beckh, H.G., 'Reuniting of Families in Europe during and after the Second World War' in *International Review of the Red Cross*. No. 211, 1979. pp. 171–183; No. 216, 1980. pp. 115–128; No. 227, 1982. pp. 71–85.

Bey, D.R., and Lange, J., 'Waiting Wives: Women under Stress' in *American Journal of Psychology*. Vol. 131, March 1974. pp. 283–286.

Crang, J.A., 'Welcome to Civy Street. The Demobilization of the British Armed Forces after the Second World War' in *Historian*. Vol. 46, 1995. pp. 18–21.

Davin, A., 'Imperialism and Motherhood' in *History Workshop Journal*. No. 5, 1978. pp. 9–65.

Davis, G.H., 'Prisoners of War in Twentieth-century War Economics' in *Journal of Contemporary History*. Vol. 12, 1977. pp. 623–634.

Fishman, S., 'The Cult of the Return: Prisoner of War Wives in France During the Second World War' in *Proceedings of the Annual Meeting of the Western Society for French History*. Vol. 17, 1990.

Fowler, S. 'War Charity Begins at Home' in *History Today*. September 1999. pp. 17–23.

Harris, J. 'Britain and the Home Front during the Second World War' in *Contemporary European History*. Vol. 1, No. 1, 1992. pp. 17–35.

Hartmann, S.M., 'Prescriptions for Penelope: Literature on Women's Obligations to Returning World War II Veterans' in *Women's Studies*. Vol. 5, 1978. pp. 223–239.

Humphries, J., 'Class Struggle and the Persistence of the Working Class Family' in *Cambridge Journal of Economics*. Vol. 1, 1977. pp. 241–258.

McCubbin, H.I., and Dahl, B.B., 'The Returned POW: Factors in Family Reintegration' in *Journal of Marriage and the Family*. August 1975. pp. 471–478.

McCubbin, H., Dahl, B.B., Lester, G.R., Benson, D., and Robertson, M.L., 'Coping Repertoires of Families Adapting to Prolonged War-induced Separation' in *Journal of Marriage and the Family*. August 1976. pp. 461–471.

McCubbin, H.I., Hunter, E.J., and Dahl, B.B., 'Residuals of War: Families of Prisoners of War and Servicemen Missing in Action' in *Journal of Social Issues*. Vol. 31, No. 4, 1975. pp. 95–109.

MacIntosh, H., 'Separation Problems in Military Wives' in *American Journal of Psychiatry*. Vol. 125, No. 2, 1968. pp. 260–265.

MacKenzie, S.P., 'The Treatment of Prisoners of War in World War II' in *Journal of Modern History*. Vol. 66, September 199. pp. 487–520.

Maitland, M.D.D., 'The Care of the Soldier's Family' in *Journal of the Royal Army Medical Corps*. August 1950. pp. 107–125.

Moore, B., 'Turning Liabilities into Assets: British Government Policies towards German and Italian Prisoners of War during the Second World War' in *Journal of Contemporary History*. Vol. 32, 1, 1997. pp. 117–136.

Nelson, H., 'The Nips Are Going for the Parker' in *War and Society*. Vol. 3, No. 2, September 1985. pp. 127–143.

O'Bierne, K.P., 'Waiting Wives' in *United States Naval Institute Proceedings*. Vol. 102, September 1976. pp. 28–37.

Riley, D., 'War in the Nursery' in *Feminist Review*. No. 2, 1979. pp. 82–108.

——'Free Mothers: Pro-natalism and working women in industry and the end of the last war in Britain' in *History Workshop*. No. 11, Spring 1981. pp. 58–118.

Roland, C.G., 'Allied POWs, Japanese Captors and the Geneva Convention' in *War and Society*. Vol. 9, No. 2, October 1991. pp. 83–101.

Rolf, D., 'The Education of British Prisoners of War in German Captivity, 1939–1945' in *History of Education*. Vol. 18, No. 3, 1989. pp. 257–265.

Rundell, W. Jr, 'Paying the POW in World War II' in *Military Affairs*. Vol. 22, 1958. pp. 121–138.

Shephard, B., 'A Clonded Homecoming' in *History Today*. Vol. 46, August 1996.

Sheridan, D., 'Ambivalent Memories: Women and the 1939–45 War in Britain' in *Oral History*. Vol. 18, No. 1, Spring 1990. pp. 32–40.

Smith, H., 'The Problem of Equal Pay for Equal Work in Great Britain during World War II' in *Journal of Modern History*. Vol. 53, December 1981. pp. 652–673.

Sokoloff, S., '"How Are They at Home?" Community, State and Servicemen's Wives in England, 1939–45' in *Women's History Review*. Vol. 8, No. 1, 1999. pp. 27–51.

Summerfield, P., 'Women Workers in the Second World War' in *Capital and Class*. Vol. 1, 1992. pp. 27–42.

Summerfield, P., and Crockett, N., '"You Weren't Taught That with the Welding": Lessons in Sexuality in the Second World War' in *Women's History Review*. Vol. 1, No. 3, 1997. pp. 435–454.

Summerskill, E., 'Conscription and Women' in *The Fortnightly*. Vol. 151, March 1942. pp. 209–214.

Swindells, J., 'Coming Home to Heaven: Manpower and Myth in 1944 Britain' in *Women's History Review*. Vol. 4, No. 2, 1995. pp. 223–234.

Vance, J.F., 'The Politics of Camp Life: The Bargaining Process in Two German Prison Camps' in *War and Society*. Vol. 10, No. 1, May 1992. pp. 109–126.

——'Canadian Relief Agencies and Prisoners of War, 1930–45' in *Journal of Canadian Studies*. Vol. 31, No. 2, Summer 1996. pp. 133–147.

Vormbrock, J.K., 'Attachment Theory as Applied to Wartime and Job-related Marital Separation' in *Psychological Bulletin*. Vol. 114, No. 1, 1993. pp. 122–144.

Index